PROACTIVE COMPANIES

PROACTIVE COMPANIES

How to Anticipate Market Changes

LEONARDO ARAÚJO
Professor of Marketing, Fundação Dom Cabral
ROGÉRIO GAVA
Associate Professor and Researcher, Fundação Dom Cabral

FUNDAÇÃO DOM CABRAL

FDC

DEVELOPING EXECUTIVES AND COMPANIES

First published 2012 by
PALGRAVE MACMILLAN

Palgrave Macmillan in the UK is an imprint of Macmillan Publishers Limited, registered in England, company number 785998, of Houndmills, Basingstoke, Hampshire RG21 6XS.

Palgrave Macmillan in the US is a division of St Martin's Press LLC, 175 Fifth Avenue, New York, NY 10010.

Palgrave Macmillan is the global academic imprint of the above companies and has companies and representatives throughout the world.

Palgrave® and Macmillan® are registered trademarks in the United States, the United Kingdom, Europe and other countries

ISBN-13: 978–0–230–28922–2

This book is printed on paper suitable for recycling and made from fully managed and sustained forest sources. Logging, pulping and manufacturing processes are expected to conform to the environmental regulations of the country of origin.

A catalogue record for this book is available from the British Library.

A catalog record for this book is available from the Library of Congress.

10 9 8 7 6 5 4 3 2 1
21 20 19 18 17 16 15 14 13 12

Printed and bound in Great Britain by
CPI Antony Rowe, Chippenham and Eastbourne

Dedicated to Adriana and my children Bernardo and Júlia, with love and admiration. May this book inspire them to create their future.

Leonardo Araújo

Dedicated to my children João Pedro and Anna Laura, source of all meaning and happiness, to my wife Clarisse, for her support on this long journey and to my parents, Enio and Dione, with admiration and respect.

Rogério Gava

Contents

Figures and tables

FIGURES

TABLES

Acknowledgments

It would not be possible to produce this book without the help of many persons and companies. We owe them all for this precious, invaluable support.

Assistance from Fundação Dom Cabral (FDC) was decisive in helping us to overcome obstacles along the path. FDC's belief in the generation of managerial knowledge, inspired by the long-range vision of Dean Emerson de Almeida, created the necessary conditions for the development of our research. The incentives and help we received from this renowned institution were critical.

Besides institutional support, we were honored to received innumerable and invaluable comments from peers at FDC, with whom we shared chapters of this book. Specifically, we gratefully thank professors Aldemir Drummond, Anderson Sant'anna, Carlos Arruda, Haroldo Motta, and Mozart Pereira. Colleagues in FDC's technical support unit have actively helped us contact the companies and executives who generously contributed to the research. We thank them all for their ever-present professionalism and commitment. In particular, we thank our colleague Sônia Diegues for her continuous involvement with and encouragement of our work.

We also warmly thank Professor Philip Kotler, for his great interest in this work. Professor Kotler's gentleness, commitment, and availability left an indelible impression on us.

In addition, we had the privilege of counting on support from a number of very special readers, who helped us improve the text with their opportune suggestions and thoughtful corrections. We thank especially Alexandre Majola Gava, Eduardo Valério, Fabiano Larentis, José Salibi Neto, Salim Mattar, and Sílvio Guerra.

Forty-seven chief executive officers wholeheartedly agreed to take part in our research, and gave us useful comments. Long conversations with these professionals about market proactiveness have been extremely relevant to our work on this book. We were also grateful for the help and interest of more than 300 executives who participated in different research stages during the last five years. We especially thank those who supported us during the systematic examination of all the proactiveness case studies we present in this book, for tirelessly making themselves available to us, and for their courtesy in providing data and information which was essential to the research.

We were also fortunate to be able to bring the subject of market proactiveness before innumerable participants in classes, workshops, and lectures, with whom we had the opportunity to openly debate the concepts and tools presented in this book. We thank all of them for their constructive and interesting insights and comments. Without a doubt this book is, in part, a product of these interactions.

We also acknowledge the professionalism, exemplary behavior, and support from our editors and their teams at Editora Campus, publishers of the Brazilian edition of the book. Especially we thank José Antonio Rugeri for his guiding comments, which were always judicious and opportune.

We would also like to thank our close friends for their assistance, support and never-ending belief in the project. We are thankful for and proud of their friendship.

Finally, we especially acknowledge our families, for their unconditional support along this journey. The tolerance and generosity of our wives and children provided a sound foundation for the construction of this book. Their very existence is a blessing for us.

Preface

Since we first enthusiastically embraced the idea of writing this book, five years ago, we have shared an increasingly stimulating interest: the possibility that companies can anticipate the future. Like fine wines, whose personality gradually emerges as you sip them, bringing you increasing pleasure, market proactiveness has grown on us. The subject has proved to be fertile soil in which we were able to cultivate new ideas in the field of management. This pursuit changed what had previously been an academic partnership between us into a close friendship.

Proactive Companies is a fruit of this journey of ours. We believe that this is not a book for organizations that are content simply to react to the market, like cornered rabbits that flee into their burrows at the first sign of danger. Neither is it aimed at companies that are only trying to survive the tides of change. This is a book for ambitious companies that believe in the possibility of building the future here and now, forging their own path. It is a book to help companies formulate new questions, rather than simply looking for the answers to the same old questions they have always been asking.

We believe that a market strategy has to transcend mere adaptation to a world where changes bombard companies like a shower of meteorites. It is time managers overcame the competitive analysis paradigm, in which the market is regarded as a reality that determines how companies should act. It is time they understand that companies are not puppets driven by their environment, guided by the apparent threats and opportunities in their market. It is time instead for executives to start to anticipate change, and make their companies follow the market proactiveness track.

One of our strongest and most unequivocal beliefs is that the major purpose of the academic field of business administration is to concern itself with business practice, and that a book written in this field should be practical in orientation. A book that does not help managers in their daily activities does not deserve room on their bookshelves. One of our earliest concerns, therefore, was to construct a set of models and tools that could bring the idea of market proactiveness into managerial practice. That is why this book not only explains the market proactiveness concept, it shows how it can be applied in actual business strategies. Actionless ideas are like daydreams; actions without ideas are nightmares.

However, it is not possible to create and enforce any strategy by dictate, let alone a proactive strategy. In order to put proactive strategies into practice, first we have to foster a culture of market proactiveness within the company. This will be a culture that includes a novel way of regarding the future. It will be a culture based on a set of capacities, a true passport to proactive action. Without these capacities, attempts to anticipate future needs will be as ephemeral as a morning breeze. We have not only identified the required capacities, we have organized them into a managerial structure. Accordingly, our approach to market proactiveness extends beyond an idea, or a method to put an idea into practice. It also emphasizes the prerequisites every company has to meet in order to develop the idea.

Proactive Companies is based on the path we have been travelling along for some time in the field of orientation to the market. During this period, we dived into theory, surveyed some 300 companies, talked to executives and CEOs of many different types of organizations, exchanged ideas with peers both in academia and outside it, tested concepts, and applied the tools we describe here. We are certain that the ideas we outline here can be useful in times of uncertainty. We are also aware of the fact that the decision to implement a market proactiveness policy is, above all, a matter of belief. To be proactive, before any other consideration a company has to believe that it is feasible to do so. From the moment when it embraces that belief, it needs to start developing the necessary capabilities.

This is the challenge we are presenting to our readers: to believe that change can be anticipated, and to start to act on that belief. We think this book can be of use to companies in the process of choosing new courses of action. We encourage readers to work through its pages and understand how this can be done. We hope you have as much pleasure reading as we had writing it.

Leonardo Araújo and Rogério Gava
August 2011

INTRODUCTION
A Model for Market Proactiveness

Why do some companies succeed better than others? Here is the essential question of competitive strategy. Its answer is the Holy Grail of strategic management. CEOs, directors, managers, businesspeople, and consultants, in fact all those involved with the routine of organizations and their strategies, long for the answer to this question. Many academic papers and books have been already written attempting to unravel the enigma of competitive advantage. The answer does not come easily, however. If you are intrigued by this question, this book has something to tell you.

It is well known that innumerable variables, and difficult-to-measure factors such as company culture and degree of innovation, can impact on a company's performance. For instance, performance is highly affected by the economic and sectoral context of a company's operations. External events – many of which are genuinely unpredictable – can easily drive results beyond expectations or annihilate planned strategies. Hence, the most suitable metaphor to describe enterprise performance is a mosaic, a heterogeneous picture built out of many interconnected and mutually influencing pieces.

This book was written because the authors believe they have found a concept that may help us understand why some companies really do stand out from the average performance of their competitors. The concept we found is called market proactiveness. Proactive companies anticipate change and respond to it before they are forced to do so, or even deliberately create change.

Thus, we are firmly convinced that many companies are more successful than others, at least in part because they deal with markets in a proactive way. This conviction is not a mere belief. The market proactiveness model we developed is grounded in knowledge in the fields of organizational theory, environmental theory, strategy, marketing, theory of marketing orientation and innovation, and in specific areas of study such as uncertainty theory, managerial decision making, proactive behavior, managerial approaches to the future and, most importantly, studies on proactiveness in organizational environments.[1]

But we went beyond theory. We tested the model that we developed based on the theory outlined above in the field. In a first stage, we interviewed more than 50 top executives from 27 large companies operating in Brazil, presenting and discussing our model and its practical validity. Next, we quantitatively studied the strategic behavior of 260 companies operating in different sectors, such as hotels, transportation, automotive, retail, energy, data processing, teaching, food, health, civil construction, telecommunications, and steel. In our research we tried broadly to evaluate at what level companies implement proactive actions in regard to the market, and up to what level (in terms of capacities) they are prepared to act proactively. In a third stage, we combined this qualitative and quantitative information with insights gathered during intensive interviews with 47 CEOs of large national and multinational companies operating in Brazil. We took the theme of market proactiveness to MBAs and other executive development programs as well as to management congresses. We published details of our model in academic journals and corporate magazines. This book is based on this work, and it sets out in a narrative all the ideas and insights we accumulated as a result of our efforts. We believe this work resulted in the creation of an innovative approach to market strategic orientation.

OUR APPROACH TO MARKET PROACTIVENESS

The research we carried out revealed a paradox: although companies consider proactiveness a fundamental strategic capability, most organizations still follow the traditional reactive pattern when establishing their strategies. Since we were curious about the underlying reasons for this, we designed an application model to enable companies to change this reality and start acting more proactively with regard to the business environment.

Market proactiveness is a long-established subject of business authors, although it is often dealt with indirectly. Many authors have produced excellent books and articles on what we have termed business proactive logic, although they might not call it by that name. We recognize the importance of all this work, but we would like to draw the reader's attention to the distinctiveness of our own book. We believe that no previous author has developed an application model that is capable of turning the the theoretical concept of market proactiveness into a recipe for action. We tried to fill in this blank, and what this book offers is a a practical method that organizations can use to develop their market proactiveness.[2]

Three fundamental pillars support our application model and constitute the bases for this book: comprehension, management and execution (see Table I.1). First, it is necessary to understand what market proactiveness means and why we believe it could become a novel path to a company's strategic development. It is also necessary to understand how market proactiveness works. It is not enough to assimilate what a strategy is, it is necessary to carry it out in practice. Part I deals with these issues. Chapter 1 introduces and defines the concept of market proactiveness, and pinpoints its importance and what distinguishes proactive from reactive companies. It also presents two fundamental issues. The first addresses the essential element of market proactiveness – anticipation – and the second addresses the concept of moment zero, which is crucial to understanding the mechanism of anticipation and the whole approach to market proactiveness as we have conceived it. Chapter 1 ends with a matrix depicting the four types

Table 1.1 The book's structure

	Understanding market proactiveness	Managing market proactiveness	Executing market proactiveness
Part I			
Market proactiveness: anticipating moments zero	Chapter 1		
Action tools and models: the DNA of market proactiveness	Chapter 2		
Part II			
Organizing the company for market proactiveness: the capacities of a proactive company		Chapter 3	
Future-today management: believing in what does not exist (yet)		Chapter 4	
Uncertainty management: learning to deal with risk and error		Chapter 5	
Proactive innovation management: innovating to change the market		Chapter 6	
Proactive behavior management: developing personal proactiveness		Chapter 7	
Part III			
Building a proactive market strategy: how to put market proactiveness into practice			Chapter 8
Offer proactiveness: creating a moment zero for an offering			Chapter 9
Industry proactiveness: creating moments zero in competitive environments			Chapter 10
Customer proactiveness: creating moments zero in customer behavior			Chapter 11
Conclusion: a strategy to anticipate the future	Chapter 12		

of companies and showing the different market orientations organizations may adopt and their consequences.

Chapter 2 completes this approach and describes how proactive market strategies work in the real world. It also introduces the DNA analysis model, decomposing proactive market strategy formulation into its dimensions, levels, and actions. Chapter 2 also introduces two tools necessary to formulate a market proactive strategy, completing the DNA model described: the generate-modify matrix and the moments-zero matrix.

Part II addresses an issue that is essential to the scope of our concept: the capabilities that are needed to support the implementation of a market proactiveness strategy. As we always say, it is not enough to be willing to be proactive; the company must be organized in way that enables it to achieve market proactiveness. The capabilities we list here are prerequisites to a successful implementation of market proactiveness; they pave the way to more proactive actions. Chapter 3 introduces the four dimensions of management within which all the capabilities mentioned must be managed, preparing and organizing a company to turn market proactiveness concepts into action. These dimensions constitute what we call *proactive management*, a managerial posture focused on the development of the capabilities necessary for market proactiveness. The four dimensions are individually discussed in Chapters 4 to 7.

Chapter 4 introduces *future-today management*, a concept we developed to represent a new way of thinking and acting relative to tomorrow. There is no way to develop more proactive strategies that does not involve a new vision of the future. Chapter 5 explores what we call *uncertainty management*, addressing risk and error and their influence on the formulation and execution of a market proactiveness strategy. Risk and error are real paradigms in management, and can strongly inhibit the development of market proactiveness. In Chapter 6 we introduce the concept of *proactive innovation management*. We believe that a new approach to innovation practices is necessary, aimed at anticipating market changes and breaking prevailing consumption patterns. Chapter 7 completes the discussion of the four dimensions of management in our model, introducing *proactive behavior management* and explaining how it works. An early and fundamental discovery we made is that proactive companies are made up of proactive people.

Finally, Part III deals with the execution of a proactive market strategy in all three dimensions of the model: the *offer*, the *industry* and the *customer*. We are convinced that market strategies are always constructed in at least one of these dimensions. We apply our DNA model to show how market proactiveness may give rise to actions in each of these dimensions. Thus, Chapter 8 draws on all the tools that have been presented, and offers a basic script for the construction of a proactive market strategy (PMS). Here we explore the four steps that are essential to implement this strategy. This structure will guide the reader's understanding of the material in the chapters that follow.

Chapters 9, 10, and 11 focus on describing successful cases of market proactiveness. Our intention is to illustrate how some companies have anticipated change in a remarkably effective way, building a proactive market strategy in the three dimensons of offer, industry, and customer, and dramatically changing market conditions as a result. Chapter 9 addresses what we call *offer proactiveness*. In other words, it outlines a number of proactive strategic actions that can be put to work in regard to what we have called standard supply and complementary supply. Chapter 10 introduces *industry proactiveness*, and describes how proactive actions relative to the market can be carried out to change existing competitive rules. Industry proactiveness is related to actions that concern suppliers, distributors, competitors, and sectoral regulatory mechanisms. Finally, Chapter 11 develops the dimension we call *customer proactiveness*. Here, we observe marketing's fundamental idea from a new viewpoint: companies should not exist exclusively to satisfy customers' needs. We demonstrate how is it possible to act proactively to change customers' needs and preferences.

Chapter 12 concludes the book, presenting five fundamental issues of market proactiveness. They synthesize essential aspects for a correct understanding of what this strategy really represents, as well as its potential as a new way of competing.

A WORD ABOUT THIS BOOK

Try to act *in* the future. What do we mean by this? For instance, try to point your finger in the future. So you point your finger – and what you meant for the future happens now. The present is in reality the only site of action, of change. We can only act in the present; only the present exists. That is why we often say that the future is not tomorrow; the future is today. It is not something to be foreseen, but rather something to be built. It is something not to expect, but to be made real. This is the cornerstone of market proactiveness: to anticipate the future, based on action performed here and now.[3]

If everyone is looking for adaptation, who is ahead? If everyone answers to what everyone hears, who will answer differently? Our studies on market proactiveness revealed that, when managing either our personal life or a company, we have only two options. Either we resign ourselves to the fact that change will happen, and adapt when it does so, or we anticipate future change and act proactively to shape it. The market proactiveness approach is based on the latter option.

We are certain that market proactiveness can become the beginning of a new strategic path, a vigorous option that enables companies to compete successfully in the third millennium. Our research, based on intensive discussions and studies on market proactiveness, supports this belief. We hold the opinion that every company, regardless of size or economic sector, has the opportunity to build its own destiny. But as the maxim goes, opportunities only favor those who are ready for them. In the course of our research we discovered how and why proactive companies are differentiated from their competitors. In this book we share these findings.

We would like to be able to say that every strategy comes with its own user's guide and is easy to understand, formulate, and execute on a Monday morning. The Monday metaphor represents the real world of competition, of turbulence, where time cannot be wasted in elegant but practically inefficient strategies. We have tried to offer a feasible strategic option, which capable of being turned into concrete actions by those who routinely deal with corporate strategy. If this book is able to help companies and their managers see market proactiveness as a new strategic possibility and to support their Monday morning decisions – and many others – it will have been a worthwhile book to write.

Part I
Understanding Market Proactiveness

MARKET PROACTIVENESS

1 Anticipating Moments Zero

One day in August 1856, workers digging in search of limestone in a quarry close to Düsseldorf, western Germany, suddenly came across some old bones. At the time, they did not realize that their finding would revolutionize the history of human evolution: the world had found the Neanderthals.[1] Vigorous and resistant to extreme environmental conditions, the Neanderthals survived for a long and difficult 150,000 years before they disappeared from the face of the earth; they were one of the most successful species in the history of evolution. Reasons for their extinction are still hazy and another fact contributes to the enigma: Neanderthals died out exactly when they confronted a strange unknown, *Homo sapiens*.

We know today that Neanderthals, like primitive *Homo sapiens*, were able to make tools and weapons, and were physically better suited to face the extreme environmental conditions of their time. In addition, the brain of a Neanderthal was 10 percent larger than that of our direct predecessors. This indicates that biological handicaps were not among the reasons why the Neanderthals disappeared. So what was the reason?

We could speculate that *Homo sapiens* developed a kind of ability the Neanderthals never mastered: the ability to plan for the future, and more importantly, anticipate actions. Planning and anticipation versus adaptation: while Neanderthals would simply adapt to the environment, *Homo sapiens* was additionally able to plan ahead and speculate on what might or might not happen Understanding how periods of high and low rainfall occur and that water can be stored, for instance, is a kind of reasoning peculiar to *Homo sapiens*, that Neanderthals apparently did not possess.[2] Another important aspect is the level of innovation gradually achieved by *Homo sapiens*, which is considerably higher than that of Neanderthals.

There are strong indications, therefore, that *Homo sapiens*' ability to create and anticipate was decisive to the survival of our species. Our forebears' imagination gave them the ability to literally see ahead of their time. To see ahead of time; anticipate; create; shape the environment: these are characteristics that synthesize proactive behavior. Neanderthals paid a high price for their reactiveness, whereas *Homo sapiens* survived thanks to the ability to create and anticipate, and to a constant attempt to change their environment.[3]

We have started this book by mentioning the Neanderthals because of an emblematic motive: we have reasons to believe that we would not have written these lines – and you probably would not be reading them – if *Homo sapiens* were not proactive.

MARKET REACTIVENESS: THE COMPANY REACTS TO THE ENVIRONMENT

In the simple story we have just told, it was neither a drastic change in the environment nor an inability to adapt that caused the end of Neanderthals. It was the competition brought about by a rival who not only reacted to facts but also tried to proactively anticipate changes that might come. This is what happened to Neanderthals and, we believe, it is what happens to many enterprises today, 30,000 years later. We believe that a major cause for the poor performance of these organizations is embedded in an essentially reactive posture toward environmental demands. We call this posture *market reactiveness*. In other words, it leads to a strategy based exclusively on adaptation to existing market conditions. Market proactiveness exactly counterpoints this adaptive posture. Hence, we will first describe the market reactiveness paradigm, its origins and implications. Understanding why companies act reactively is the first step on the way to market proactiveness.

History is full of examples of companies that, at some point in their trajectory, made the mistake of being market-reactive. The computer giant IBM, for instance, experienced the sour taste of market reactiveness in the 1980s. The Big Blue neglected the advent of personal computers (PCs) and their widespread use by companies, and quickly felt a strong impact on its three-decade absolute leadership of the computer industry. Valuable market space was opened to competitors like Microsoft and Intel, which are now market leaders. Louis Gerstner – who in 1993 assumed the position of CEO at IBM and later guided the company's major strategic change to become a service provider (later in this book we will analyze this market proactiveness case) – commented, "PCs would be soon used by companies too, not only by students and aficionados; we failed to properly read the market; we did not see it as top priority."[4]

At that time, IBM imagined it would be enough to keep on responding to the market's needs and that these needs would not change. In other words, IBM acted reactively: that is, it just adapted its offers to the apparent patterns of the market, underestimating the growing charm of personal computers, a strategic mistake other companies would soon repeat.[5] When, in 1982, IBM finally decided to invest in the PC market, more than 2 million PCs had already been sold. A decade later, 110 million had been. The rest is history.[6]

Companies excessively focused on responding to the market end up being victims of change. This is what happened to Kodak, an icon of the photographic industry that drastically lagged behind competitors like Sony, believing that the traditional photographic film market would never change. Kodak paid a high price for this reactive posture: in the period between 2004 and 2008, the company's revenue fell from US$13 billion to US$9 billion, and a US$69 million profit vanished into losses of US$727 million. In the mid-1990s, the digital machines market achieved sales of 12 million units in the United States alone.[7]

As we can see, reactiveness may lead companies to the dangerous strategic attitude that responding to the market's demands will be enough to ensure survival in the competition game. That is not always the case. Consider now the internet search engine industry toward the end of the 1990s. Pioneer companies such as AltaVista and Yahoo! regarded web search as simply another option for internet surfers. Purchases, e-mail access, and news seemed to be much more interesting offers. With their websites loaded with advertisements and external links aimed at selling rather than helping 'internauts' lost in a maze of information, these pioneers never imagined being eclipsed by Google, let alone losing out as overwhelmingly as they actually did. Their disbelief reached such high levels at that time that both companies rejected low-priced offers to buy the as yet unknown search engine with the strange name.[8] Even giant companies such as Microsoft were not able to perceive signs of the huge potential market for search engines. Google is very thankful for that: with a global market share around 90 percent, the company proactively revolutionized the way we search for information on the web. Its brand is now worth more than US$40 billion.[9]

Despite being well known and classic, these examples point up a common fact that we think is often neglected when such cases are studied: the reason that IBM, Kodak, AltaVista, Yahoo! and many other companies experienced sudden market failure was because they were all exceedingly reactive to the market. Just like modern Neanderthals, they acted only adaptively, neglecting the latent possibilities for creating change and transforming the market. When they finally noticed what was going on, it was already too late.

We believe that most companies are reactive, most of the time, just like those we have described. Our research, including more than 350 executives in more than 250 organizations, found low to average levels of proactiveness in 95 percent of them. (You will have the opportunity to diagnose your own company's level of proactiveness by applying the Promark scale presented in Appendix A at the end of this book.[10]) Almost a hundred interviews with CEOs and executives support our understanding: few companies are able to anticipate the market and act before changes take place, or even create change in a revolutionary way. We wondered why this occurred. Why do most strategic actions still try to respond to the market's demands? You are probably asking the same question yourself. Maybe the company you work for fits our description. After all, why should companies only respond to markets when they can shape whole environments to their benefit?

WHY ARE COMPANIES REACTIVE?

You might like to observe your company's reality from three different standpoints. First, how does your company usually design its strategy? Does it simply adapt itself to circumstances, or is the strategy aimed at building new market realities? Second, what type of market orientation has guided your company's marketing actions lately? Was your company oriented to respond to consumers' needs and competitors' moves, or does it try to create entirely new needs and to change the rules of the competition game? Third, how does your company deal with innovation? Does it see it as a process based on market demands and on clients' requirements, or as an action based on a proactive interpretation of something not fully revealed by the market as yet, which could create a marked rupture in current supply patterns?

If your answers indicate a strong reactive orientation, don't worry too much; your company is doing what the market on average does. It is easy to explain why: actions in the realms of strategy, marketing, and innovation are the best mirror for market reactiveness. They are the very sources of the reactive posture (see Figure 1.1). What we are trying to say is that reactive attitudes did not appear by chance, but are rather a consequence of the adaptive nature that pervades most of what has been studied and practiced in three areas of management in the last 50 years. These sources have strongly contributed – and still do contribute – to making market reactiveness a true paradigm in management.

THE SOURCES OF MARKET REACTIVENESS

Strategy reactiveness

The concept of business strategy has its origins in the 1960s, and its essence has not changed much since, in our opinion. It is an attempt to better position a company in relation to the environment, adapting it to circumstances. If you have ever taken part in a strategic planning process, you should know what we are talking about! An accurate environmental analysis guides the establishment of strategies and objectives capable of responding to the perceived reality and of achieving expected results; just like a symphonic cadence. The market and its conditions are the starting point (just about every manager must have participated in some kind

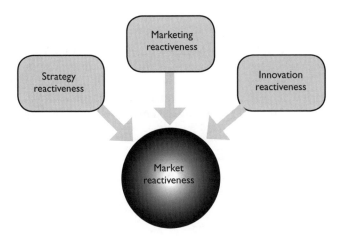

Figure 1.1 The sources of market reactiveness

of diagnosis of threats and opportunities) of every action planned. We often say that if classic strategic management had a motto, it would be: adapt or die!

Why do strategies follow this reactive paradigm? We do not need much theory to explain that the reactive perspective descends from contingency theory. Simply said, this school states that companies, in order to survive, must adapt themselves to the surrounding environment or circumstances. This is what academics call "environmental determinism."[11] The deterministic paradigm exerted enormous influence on everything that was, and still is, thought about business strategy. It is enough to say that its principles support most theories on strategic planning and competitive strategy that were introduced later on. Thus, the process of strategy building – as both taught and practiced – resulted in an overestimation of market conditions and prevailing competitive patterns, as if they were compasses determining the right direction for companies' strategies. This is the basic thought that permeates established marketing and strategy models and tools, with strategy always being treated as a variable depending on market conditions.[12] Such intense influence could only lead companies and their strategists to a position favoring adaptation to environmental requirements. This is the origin of the reactive nature of strategic management.

Marketing reactiveness

Modern marketing was born in the 1950s, brought about by Peter Drucker, author of a famous and inspired statement, "there is only one valid definition of business purpose: to create a customer."[13] Though it may sound obvious and even commonplace today, it was a warning against the negligent way customers were regarded at that time. Drucker ultimately reveals that only a company's changing action can create markets and their needs. But evidences indicate that Drucker's impacting statement was misinterpreted: the expression "create a customer" was taken to mean "satisfy a customer." This misinterpretation eventually became one of the cornerstones of the marketing construct: companies exist to satisfy customers, guiding them through their demands and wishes. To be successful, organizations should constantly and exclusively consider the possibilities of effectively satisfying consumers' needs. And so was born the mantra of strategic market orientation, which has dominated the theoretical development marketing ever since.

It is true that in the 1990s, the theory of marketing orientation brought fresh air to strategic marketing. It pinpointed the importance of new players, other than customers, in the competition scenario, such as competitors, suppliers, and even governments. In other words, instead of being exclusively customer-oriented, companies should also be oriented to other players that are capable of influencing consumer behavior. Thus, a strong market orientation became marketing strategy's state of the art. However, this new line of reasoning did not change the reactive nature that had been embedded in marketing since its very birth. What do market-oriented companies do in essence? They gather information on the environment, process them and respond to the market according to the diagnoses they make. Though market-oriented companies have widened their field of view to reach beyond customers, this does not mean they did not remain reactive.[14]

Hence, marketing strategy, either customer-oriented or market-oriented, has always reflected an adaptive posture to prevailing market conditions. Customer-oriented and market-oriented companies are still being led, rather than leading the environment and its variables. They seem to forget, as we have said, that the market does not provide much reliable guidance to success, and that many times profit comes from guiding customers instead of only responding to their demands.[15] Marketing reactiveness thus became the second pillar of the reactive posture toward the market.

Innovation reactiveness

Our last source of reactiveness is related to innovation generation. For a long time now, in most companies the innovation process has been reduced to a mere question of responding to market requirements. This reactive posture has certainly been remarked on in the past.[16] Innovation based on technology, research, and development is almost invariably subordinated to market demands. This limits innovation generation to what is strictly known, familiar, and accepted as viable. This is what we call "reactive innovation."

Reactive innovation occurs because most of the time companies insist on adopting the market as a guideline for their innovation processes. However, the ability of consumers to imagine innovation is known to be low. Generally speaking, people do not have insight to create really revolutionary products and services. Try to imagine a need – a product or service – that does not exist yet, but that you wish existed. Can you be sure it would be technologically feasible today? What we are trying to say is that companies should not expect consumers to help them generate real innovations. As Steve Jobs once said, consumers only decide what they want after someone shows them what they might want.[17] But it was Henry Ford who maybe first captured the dilemma of reactive innovation with his famous statement, "If I had asked my customers what they wanted, they would have answered they wanted a faster horse."

The three sources of reactiveness we presented continue to shape reactive postures toward the market. These are postures that dominate business thinking and lead to a narrow vision of what strategy is able to do for companies. That vision, we believe, is not sufficient in times of hypercompetition like today.

MARKET REACTIVENESS IS NOT ENOUGH ANY MORE

Market reactiveness is and will long remain a feasible strategic option, and even the one that is the most efficient on many occasions. Alignment with the market will always be important, no doubt. Reaction is an undisputable reality in the construction of business strategies. The point is that the reactive posture too easily becomes the single strategy to be pursued. This is the problem. The question is not the remedy, but the dose that needs to be taken. We usually say that in a strategic construction, like life itself, "nothing is more dangerous than an idea, when it is the only one we have."

To limit strategic construction to a permanent search for adaptation puts companies, sooner or later, under the well-known "tyranny of the served market."[18] In other words, in a given context, the environment gives orders, and organizations try to do the best they can to fulfill them. It is like conceiving the market as a game with preestablished rules. In this context, players have two options: either they strive to quickly learn the rules of a game created by others and be the best, or they create a new game, with rules established by themselves. Successful companies have usually preferred the latter, because the one who creates the rules gains more advantage from them.

We believe now that it is not enough to be only reactive; the examples we have examined showed this truth. "Best in class" companies demonstrate that the market needs to be guided, shaped to the interests of the company, and business environments must be transformed accordingly. This move, clearly seen today in some of the companies we have studied, signals a proactive business logic: that is, a strategic orientation posture that does not only respond to the contingencies – and demands – of the environment. In other words, it points up what we call market proactiveness.

Proactive companies go beyond mere adaptation to market conditions. They try instead to anticipate changes, acting before they are forced to do so. This is the fundamental difference between market proactiveness and the market reactiveness we have so far described. While reactive companies try to learn the rules of the competitive game (as created by others), proactive companies understand that these rules are not fixed and immutable, and can be changed by means of a strategic choice. This proactive strategic choice is not subject to current competition paradigms and patterns. It rather tries to subvert the order of the game and generate enduring competitive advantage.

Anticipation is clearly the essential element of market proactiveness. To understand how market proactiveness works, it is necessary to understand the meaning of market and change anticipation, and ultimately understand how anticipation manifests itself and how can it be changed into a real strategy.

ANTICIPATION: THE ESSENTIAL ELEMENT OF MARKET PROACTIVENESS

Although it is a commonly used expression, the term "proactiveness" was only recently conceived, and it is therefore sometimes misunderstood.[19] We agree that proactiveness is one of those words frequently used and rarely understood.[20] Despite all this, we could say that proactiveness is consensually recognized to mean taking action that anticipates change: it means acting before the effects of change appear, or even deliberately causing change.[21] Being proactive means causing change, anticipating it instead of waiting for change to occur and acting afterwards.

Knowing that anticipation is the essential element of market proactiveness, we started to identify ways to carry out this anticipative action in practice. To ease the analysis, we prepared a mechanism of anticipation, a graphic scheme to help understand how anticipation – and consequently market proactiveness – occurs (see Figure 1.2).

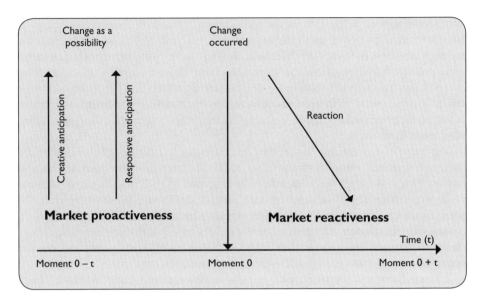

Figure 1.2 The mechanism of anticipation

MOMENT ZERO

To understand the mechanism of anticipation, we started with what we call moment zero (MZ) of the market. This moment is the very instant when a change takes place in the environment. Therefore, every change that takes place in the environment has its MZ. Consequently, the MZ is the moment of change. Acquisition of a competitor by a large player, new consumption habits, new legislation that substantially impacts a given market, new distribution channels, the launch of products that end up creating new consumption categories: these are all examples of MZs of the market. Obviously, the impact of MZs will vary greatly in strength and breadth. Metaphorically, we could say that while some MZs constitute earthquakes of considerable proportions and effects, others cause only slight trembling or are not even felt, remaining forever unnoticed.

The effects of a MZ result from two distinct dimensions: its breadth or reach, and its intensity. When we say that a company has anticipated a broad and high-intensity MZ, we mean that the change generated by this MZ impacted a large number of market players (reach) with great magnitude (intensity). The stupendous efficiency of Google's search engine and Dell's online sales model are known examples. On the other hand, a company may anticipate an MZ that will later prove itself to be unfruitful in regard to its impact, because of its low intensity or short reach. Think, for instance, of the more than ten web search sites that failed to gain significant market share in the pre-Google era. Two or more companies operating in the same market might both be proactive, but one of them will certainly be more efficient in its proactiveness and will generate more significant MZs.

Let us go back to Figure 1.2. Anticipation – and consequently market proactiveness – will always and only take place in the period of time (t) before the described MZ (moment 0 – t). It is as if the company had brought the MZ to a time before its very own occurrence. Conversely, every action stimulated by an MZ and taken after its occurrence (moment 0 + 1) constitutes a typical reactive move. Market reactiveness is a clear process of stimulus and response. Observe the direction of the arrow: the occurrence of a change triggers a delayed action; in other words, a reaction. Thus, reactive companies only act when they are forced to do so, when the MZ has already occurred, when change has already taken place and there is nothing else to be done except respond to its effects. In brief, a reactive response (or reactiveness), to something that invariably has taken place in the past, is the antithesis of an anticipated response. This is the subtle difference between responding before or after a change. That small difference can have a huge impact on the competitive performance of companies.

THE TWO TYPES OF ANTICIPATION

While reactions act on an already established change, anticipation acts when change is still a possibility. We could say that anticipation always occurs when change is latent, while reactiveness operates after its manifestation. Within this latency zone, anticipation may assume two different forms, which are the two anticipation types we conceived. A company may act on change symptoms, tuning in to MZ signals that no one else (particularly its competitors) perceives. This is what we call *responsive anticipation*. This same company, on the other hand, might itself create change, configuring what we call *creative anticipation*. The change, in this particular case, results from an action taken by the company in an attempt to shape the surrounding environment and to create entirely new, so far unimaginable, market realities.

Responsive anticipation constitutes a strategy focused on what others are (still) not seeing. The market often broadcasts signals that are true symptoms of future changes. Action based on these market hints or clues – before change actually takes place – constitutes a proactive behavior. When addressing this matter, we usually use an illustrative analogy: although signals do not appear painted on the walls, companies are able to read and interpret them, and to start acting in a proactive way, anticipating what will happen. Consider what Toyota did when conceiving the Prius hybrid car toward the end of the 1990s. The company was able, one decade earlier, to tune in to signals that pointed to society's growing concern with gaseous emissions by vehicles, and to devise a large latent market of consumers sensitive to ecologically appealing products. This anticipated vision gave Toyota a leadership position in the hybrid (gasoline and electricity-driven) car segment, placing the Japanese company ahead of giants like GM and Ford. While competitors were still trying to respond to demands, Toyota created a new market, anticipating future needs.

Note that responding to market signals, like Toyota did, does not mean the company is reactive: there is a fundamental difference between early and late responses. Observe that an anticipated response comes always before MZ (Figure 1.2); delayed, or reactive, responses, no matter how quick they are, always come after it. We could say that while reactive responses are responses in the past (they respond to a present that has already changed), anticipated responses are responses in present time (to a future that has not arrived yet). It is a matter of acting in anticipation of a future and predictable event, before being forced to act by it. Many auto makers produce hybrid cars today (a reactive response), but Toyota acted before them, based on signs of change (an anticipated response).

Let us now discuss creative anticipation. Here, companies create changes that were previously unimaginable, impacting on the market in an original way. Danone's introduction of Activia yogurt in Brazil in 2004 is an example of creative anticipation. It was a product that ended up remarkably changing consumers' needs (and is another outstanding market proactiveness example which we explore in this book). Danone did not firm up the idea of the product in response to market signals; rather the trigger was the company's strong orientation to changing customers' perceptions of when and why they should consume yogurt. They achieved this by constructing a new value proposal (that yogurt has therapeutic benefits to intestinal functions). Shortly after, Activia became a best-seller in the functional yogurt segment, a new product category Danone proactively created in the Brazilian market.

In brief, a company will be proactive if it is able to anticipate the MZ of the market, to respond to signs of change before the competition or to intentionally create change. That is why we define market proactiveness as the ability to anticipate a change in the market, deliberately creating it or acting on its first signs. A proactive market strategy always and invariably involves an anticipative action aimed at change.

We have developed a typology of four different categories of company, based on the way in which companies in each category act relative to the market's MZs. Let us now go on to consider this typology.

COMPANIES AND THE MOMENT ZERO

Companies do not all deal with the market's MZs in the same way. While some companies are well focused on anticipation, others, more reactive, usually establish their strategies around attempting to respond to environmental demands. A third kind, surprised by changes, responds too late to, or is even paralyzed by, the dynamics of the environment. We can use these different attitudes towards market's MZs to establish a typology of four different categories of companies (see Figure 1.3).

Let us start with those we call *afflicted companies* (who fall into the upper-right quadrant in the matrix). Such companies are not able to anticipate or respond to market changes. They are not even able to provide a late response. In other words, most of the time they cannot even be reactive, remaining inert and passive in face

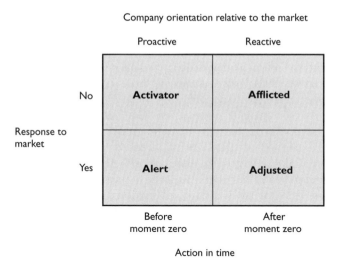

Company orientation relative to the market

	Proactive	Reactive
No	**Activator**	**Afflicted**
Yes	**Alert**	**Adjusted**

Response to market

Before moment zero   After moment zero

Action in time

Figure 1.3 Market proactiveness and four types of company

of the environmental dynamics. We call these companies "afflicted" because they suffer from their inability to respond to market moves. We could also say that an afflicted company is a reactive company that is unable even to respond (observe the matrix: despite the reactive orientation, it does not respond to the market). The question most relevant to afflicted companies is "What happened?" (See Box 1.1). These companies become afflicted because they are incapable of responding to change, reluctant to do so, or indifferent. When change comes, they remain inert, because they do not have the resources to adapt, because they are unwilling to accept the new reality or even because they want to hide from the change. Think of companies that have lost considerable market share or even disappeared: you will certainly be able to identify a moment of affliction in their trajectory.

Box 1.1 Four questions about change

Afflicted companies: What happened?
Adjusted companies: What is happening?
Alert companies: What will happen?
Activator companies: What do we want to happen?

It is important to note that the behavior of afflicted companies reflects more a lack of strategy than a genuine attitude to the environment (this is the reason we talked of three strategic attitudes and four types of company). This strategic dysfunction has a fundamental consequence for the meaning of market proactiveness. It discloses the fact that the opposite extreme to proactiveness is not reactiveness, as we might be inclined to think, but rather passiveness or inaction –

in other words, inability to adapt to environmental conditions. Reaction to market is a typical strategic posture which, in many situations, may be the best choice. Market reactiveness – as we will see – is not a negative approach in itself. How it works will depend on the administered dose and when it is applied.

Observe now what we call *adjusted companies* (those in the matrix's lower-right quadrant). Adjusted companies also act only after the MZ occurred, but differently from the afflicted, they do manage some action. Generally speaking, they try to respond to clients, competitors, and environmental movements as a whole, when the effects of these dynamics are already being intensely felt. They act only when forced to do so (as did all the large auto makers after being surprised by Toyota). It is true that there are extremely agile adjusted companies, capable of rather efficient adaptations. In many cases, a quick adaptation may be the best strategy. The problem with adjusted companies is that they are permanently on "red alert," a condition that may lead to precipitate decisions and expenditures.[22] Confronted with change and facing an unanticipated situation, adjusted companies can only ask themselves, "What is happening?"

Companies of a third type have the ability to detect signs of change well before their competitors. We call them *alert organizations* (they fall in the matrix's lower-left quadrant), because they are permanently monitoring the environment in search of hints and symptoms of change. This ability enables alert companies to guide themselves proactively in regard to the market, responding to MZs before they actually occur. Alert companies' sensitive radars become evident in their characteristic question, "What will happen?" Note that alert companies practice responsive anticipation: in other words, they respond to the market before they are forced to do so. Alert companies filter market noise to obtain relevant information, anticipating responses to opportunities or getting ready for threats brought about by MZs, and they do it before and better than their competitors. (In Chapter 4 we describe in detail how alert companies act to detect market signs.[23])

Finally, there is a type of company we call an *activator*. Observe that they act before MZs too, but not in response (they are in the matrix's upper-left quadrant). On the contrary, they literally try to create change in the market. Activator companies act in the present trying to create the future, generating their own MZ and revolutionizing markets from then on. They practice creative anticipation. Activators are guided by their strategists' strong beliefs in audacity, ambition, and the courage to pursue new opportunities. Accordingly, their characteristic question is "What do we want to happen?" (See Box 1.2). Instead of being taken by surprise, activator companies surprise, create options even before they are needed. Activator companies are the very epicenter of change. They ask novel questions, instead of trying to answer the same old questions. Instead of matching bets, activator companies deal the cards and command the game.

Obviously, the four types of company we have just presented should not be taken as perfect categories. Reality is made up of hues, not precise colors, and the exact position of any organization in the matrix will depend on its history, context, and specific contingencies. No company should be labeled afflicted, adjusted, alert, or activator simply because it adopted one of these positions in a given situation.

> **Box 1.2 Market proactiveness: what do CEOs think of it?**
>
> What does market proactiveness mean? We put this question to CEOs of many large companies operating in Brazil. It became clear that proactiveness before markets change represents a strategic asset for companies, and as such, it must be stimulated and developed. Besides the essential connotation of *anticipation*, market proactiveness was frequently related to attitudes connected to *audacity*, *ambition*, *courage*, and also to a certain *discomfort* in the behavior of top managements, indicating a strategic wish to perform more and to look for new challenges. Sérgio Chaia, CEO of Nextel – a mobile telephony operator with a very differentiated value proposal in the market – said, "proactiveness is the consequence of a positive nonconformism." For Gustavo Valle, Danone Brasil's former CEO, this nonconformism leads to the question, "Why shouldn't we want more?" For Romero Rodrigues, the young businessman who directs Buscapé – the most popular price comparison website operating in Brazil, acquired in 2009 by the South African media group Naspers for US$340 million – this nonconformism represents "ambition for projects." Finally, we believe that nobody has ever so precisely reconciled *audacity* with *anticipation* as Salim Mattar, CEO at Localiza Rent a Car, one of the world's most profitable and Latin America's largest car rental company: "Some companies wait until things happen to act. Others foresee what is going to happen and take the risk of acting before change." That is a statement in perfect harmony with the essence of market proactiveness.[24]

In other words, the categories we highlighted are not permanent and exclusive states or conditions: a company may be reactive at a given moment and proactive some other time, or even put both strategies into practice simultaneously (as we will see throughout this book). Much in the same way, a state of affliction may redirect a company's strategic thinking to more proactive horizons. We have observed, however, that companies end up showing a certain prevalence of one type of behavior when they orient themselves to the market. Proactive companies are those that, most of the time and most frequently, are able to behave in an anticipative way towards market conditions, showing traits and characteristics that are both proper and differentiating relative to competitors. We end this chapter by discussing this issue.

THE PROACTIVE COMPANY

Alert and activator companies are the main subjects of this book. They represent what we understand by proactive companies. They possess some fundamental characteristics that make them different from reactive companies (see Table 1.1), and synthesize everything we have discussed so far.

Proactive companies anticipate events, instead of reacting to them. They have a voluntaristic view of facts: that is, they believe that the environment can be shaped

Table I.I Fundamental differences between reactive and proactive companies

Reactive company	Proactive company
Reacts to events.	Anticipates events.
Is deterministic: the environment establishes the norms.	Is voluntarist: the company establishes the norms.
Sees the future as something to be forecast. The future happens tomorrow.	Sees the future as something to be built. The future happens today.
Tries to be the best player.	Tries to break the rules of the game.
Protects markets.	Defines markets.
Listens to the market.	Talks to the market.
Follows the market.	Guides the market.
Key words: adaptation, response, adequacy, complacency, protection, contingence, reaction, determinism, conformism, necessity.	Key words: anticipation, creation, conduction, transformation, choice, influence, stimulus, voluntarism, initiative, opportunity.
Motto: Seeing is believing.	Motto: Believing is seeing.

according to market strategies. In other words, reality can be constructed rather than simply accepted as something determined. Proactive companies' concept of the future is also different. For them, the future happens today, not tomorrow; hence it can be deliberately constructed. As we said, proactive companies try to break the rules of the competitive game, and in doing so, they automatically create a new game (whose rules they themselves dictate), where the chances of dominating the market grow exponentially.

In consequence, proactive companies end up defining markets, instead of only investing efforts in maintaining market share. They acquire the ability to speak to the market, instead of only hearing its demands. They guide, instead of being guided. Accordingly, the best definition of market proactiveness – which exposes a huge difference between proactive and other companies – is that of Fábio Barbosa, former president at Santander Brasil and now executive president at Abril S/A: "Contrary to the popular saying, for market proactiveness believing is seeing."[25] This definition presents, in a singular way, the motto of proactive companies.

Companies, however, do not become proactive by decree or simply because they wish to do so. The implementation of a proactive strategy requires the previous development of certain capabilities as well as the use of analytical tools and models to transform market proactiveness into concrete actions. This is our subject in the next part of this book.

ACTION TOOLS AND MODELS

2 The DNA of Market Proactiveness

So far, we have learned that anticipation is an essential element of market proactiveness. Proactive companies anticipate moments zero (MZs) in the environment, either responding to signs of change before it actually happens or intentionally creating change. The question now is how to change the anticipation mechanism we described into a real and tangible strategy. Strategy formulation and execution are the most important tasks in the scope of both managerial activities and market proactiveness. This is the main reason that we have always been engaged in the development of analytical tools that could help guide the development of proactive actions in the market, showing executives the path to construct and exercise their anticipatory strategies.

In essence, the formulation of a proactive market strategy differs from that of classical strategy in that it deals with what does not exist yet: that is, with a change that still has not occurred. Consequently, traditional strategic tools – the kind repeatedly presented in strategy and marketing books and manuals – are inadequate to support action based on proactive business logic.[1] While they are valuable instruments to help diagnose and analyze market structures, they are of little help when changing those structures is our goal. They are efficient tools in the hands of reactive strategists, but almost useless for managers interested in leading their companies on courses other than adaptation.

For that reason, we decided to elaborate a specific method of analysis that could effectively help those wishing to adopt the strategy to anticipate MZs in the market. To achieve that, we studied many different types of companies, from different economic sectors, trying to find out what made proactive companies different from others. We tracked successful progressions in regard with market proactiveness, closely evaluating how proactive strategic moves were constructed. We had the opportunity to field test the tools we developed, checking how they performed in the companies we studied. The resulting method includes practical tools and models to support the formulation of proactive strategies that can help companies escape a commonplace strategy of reactiveness. If your company is to abandon an exclusive focus on reactiveness and embrace more proactive strategies, you will need an integrated comprehension of the anticipatory mechanism presented in Chapter 1 and the models and tools presented in this chapter. We start by introducing the first action tool we have developed, the DNA model of market proactiveness.

THE DNA MODEL

The DNA model is the fundamental instrument in the formulation of proactive market strategy. More specifically, it represents the basic structure of a proactive strategy, combining **dimensions**, **levels**, and **actions** (which in our native Portuguese, produces the acronym DNA) to construct a strategy capable of anticipating the market's MZs. Just like biological DNA, which contains all the information necessary to generate living beings and make them functional, the DNA of market proactiveness contains all the essential information to formulate and execute a proactive strategy. It is our prescription for changing the concept of market proactiveness into an actual strategy, and it will be used throughout this book.[2] Once you understand the mechanism of the DNA model, you will understand how a proactive market strategy is formulated and effectively put into practice.

In the construction of a proactive market strategy (PMS), the DNA model answers the three most fundamental questions faced by managers when they try to anticipate MZs (see Figure 2.1). First, they must ask themselves from what perspective the company should act. In other words, in what direction should the strategy aim? At products? At competitors? At clients? At the business model? Put differently, in what field should the company act to proactively impact the market? Second, they must ask themselves how to identify the elements that compose each individual perspective. For instance, it is relatively simple to determine that the company will try to be proactive regarding its offer, but what does it mean precisely? What elements ultimately compose a company's offer, and what can be proactively developed in regard to them? Or else, what can be anticipated concerning competitive forces acting on the sector a company operates or with regard to clients? Finally, those responsible for a company's strategy have to decide on actions capable of putting strategic thinking to work. Accordingly, they ask themselves, what actions differentiate a proactive company from others?

As you can see from Figure 2.1, the three stages of the DNA model correspond to these three fundamental questions. The dimensions are related to the perspective from which the company will act in order to be proactive; the levels, to the elements

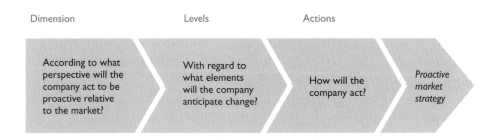

Figure 2.1 The DNA of market proactiveness

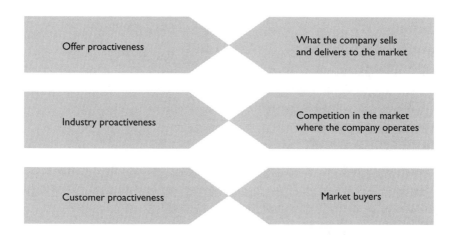

Figure 2.2 The three dimensions of market proactiveness and focus of action

to be worked at in each dimension; and actions, to the way the company will act to carry out a planned strategy. Consequently, the formulation of a PMS ultimately expresses a company's strategic choice in terms of dimensions, levels, and actions. In this book we will identify generic dimensions, levels, and actions – applicable to any context and any type of company – capable of putting market proactiveness into practice.

DIMENSIONS OF MARKET PROACTIVENESS

As we just explained, the first question to be answered when formulating a proactive market strategy is related to the company's focus of action. We identified three distinct dimensions where market proactiveness may be activated, and named them *offer proactiveness*, *industry proactiveness*, and *customer proactiveness*. These dimensions constitute the three ways through which market proactiveness can be put into practice. They represent the backbone of every anticipatory strategy. Each dimension concentrates the company's strategic effort on a particular focus of action (see Figure 2.2).

Hence, the focus of offer proactiveness is on what a company sells and delivers to the market: in other words, what it offers to buyers. The focus of industry proactiveness is competition in the market in which a company operates.[3] Finally, the focus of customer proactiveness is buyers in the market supplied by the company and its competitors.[4]

The three dimensions described are independent and exhaustive. They are independent because they can occur individually. That is, despite the fact that the three dimensions are important to understand the full extent of market proactiveness, a proactive company does not necessarily need to make strategic efforts in all three dimensions. And they are exhaustive because we believe they encompass every conceivable proactive market strategy. Although the exact distinctions between the dimensions is sometimes uncertain – between offer proactiveness and customer proactiveness, for instance – what is important here is that anticipation of market's MZs will always take place in one of the three dimensions described. We find difficult to imagine any market-oriented strategic action that cannot be classified in one of these three dimensions. Out theoretical and field research has convinced us that there is no fourth dimension of relevance here.

WHY THREE DIMENSIONS?

We often asked executives to describe the market strategy their companies had elaborated in the previous year.[5] They almost always mentioned actions related to services and products, to competitors, to business partners (suppliers and distributors), and to customers. We then encouraged executives to indicate a market strategy that could not ultimately be reduced to one of these categories. We consistently received confirmation that these paths encompass all marketing strategies. We have a very simple explanation for the difficulty executives find in conceiving different paths to market strategy formulation: they simply do not exist. All that can be done in terms of market strategy is ultimately restricted to actions related to what the company offers, the industry where it operates, or the buyers in its market.

This is also true with respect to market proactiveness. In our interviews, we asked almost 100 executives and CEOs how would it be possible to carry out a proactive strategy in practice. Invariably, their answers converged on products and services, competitors, suppliers and distributors, and customers. We also noticed that all the actions that are usually considered as sources of proactiveness by the specialized literature – although it often uses different terminology – turned out to be related to at least one of these three dimensions.[6] When we look past the apparent diversity implied by the variety of terminology, we can clearly see that the paths to strategy building are not as diverse as you might imagine. Hence, a proactive market strategy deals, ultimately, with what a company offers to the market and the forces that immediately act on that offer; in other words, the players in the segment or industry in which a company competes, and the buyers targeted by the offer.

The notion that market proactiveness is a strategy focused on offer, industry, or customer has four important implications. First, it avoids any waste of managers' strategic energy and the time they have available to formulate strategy, both of which are valuable and limited resources. Second, it concentrates the flow of resources and competencies exclusively on the chosen field of action, maximizing them and literally helping the company to do more with less. Third, it keeps the attention of those involved with the company's strategy coherently directed to the planned focus. Fourth, and lastly, it conveys a clear and easily understandable reasoning, avoiding what we call "complexity distancing," a posture of subtle withdrawal from responsibilities people adopt when they interpret a company's strategy as complicated or confusing.

To put proactiveness into practice, however, we need to do more than merely delimit a company's focus of action. It is also necessary to recognize the formative elements of each dimension, choosing one or more dimensions that give the company better chances to carry out the chosen proactive strategy. To accomplish that, strategists will have to make use of the DNA model's second stage, which we call "levels of market proactiveness."

LEVELS OF MARKET PROACTIVENESS

If dimensions are the main stem of the DNA model, levels represent its ramifications. In other words, they represent the specific paths or alternatives a company has to define its proactive strategy with regard to offer, industry, or customer. In our model, these paths amount to six levels of action, two for each dimension of market proactiveness (see Figure 2.3).

Initially, proactive actions might be designed in the realm of standard and complementary supplies, the two levels we have defined for the offer dimension. In the industry dimension, market proactiveness could be conducted on the levels of competition dynamics and regulatory mechanisms. Finally, for the customer dimension, the company might act on the levels of customers' preferences and needs.

As far as the levels are concerned, a proactive posture refers to two questions that are fundamental to enable anticipation of the market's MZs. The first question makes companies think of what is within the analyzed level, and at the same time, ask what can be changed there. This focus on "existing reality" leads companies to the first basic action of market proactiveness: the **change**. The second question focuses on what we call "nonexistent reality." We use these apparently incongruous words because we understand that reality often does already exist, but it does so latently, waiting to be unveiled. The focus on nonexistent reality calls for a second fundamental action of market proactiveness: **generation**. Thus, change and generation constitute the two fundamental actions of market proactiveness: that is, the third stage of the DNA model.

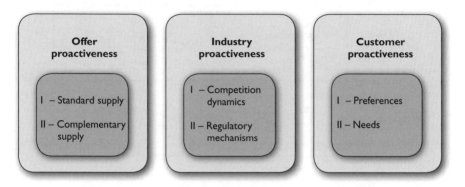

Figure 2.3 The six levels of market proactiveness

MARKET PROACTIVENESS ACTIONS

We have already described market competition as a game with established rules that reactive companies do their best to follow (always responding to given rules, however). Generation and change actions prompt companies to do exactly the opposite. When a company focuses on the existing reality, trying to change it, it is in fact trying to redefine old rules in a completely new way. It then asks itself what exists and what can be changed. At the same time, when it focuses on what does not exist yet, trying to create new market realities, the company is in fact trying to define novel rules and subvert those currently practiced. It asks itself what there is that does not exist yet but could be generated. (See Box 2.1.)

Box 2.1 The two fundamental questions of proactive actions

What does not exist but could be generated?
   (Define new rules)
What does exist and could be changed?
   (Redefine old rules)

While these two fundamental questions of proactive action lead companies to think of the reality that surrounds them and the realities that could possibly exist, the related actions of change and generation stimulate companies to act effectively. Laid over each dimension's described levels, the questions and actions synthesize the possibilities of acting on the market proactively. These possibilities can perhaps better visualized with the help of the generate–modify matrix we have developed (see Figure 2.4).

As we can see, generation actions act on the nonexistent reality, stimulating the company to think of what could be generated in the two levels of dimension under analysis. Change or modification actions, in their turn, focus on the existing reality

	Existing reality	Nonexistent reality
Level I (offer, industry, customer)	What does exist and can be changed?	What does not exist and can be generated?
Level II (offer, industry, customer)	What does exist and can be changed?	What does not exist and can be generated?
	Change	Generation

Figure 2.4 The generate–modify matrix

and on what can be changed in regard to these levels. Besides helping companies make a diagnosis of proactive strategic possibilities on each level, the generate–modify matrix unveils to the company its own mental strategic model. In practice, this means that executives, when attempting to fill out the matrix's quadrants, are not only analyzing opportunities for proactive action, but also sensing the inherent difficulties of the process, and consequently asking themselves what these difficulties mean. In one of the companies we worked with, for instance, it became very clear that the managers and leaders had difficulties in conceiving of potential realities and articulating the possibility of their existence. This urged the company to review the way it managed competencies, aligning management with more proactive strategic practices (In Part II of the book we address more specifically the capabilities needed to pursue market proactiveness.) Exercises like this make companies aware of reactive paradigms and ways of acting, which might otherwise not be clear. They usually constitute hidden barriers to the construction of challenging strategies such as proactive market strategies.

We will now analyze the application of the generate–modify matrix in all three dimensions of market proactiveness; in other words, how generation and change proactive actions can be put into practice effectively in the realms of offer, industry, and customers.

PROACTIVENESS ACTIONS CONCERNED WITH THE ORGANIZATION'S OFFER

Offers are the way to deliver a benefit to the market. The bigger the benefits appear to buyers – that is, the greater the advantages and gains buyers associate with a given product or service – the higher the value proposal of the offer.[7] Thus, we could say that benefit is the essence of what we usually call offer. Proactive strategies operate on benefits delivered to the market, by means of what we call *standard supply* and *complementary supply*. The standard supply represents the main benefit delivered to the market by a company's products and services; it is what is commonly meant by a by sectoral basic offer.[8] People go to bookstores to buy books; guests expect above all that a hotel will offer them comfortable beds and good showers. But the value of an offer has other components besides the main benefit. The customers of a bookstore might have the additional benefit of buying books in a pleasant and cozy environment that invites them to stay for a couple of hours, absorbed in reading and enjoying a cappuccino. A hotel stay can also be complemented by facilities that range from a choice of cable TV stations to an international restaurant operating 24 hours a day. Thus, the complementary supply represents benefits that are linked to the standard supply and impact on the value a company delivers to the market.

We will use some preliminary examples to clarify this point. First, think of the iPad, an innovative offer conceived by Apple, which launched at the beginning of 2010 and sold a million units in the three months following its introduction to the market. Customers ran to shops to buy it because the iPad represented a new category of tablet computer; it was not just another laptop, with a few additional features. It was "Much more personal than a laptop; much more powerful than an intelligent telephone," according to its creator Steve Jobs. The iPad generated a new standard offer in the computer industry, confirming Apple's ability to anticipate the market.[9]

Consider now the Havaianas rubber sandals produced by Alpargatas, one of the most successful products in the history of the Brazilian shoe industry (in the 1990s, the company achieved the landmark of 60 million pairs sold per year). Despite this huge success, Alpargatas did not resign itself to simply keeping on supplying the market in the same way (as is perhaps a typical behavior of reactive companies). Proactively challenging the reality of the offer, the company repositioned the brand Havaianas in a completely innovative way, creating models, shapes, and colors that changed what had been a popular utility product into a fashionable item. This proactive strategy changed the sectoral standard supply, renewed the brand's success in Brazil, and opened doors for Alpargatas abroad. Márcio Utsch, Alpargatas's CEO, emphasized the power of this proactive innovation: "we invented and reinvented the Havaianas and no one is able to imitate us."[10] Note the distinction between these two examples: while Apple created and introduced a new offer to the market, Alpargatas changed an already existing offer. These are two distinct types of action, but the intention is the same in both: to anticipate market change.

In the sphere of complementary supply, observe the case of the McCafé. Developed at the beginning of the 1990s by giant food chain McDonald's, this proactive strategy generated a new complementary supply in the highly competitive fast-food market. The McCafé offered consumers a varied menu of beverages based on gourmet coffee and side orders of tarts, croissants, brownies, and cookies. It provided appealing rooms with comfortable seats, located next to the chain's traditional restaurants, charged prices slightly below those of competitors such as Starbucks, and generated higher margins than McDonald's established offer of burgers and savory snacks. The McCafé concept opened a door to the profitable coffee shop market for McDonald's. The McCafé chain has now approximately 2,000 locations in more than 30 countries.

Now let's think of the activities of the French group Accor, which operates in the hotel industry. Accor innovated by segmenting its offer, providing a range of different brands, and starting from a lower price/offer level than other chains. For Formule 1 and Ibis, the two lowest-priced chains, it chose to drop complementary benefits, such as room service and porters to carry guests' luggage, which had been regarded as indispensable. By creating a new perception of value and benefits, Accor constructed an important MZ in the hotel industry.

You will notice that the examples we have presented can be classified according to the four distinct quadrants of the generate–modify matrix (see Figure 2.5). Alpargatas and iPad acted proactively on the standard supply, although they started with different types of action: for Alpargatas, modification of an existing product, and for Apple, presenting a new product category. The same happened with McDonald's and the Accor group in the realm of complementary supply: McCafé could be considered as a new type of complementary offer, and the Accor branding as modification of the existing complementary offer.

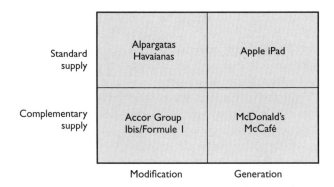

Figure 2.5 Examples of proactive actions concerning the organization's offer

Major MZs in the sphere of the offer can end up determining the rules of demand in that sector for a long time, until they are overtaken by another proactive generation or modification, perhaps launched by a different company – that is, by a new MZ. This happened, for instance, in the domestic videocassette industry towards the end of the 1970s, when Sony's Betamax standard was supplanted by rival Matsushita's offer, the VCR system. In other situations, however, the offer MZ so unequivocally determines the rules of demand that it might seem almost impossible to replace the corresponding product: think for example of the Microsoft Windows operating system. Today, the life-cycle of a standard supply seems more and more ephemeral in many fields. Consumers are conditioned to expect quick changes in the offer in economic sectors such as mobile telephony, automobiles, and digital music. Here, the craze for innovation seems to grow geometrically.[11] In the pharmaceutical industry, the development of specific market niches such as the third age segment makes the sector's standard supply more and more volatile: it is marked by a continuous introduction of new medicines.

So as we have seen, the offer battlefield is a fertile terrain for market proactiveness. The offer dimension is where proactive companies are able to anticipate market MZs in intentional and unusual ways. In Part III of this book we discuss in more depth the types of proactive action concerned with offer, but let us now go on to explain how to apply the generate–modify matrix in the realm of industry.

PROACTIVE ACTIONS CONCERNED WITH THE INDUSTRY

If competition starts with companies' offers, it is in the industry dimension that it develops. The industry – or sector – is the arena where companies compete for buyers. Historically, the structure of an industry has been seen as a determining force in the strategic behavior of companies, one of the causes of the reactive nature of a typical strategy, as described in Chapter 1.[12] With the concept of market proactiveness, we propose a new approach to the matter. We would suggest that the definition of an industry is no longer an absolute that determines strategic positioning, a kind of environmental straitjacket which ultimately defines how companies compete. The logic of proactiveness does not condemn managers and strategists to simply ensure that a company adjusts to the conditions prevailing in the sector it which it operates. Let us see how it can take a different approach.

For almost any company, in any industry, there will be three types of key player it must consider: its competitors, suppliers, and distributors. The structure and behavior of these players in the industry determine what we call the dynamics of competition. In addition, another force acts on the dynamics of competition: regulatory mechanisms. Thus, the dynamics of competition and regulatory mechanisms are the two levels on which market proactiveness influences the industry dimension. In the domain of the dynamics of competition, proactive actions focus on the structure and behavior of competitors, suppliers, and distributors. In the sphere of regulatory mechanisms, the focus falls on the obstacles and facilitating factors that normalize activity in the industry. It is with regard to these elements that the two key actions of market proactiveness – which are, of course, generation and change – will be implemented.

Let us first analyze competition, starting with competition dynamics, the most obvious issue to be evaluated when formulating a strategy. The structure and behavior of competitors are modified, for instance, when a company adopts a vigorous strategy that ends up "forcing" competitors to act in the same way. This happened when traditional bookstores were forced to enter the online book sales market following the arrival of Amazon.com. This also happens when a major competitor adopts an aggressive strategy of acquisition, dominates the market and then dictates its rules. It happens too when two powerful competitors join forces and create a new reality in the market. The reconfiguration of the Brazilian beverage market after the creation of Ambev illustrates this idea. The new company dramatically changed the prevailing competition model, heavily impacting on the structures and behavior of the competition from then on. Finally, the generation of new competitive structures may be also detected in what we call "competition creation," when a company introduces a new brand name in an extremely concentrated industry. This is usually aimed at inhibiting participation in the market by potential competitors that are attracted by the low level of competition. The strategy makes the company a competitor against itself before new entrants can compete with it.

In the sphere of distributors, structures and behaviors are changed when a company advances in the value chain and starts to distribute its own offers. This can be observed in own-store and franchise models in sectors such as cosmetics and perfumes, clothing, and designer furniture. Hering, a very well-known centenarian Brazilian company, famous in the country's clothing industry, did exactly that (as of 1997, more than 5 billion units of a traditional cotton T-shirt, one of the company's iconic products, had been produced). From 1993, the company dramatically redefined its distribution model and started to retail its products through a chain of franchised stores. Hering Store has now more than 250 shops, a proactive action that strongly and positively impacted both brand penetration and the organization's results, as was confirmed by CEO Fábio Hering: "control of points of sale meant stronger market presence of the brand and higher profitability."[13] The generation of new distribution structures and behaviors can also be noticed in innovations such as the online selling of music, videos, books, and computers, a proactive action targeted at distribution that has remarkably changed the previous business models prevailing in these markets.

A marked example of generation of new behaviors in distributors – a term that includes other agents such as producers and end consumers – is the Swedish Tetra Pak, at the time when it introduced long-life milk containers in Brazil, 20 years ago. These containers enabled a milk distribution process operating at ambient temperatures, while previously pasteurized milk had had to be chilled for distribution. To implement the new concept, the company had to overcome barriers and generate favorable behaviors along the several stages of the supply chain. Tetra Pak's proactive action changed reality and secured more than a 90 percent share of the huge Brazilian market. This hegemonic position was achieved by means of a decision to change the established rules of competition dynamics. Paulo Nigro, Tetra Pak's CEO in Brazil, explained, "we have been long-life milk's category driver in Brazil and moved the whole value chain in this direction."[14]

In the supplier field, new structures and behaviors may be generated when companies integrate their supply chain. This can be implemented by simply acquiring a supplier or by integrating functions previously performed by suppliers. Casas Bahia, a large Brazilian retail chain, adopted this strategy and now produces most of the furniture it sells. At the same time, suppliers also change their structures and behaviors in response to substantial modifications by companies of their supply policies. The Japanese Toyota and the Swedish IKEA, for instance, are good examples of companies that radically changed the supply model in their sectors, introducing a collaborative relationship strategy with suppliers.[15]

Competition dynamics, however, is not entirely a free for all. Regulatory mechanisms constantly exert a sensible influence over the structure and behavior of competitors, suppliers, and distributors. The government provides the most obvious and relevant regulatory mechanisms, but the growing impact of actions by other bodies that can act as regulators, such as labor unions, consumer protection entities, non-governmental associations, and interest groups, should not be neglected. Obstacles and facilitation are the two basic types of sectorial regulatory mechanism a company may proactively act upon.

By obstacles, we mean everything that limits competition. This is most apparent in very heavily regulated industries such as the tobacco, health care, and pharmaceutical segments. Think, for instance, of the role played by regulatory mechanisms in the behavior of the pharmaceutical industry, and of the growing restrictions imposed on cigarette and alcoholic beverage advertisements. By facilitation we mean the opposite, mechanisms that promote and stimulate competition. The deregulation of sectors such as aviation and telecommunications provides recent examples of facilitation.

Proactive companies may promote the modification of existing obstacles, as Southwest Airlines did in the North American aviation market, when it succeeded in changing the regulations that limited its activities in the segment.[16] Sometimes proactiveness in regard to regulatory mechanisms results from the joint action of companies in the sector. This happens, for instance, when a group of companies combine and try to persuade governments or other representative organizations to create obstacles that will protect their market against attacks from foreign competitors, or to obtain other benefits. As for facilities, facilitators may be created to promote the growth of a company's market share. The multinational WEG, one of the largest Latin-American electric motor producers headquartered in Brazil, did exactly that. Towards the end of the 1960s the company was able to introduce metric-standard motors in the Brazilian market, while until then the market would only accept the North American standard, in inches. It achieved this by prompting the industry's regulatory agency to introduce new regulations.[17] Changes in facilities happen when a company is able to favorably modify an existing facilitator, for instance extending exploitation licenses, improving the conditions of an incentive, or obtaining deferment for payments to the government.

We can analyze the examples mentioned using the generate–modify matrix (see Figure 2.6). On the level of regulatory mechanisms, note that while WEG acted to create facilities to enable its operation in the market, Southwest removed a legal obstacle that hindered its activities. On the level of competition dynamics, observe that Tetra Pak generated favorable behavior towards its new packaging, while Ambev modified the current market structure. So we have four distinct examples but one common objective: to anticipate an MZ in the market by acting on the industry.

As in the case of offer, proactive actions on an industry provide a promising area for the anticipation of market changes. In Part II of this book, we will also analyze in more depth proactive actions in this dimension, presenting other companies that were able to proactively change competition dynamics and regulatory mechanisms. Let us now finally analyze the generate–modify matrix in the customer dimension.

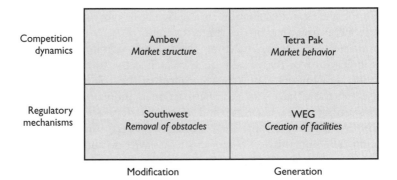

Figure 2.6 Proactive actions on an industry

PROACTIVE ACTIONS ON CUSTOMERS

In the realm of customers, organizations can be proactive by acting to change customers' preferences and needs, the two levels of the customer dimension we elaborated. By preference, we mean the choice of one product or service rather than another, as when we opt to try a certain washing powder, or when a new offer persuades buyers to change their consumption decisions. By needs we mean that there is a gap between what customers are currently offered and what they would like to purchase. For instance, a new product or service might on introduction be perceived as important or indispensable, changing consumption habits. Both preferences and needs are reflections of human behavior, and they are therefore sensitive to companies' anticipatory actions.

The Amazon.com case may be one of the most remarkable examples of a proactive strategic action on consumers' preferences. Despite the radical redesign of retail sales and distribution structures, the essential element of the company's success lies in the generation of new consumption preferences. Amazon.com changed the way people used to purchase goods and created a new and then-inexistent preference in consumption, typically adopting a proactive customer strategy based on generation.

In the same way, analyze Natura's proactive strategy. This company is a leader in the Brazilian cosmetics, fragrances, and personal hygiene markets. When it introduced the Chronos line of face creams, it acted in a way that was radically different from how the industry normally approached female customers. Advertising has historically focused on creating the appearance of youthfulness, but Chronos emphasized a more holistic concept of beauty, encouraging women to "live in peace" with their own appearance, and have a good relationship with their age. As Alessandro Carlucci, the company's CEO, says, "Natura was able to see the market through different lenses, challenging all prevailing beauty stereotypes in the industry."[18] Often, proactiveness is a matter not so much of seeing something distant, but rather of looking differently at what is close at hand.

Note that while Natura acted to modify an existing preference – in the consumption of cosmetics by women – Amazon.com awoke what had been a dormant preference, the online purchase of goods (see Figure 2.7). True, Amazon.com was not the first company to enter the online direct sales market, but it was the one that created the intensity and amplitude of a significant MZ. As we shall see repeatedly throughout this book, market proactiveness does not necessarily mean being first in the field (although many proactive companies are pioneers). Often the actual pioneers are unable to collect the fruits of what they planted, and it is a successor that capitalizes on their groundwork.

Let us now analyze the generate–modify matrix with regard to consumption needs. Here, proactive actions may focus on both existing needs and latent needs: that is, needs which had been hidden from the market. For instance, a company could create a new pattern of consumption that modifies customers' understanding of what they actually need. This is what Danone did in the Brazilian yogurt market, when it introduced Activia (Chapter 11 discusses this example in detail). People already had their own sense of how much yogurt they wanted to

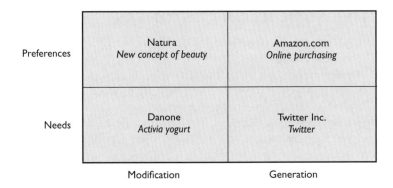

Figure 2.7 Examples of proactive actions on customers

consume, but Danone persuaded them that they needed much more, in order to help with gastrointestinal problems. Activia became a tremendous success, not only because of its proven therapeutic properties, but also because the company was so successful in influencing and educating potential consumers. Its open, empathetic, and convincing language communicated its new offer extremely powerfully.

With regard to latent needs, Twitter is an obvious example. The virtual network created by North American Jack Dorsey in 2006 is now an omnipresent reality in the life of thousands of people. Twitter seduced thousands of internauts and materialized their need – which until then had been latent – to follow people and organizations online. This proactive action was based on the generation of a new consumption need (see Figure 2.7). At the time of writing, Twitter was attracting on average more than 60 million visits per month. The example illustrates how dormant needs can be a real reservoir of opportunities for proactive action, exactly because they are unknown to both consumers and companies. They are mature needs, just waiting for companies to pick up on them, as in the case of Twitter.

We could provide many other examples of proactive actions on the levels of preferences and needs. Part III specifically analyzes customer proactiveness, thoroughly exploring the levels of preference and needs.

So now we have outlined the DNA model and given a sense of how it can be applied on the different levels of offer, industry, and customer. Different combinations of dimensions, levels, and actions correspond to different ways of acting proactively towards the market. Briefly, this outlines the strategic sequence adopted by a company in terms of the DNA model. The configuration of possible sequences might be seen more clearly in Figure 2.8.

Now that we know all the possible ways to formulate a proactive market strategy, we need to choose a strategic sequence to follow. Obviously, every company will choose the sequence – or sequences – that its executives feel present the best chances of strategic success. But how can they be sure? How will the company decide whether it will do best to focus on the offer, the industry, or the customer? And even after choosing one of these alternatives, at which level should the company act and how? What will guide the company through these choices?

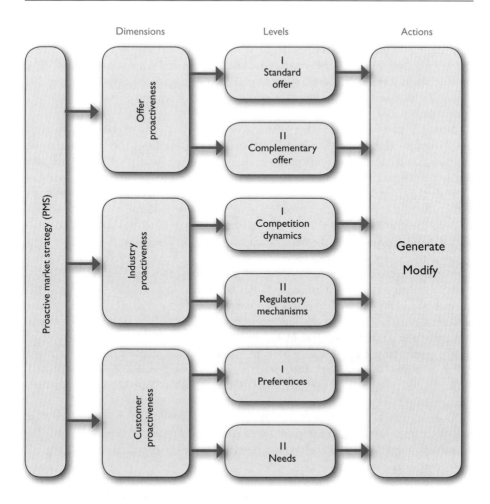

Dimensions   Levels   Actions

Proactive market strategy (PMS)

Offer proactiveness

I
Standard
offer

II
Complementary
offer

Industry proactiveness

I
Competition
dynamics

II
Regulatory
mechanisms

Customer proactiveness

I
Preferences

II
Needs

Generate

Modify

Figure 2.8 Possible sequences in the formulation of a proactive market strategy

To help companies answer these questions, we prepared a complementary tool to the DNA model and the generate–modify matrix: the moment zero matrix, a fundamental tool in the formulation of a proactive market strategy. This tool will help determine the strategic sequence to be followed by the company.

THE MOMENT ZERO MATRIX

Imagine any market: the one in which your company operates, for instance. First, consider how it is now. What products and services does it offer? How does competition play out among its participants? How do customers behave? When you do that, you are sketching the market's current reality. In doing so you will identify past MZs: that is, changes that have already occurred that are still impacting on companies. The current market reality is ultimately the mirror of all the significant changes that have occurred and that, in some way, continue to determine companies' behaviors. But we all know that reality is not static. Every market also has a past. These bygone realities encompass what we call **past MZs**: products and services that have been overtaken by new offers, extinct competitive dynamics, consumption preferences and needs that have since changed radically, and so on.

Now go on to consider what market realities could exist *beyond* the concrete and tangible reality you sketched. First, evaluate possibilities that you are aware of, but that have not yet impacted on the market: in other words, realities that are still not in existence, but that could be sending signals of coming changes. We call these undetermined realities. In other words, they are realities that we can presume will materialize at some point, but we do not know when or where, or even the impact they will have. Within this undetermined reality we find what we call **pulsating MZs**: unnoticed demands, new and latent consumer behaviors, approaching changes in the structure of competition. Finally, think of the realities that could be created by the company: that is, things that are currently no more than speculations or abstractions, but that could become realities. They are what we call uncertain realities; in effect no one knows if they will ever happen. These uncertain realities – which are today pure ideas in the heads of strategists – contain what we have named **potential MZs**.

To understand how MZs behave in its sector, a company must put many different kinds of knowledge into practice, one for each reality being diagnosed. This structure of realities and attitudes is the focus of the MZ matrix we have developed (see Figure 2.9).

The matrix's horizontal axis represents the four dimensions of reality we have just described and the corresponding types of MZ. The vertical axis represents the four cognitive attitudes the company needs to adopt, depending on the type of MZ being studied.

The company must then explore potential MZs building hypotheses about their existence. To explore potential MZs means, in brief, to believe that new realities could be created by a company's transformative action. The company must also track pulsating MZs, trying, in an anticipatory way, to detect signals they might be emitting. This means being alert to every hint of change that is sent out before the change actually materializes. The company must also analyze current MZs and examine the reality it is presently facing from an anticipatory viewpoint. This does not mean examining reality in order to respond to changes that have already occurred, but anticipating change in the reality being analyzed. Finally, the company must look at past MZs, and take in the lessons they have to offer. This activity helps strategists to recognize the pattern of changes in their market. It is like looking through the rearview mirror while also watching what is coming up on the road ahead.

When putting into practice these four attitudes, the company will be promoting an important displacement. Instead of trying to answer old strategic questions (What are the current buyers' needs? Where are competitors going now? What key factors are important for performance? What company's prices are competitive?),

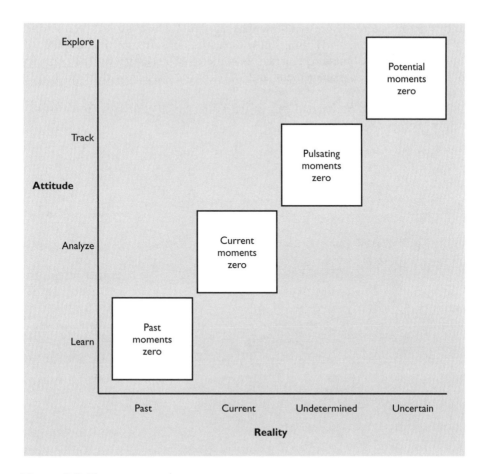

Figure 2.9 The moment zero matrix

it will pose entirely new questions. These are questions that lead to an broader and more open view of reality: they are unlikely to generate automatic and instantaneous answers. What signals indicate that changes are likely to occur? What changes can a company effect on the market? What do the past and current realities of the market teach us? These are good questions. Even if they cannot immediately be answered, they will be more valuable in the construction of market proactiveness than worn-out answers to the same old questions.

The MZ matrix, the generate–modify matrix, and the DNA model constitute the tool set necessary to formulate a proactive market strategy. In practice, market proactiveness will always involve taking action to modify the current situation or generate a new situation, after realities have been analyzed according to the six levels of proactiveness we have presented.

A mere decision, however, does not ensure that a company will be proactive. To develop a proactive market strategy is one thing; to put it into practice and make it function successfully is something else. We have found that the ability to do this depends directly on some essential capacities, which are real prerequisites for market proactiveness. Without these capacities, any attempt to anticipate will fail even before it is put into practice. It is therefore necessary for the company to practice proactive management and develop the capacities that can help it anticipate change.

We now come to the second part of the book, which addresses these issues of market proactiveness management.

Part II

Managing Market Proactiveness

ORGANIZING THE COMPANY FOR MARKET PROACTIVENESS

3 The Capacities of a Proactive Company

The implementation of planned strategies remains one of the toughest challenges faced by a company, the Achilles' heel of strategic management. Most managers and executives are convinced that it is easier to formulate good strategies than to ensure their proper execution. Historical data on the success of strategies agrees with them.[1] This is so because strategy implementation is a complex activity that depends on factors ranging from the ability to manage people and processes to the usually difficult task of promoting organizational change. This is why so many strategies fail: all the variables that impact on their implementation must be managed continuously.

The same happens to market proactiveness. Since we began our studies, we have noticed the presence of elements that can inhibit or even completely obstruct implementation of proactive strategies. Unaddressed attitudes and behaviors may lead a company to give up anticipatory ideas even before they are put into practice. Such elements act as viruses, attacking market proactiveness. Companies must develop antibodies to escape their effects and prevent them from spreading irreversibly, becoming an epidemic. These antibodies constitute what we call capacities for market proactiveness. We studied these capacities and how they could be developed.

We ended up identifying a group of capacities we thought to be essential to make market proactiveness happen. These capacities are more related to how a company "feels" and what it "believes" than to what the company actually does. Therefore, they involve more than simple operational decisions or actions, being more akin to organizational behavioral and cultural aspects. If market proactiveness were the mere result of an operational process, it would be easy to implement it in companies, but the reality is very different. Thus, we would emphasize that proactive actions will be inconsistent and lack efficacy if they are not anchored by a company's real disposition to anticipate changes in the market. This willingness to act is directly dependent on the capacities for market proactiveness. These capacities are necessary to enable a company to build what we call a *culture of proactiveness*, a condition where the organization regards proactiveness as a value to be developed and shared. Changing a proactive market strategy into concrete actions is very difficult in the absence of such cultural perspective.[2]

We often say that willingness is what determines action, and not the reverse. Willingness is essential to action. For instance, we have seen many companies formulate their proactive strategies only to eventually hesitate in assuming the inherent risks. Sometimes these companies even try to carry out a planned strategy but then retreat at the slightest sign of uncertainty. This difficulty in handling risk (one of the capacities we explore) eventually turns out to impair proactive strategic attempts. Just like a mountaineer who gives up the climb as the first challenges appear, these companies lack a real disposition to be proactive. Hence, it is fundamental that they develop the capacities necessary to give substance to anticipatory strategic actions; it is essential that they develop abilities that help them become more proactive toward the market.

THE CAPACITIES OF A PROACTIVE COMPANY

In our research, we identified eight different capacities for market proactiveness:[3]

1 Capacity for dealing with risk.
2 Capacity for dealing with mistakes.
3 Capacity for visualizing future realities.
4 Capacity for managing short-term pressure.
5 Capacity for proactively innovating.
6 Capacity for managing in a flexible way.
7 Capacity for proactively leading.
8 Capacity for identifying and developing proactive people.

The effective exercise of these eight capacities reveals a new way of thinking, a proactive mindset different from what we find in companies aimed exclusively at responding to the market's demands. This new mindset is essential to the execution of proactive strategies, and above all, to achieve positive results. Observe the differences between proactive and reactive mentalities in regard to the eight listed capacities (in Table 3.1).

First, note that proactive companies deal with risk and mistakes in a totally different way from reactive companies. In a proactive way of thinking, risk taking is considered as inherent to change processes, and is therefore encouraged. A different approach may be observed in reactive companies, where pressure for results – and fear of inherent risks – often hinders the search for opportunities for change, keeping the company stuck in the grooves of reactiveness. This dichotomy is also evident with regard to mistakes. A reactive discourse, even one advocating a non-conservative position, is no longer sustainable when mistakes and faults in execution begin to be criticized vehemently. On the other hand, companies with a more proactive mindset approach mistakes as learning and growth opportunities, and avoid expressing disapproval of them.

Proactive and reactive mindsets also correspond to very different strategic visions

Table 3.1 Differences between proactive and reactive mindsets

Capacities	Reactive mindset	Proactive mindset
How does the company deal with risk?	The urge for immediate financial results inhibits risk taking.	The company encourages risk taking in the search for change.
How are mistakes handled?	In theory faults are accepted but mistakes are actually punished.	Mistakes are regarded as learning and growth opportunities.
When formulating its strategies, does the company consider future realities?	The strategic perspective is centered on current threats and opportunities.	The company is continuously trying to imagine new market realities.
Does pressure for short-term results hinder anticipation of the future?	Future gains are less important than current results.	Current results are often sacrificed for future gains.
Is innovation a market-driven process?	Usually innovation is an answer to market demands.	Innovation is a process aimed at breaking current market patterns.
Do excessive bureaucracy and rules inhibit the free flow of ideas?	The operational *status quo* obstructs presentation of new approaches and ideas.	People are free to express their ideas and opinions.
What is the leadership style?	Traditional leadership focused on control and hierarchy.	Transformative leadership based on autonomy and freedom.
How does the company regard proactiveness at the level of individuals?	Proactiveness is an innate trait.	Proactiveness must be stimulated and developed.

of the future. While proactive mindsets produce strategies that continuously look for nonexistent realities, reactive approaches still focus on current opportunities and threats to build strategy. Reactive mindsets still regard the future as less important because of what we call short-term pressure, a reality within which present pressures end up weakening the faith in future potential gains. Proactive companies, on the contrary, understand that it is often necessary to sacrifice gains in the present to benefit from greater future profits.

The process of innovation also presents stark contrasts between proactive and reactive ways of thinking. In reactive companies, innovation is almost always a response to consumers' wishes; in other words, it is market-driven. Proactive innovation goes far beyond this responsive posture. It is a process aimed at breaking current market patterns. Differently from the bureaucratic and excessively hierarchical organizational pattern common in reactive companies, a more flexible management style that preserves autonomy and free flow of ideas favors this innovative proactive posture.

Finally, observe how the people development and leadership process occurs for each of the two mindsets under analysis. Proactive companies encourage transformative leadership, a guidance style based on autonomy and flexibility, very different from the conventional leadership style based on permanent control and supervision. With regard to people, proactive companies clearly promote the development of proactiveness at the individual level, since they believe this disposition is not innate but rather capable of being stimulated: a very different approach from that of reactive companies, which aim their efforts at the identification and development of those who have shown previous action-driven behavior.

It is important to highlight that the differences mentioned here will be more or less intense depending on the stage of development for each of the eight capacities. This will ultimately reflect each company's particular reality. In other words, capacity-related difficulties manifest in different degrees, the extremes being companies showing no capacity problems (as in developed proactive cultures) and companies with apparent difficulties in many or even all capacities (as in dominant reactive cultures). Most frequently, however, we noticed that companies are distributed over several different development levels, and as a rule they need to improve behavior in regard to one or more capacities. Regardless of the development level, however, the management of each capacity is essential for every company willing to act proactively with some efficiency. To achieve that, companies have to manage market proactiveness, as we shall explain.

MARKET PROACTIVENESS MANAGEMENT

Capacities do not develop spontaneously. They must be worked on, and become part of a company's culture. Nor are they isolated variables; the effect of any capacity will be supported – or countered – by other related capacities. In other words, capacities depend on each other, and the better they are managed as a whole, the more they will contribute to a company's objectives and goals. In order to manage capacities for market proactiveness, the company must adopt what we call market proactiveness management (proactive management): that is, a managerial posture aimed at the development of capacities for market proactiveness.

Proactive management combines all the eight capacities we described in four distinct dimensions, each focused on managing specific capacities (see Figure 3.1). Each proactive management dimension encompasses two capacities. The arrows relating to the four management dimensions indicate that the eight capacities compose a cohesive set and that the capacities are interconnected and complementary. The set constitutes a real competence in market proactiveness: that is, a higher capacity that surpasses the simple development of a particular capacity.

Distributing the capacities in four dimensions eases their management and makes clear to the company what capacities require more attention and development. Besides, action focused on pairs of capacities allows companies to visualize the relationship between their critical points and to take measures that are intended to improve two capacities at the same time. For instance, a company we studied adopted a conservative action style and avoided risk taking, a hindrance to its attempts at proactiveness. A deeper analysis showed that this resulted from a culture that stigmatized mistakes and failures. Mistakes were regarded as shameful, and they provoked a kind of unconscious organizational amnesia which blocked any attempt to raise discussion about the company's unsuccessful initiatives and lit the red light of risk every time strategic decisions were made. After uncovering this

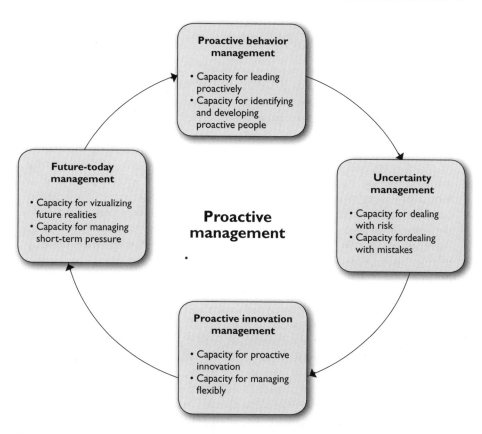

Figure 3.1 The four dimensions of proactive management

behavior, the company launched efforts to change its mental disposition toward mistakes and to build a proactive mindset for dealing with mistakes that could result in a more flexible attitude to business risks.

No capacity is more important than another in proactive management. The combined action of different capacities is more important than the performance of a single specific capacity. It is of little use, for instance, for a company to master the capacity of visualizing nonexistent realities, if it is countered by the short-term result-driven attitude of a risk-averse culture. Thus, when implementing proactive management, leaders and managers must look for synergistic results, where the resulting enhanced capacity transcends the mere addition of individual capacities. Organizing the company for market proactiveness requires a balanced development of proactive management in all four dimensions we have conceived: uncertainty management, future-today management, proactive innovation management, and proactive behavior management (see Figure 3.1). This is the biggest challenge of a proactive company, according to most CEOs we interviewed (see Box 3.1). These dimensions are dealt with in the second part of this book.

> ### Box 3.1 Capacities: the very foundation of market proactiveness
>
> "Market proactiveness does not come by chance." This was a remarkable comment in the survey we conducted with CEOs, drawing attention to the importance of capacities as true pillars of proactive action.[4] According to Alberto Saraiva, founder of Habib's – the world's largest Arab fast-food chain, with more than 300 shops in Brazil and 160 million consumers served annually – there is no way to talk of proactiveness if the company does not have the capacity for managing uncertainty: "If there is no risk and no mistake then you are not proactive." Future-today management was positively mentioned in the interview with Francisco Valim, former president of Serasa Experian and now head of Oi, leader in the Brazilian fixed and mobile telephony segment: "Market proactiveness only materializes when the company takes on board the future and brings it to the present." The need to overcome short-term pressure to achieve anticipatory vision was mentioned by Walter Schalka, president of Votorantin Cimentos, one of the world's ten largest cement, concrete, and aggregate companies: "To be proactive, a company must avoid being held hostage to the short term."
>
> The relevance of proactive innovation was also highlighted in statements made by many leaders we interviewed, such as Clóvis Tramontina of the innovative metallurgical industrial group Tramontina, with operations in more than 120 countries: "The true innovation is to deliver what the market has not yet demanded." Besides proactive innovation, a company's ability to act flexibly was summarized by Sonia Hess, leader of Dudalina, the largest Brazilian manufacturer of men's and women's shirts : "Proactive companies let people think."
>
> Comments on the importance of proactive behavior as a foundation of market proactiveness were revealing. Concerning the role of leaders, Alessandro Carlucci, president and director of Natura – a leader in the Brazilian cosmetics market – emphasized the relevance of a company leader's role in the construction of proactive postures: "Leadership is the number one factor of market proactiveness." Lastly, it is worth mentioning the importance almost all the CEOs we interviewed attached to personal proactiveness. Hence, we believe we can summarize this knowledge in an unequivocally repeated and collective statement on the importance of people for the construction of market proactiveness: "Proactive companies are made up of proactive people."

THE FOUR DIMENSIONS OF PROACTIVE MANAGEMENT

The four dimensions of proactive management are the bases for a company to develop capacities for market proactiveness.

Future-today management is the first proactive management dimension we present. We created the expression "future-today" to represent a new vision of the future, where the future is not regarded as something that is definitely coming, but rather a reality that can be constructed in the present. The belief in the future-today is a strategist's refined ability to act in the present regarding the future. However, this ability is only effective in practice when companies possess the capacities for visualizing future realities and for overcoming short-term pressures. The capacity for visualizing future realities is an essential condition for companies to track and explore the pulsating and potential moments zero (MZs) mentioned in Chapter 2. The capacity for overcoming short-term pressure, in turn, represents an attitude that is capable of balancing demands for results and goals – ever more urgent – and adopting strategies with longer reach. It is a matter of finding room in the strategic agenda to allow for non-immediate returns.

Uncertainty management refers to dealing with risk and mistakes, two elements that are always present when companies try to anticipate MZs in the market. An often repeated comment in interviews with executives and CEOs was that fear of the unknown is the biggest hindrance to market proactiveness. To them, dealing with uncertainty is a major challenge facing leaders and managers who want to make their companies less reactive. And to deal with uncertainty, it is necessary that companies reverse their mindset regarding risk and mistakes. In the realm of proactiveness, the way we deal with these two elements assumes characteristics very different from those we are acquainted with. In this context, the concept that radically distinguishes success and failure is reinterpreted. Proactive companies know that nothing is riskier than risk aversion, and that this is the biggest mistake of all.

The third dimension describes *proactive innovation management*. It refers to a company's capacities for proactively innovating and managing in a flexible way. We call proactive innovation a novel attitude toward the innovative process, which is really aimed at changing current market rules. This attitude subverts the reactive innovation pattern, described in Chapter 1, that is still present in many companies and causes market reactiveness. Besides the capacity for proactively innovating, proactive innovation management requires that companies be willing to act in a more flexible way with regard to their operations and hierarchies. Bureaucratic structures, marked by strong control and normalization, are deleterious to market proactiveness because they inhibit autonomy and the generation of innovative insights.

Finally, *proactive behavior management* encompasses a company's capacities for proactively leading, and for identifying and developing people's proactiveness. We call proactive leadership the kind of leadership aimed at promoting behaviors and actions leading to anticipation, creativity, and the construction of new ways of working. Proactive leaders are transformative, and oppose traditional leadership styles which are marked by control and supervision. This kind of style is aligned with the second capacity for proactive behavior management, the capacity for developing individual proactiveness. Proactive companies must identify, develop, and retain in their work teams employees with proactive profiles and whose competencies support the execution of planned proactive strategies, because rather than being a rare innate talent of a few privileged individuals, individual proactiveness is something that can be developed. Like any other ability, it must be worked on and trained. Proactive companies recognize the fact that people are proactive potentialities waiting to be employed.

Once they understand what capacities are necessary to implement market proactiveness, companies need to put into practice the proactive management style we have described. To accomplish that, companies have to evaluate, above all, how they behave in relation to each of the eight capacities, analyzing their own current stage of development for each one. In other words, they must make a diagnosis of their capacities for market proactiveness. This can be done by means of a check-up, an instrument to evaluate capacities for market proactiveness.

THE DIAGNOSIS OF CAPACITIES

The check-up on capacities (see the Appendix) is a tool to measure how a company acts and behaves in relation to the capacities for market proactiveness. This examination allows those responsible for strategy to visualize to what extent the company is – or is not – organized for market proactiveness.

Our field research found that a substantial number of companies reveal some degree of deficiency in these capacities. Research has also revealed what we called a "paradox of discourse": although capacities are deemed important, little is done to improve them.[5] These findings make clear the need to put a heavier emphasis on the development of the capacities needed for market proactiveness. The management of capacities we explore in this part of the book addresses just this gap.

In the next few chapters we address the four different kinds of management outlined in our model, and the capacities related to them. An integrated analysis of these four chapters is essential for understanding market proactiveness management, and for companies to successfully execute planned proactive strategies. Together with the diagnosis of capacities, proactive management will enable companies to organize to avoid falling short in their strategic attempts. This common failure becomes worse when companies are dealing with more challenging strategies such as proactive strategies. Possessing the capacities to be proactive is as necessary as wanting to be proactive.

Let us now move on to Chapter 4, which deals with future-today management and its related capacities.

FUTURE-TODAY MANAGEMENT

4 Believing in What Does Not Exist (Yet)

The anticipation approach presented in this book relies on a basic premise: that we can build the future by acting in the present. When we started our research on market proactiveness, something became readily evident: to be proactive, a company has to change its mindset towards the future and start to regard it as something it can create from its own strategies.

We noticed that the vast majority of managers still act according to the paradigm that preserves tomorrow from human influence and action. As a manager once told us: "Here [in the company] we act as meteorologists: we spend a lot of time trying to predict if it will rain tomorrow." From that meteorological perspective, all action aimed at the future basically follows the typical and traditional strategic-planning prediction mindset, which first tries to predict the opportunities and threats of the future environment, then tries to adapt the company to the market as much as possible.

We believe that this mindset – simply because it reflects a certain view – is a cognitive hindrance and must be changed. Strategists should stop regarding the future as "something that will happen tomorrow," and start to think of it as something that can (and must) be constructed today. This requires proactive management to be directed to diffuse a new conception of the future within the company: the "future-today" concept. Proactive companies invent the future instead of waiting for the future and then acting. It is a matter of acting in the present, keeping in mind the future we want to see come about.

A simple exercise should help to better illustrate what we mean by "future-today." You started reading this book some time ago, and probably expect to keep reading to the end (we're assuming that if you have reached this point, you probably see some value in the book). As seen from today, the moment you will finish reading the book is what we usually call the future. In other words, we believe that there will be a subsequent time when we have finished reading the book. But notice that this future time does not really exist: if you give up reading now, it will never come into being (we hope you will not do that!). In other words, what we call future is nothing more than a latent, unrealized possibility, and it will remain so until you take action to make it come true. In our example, this means saying that the future is being built by you; that is, any individual future is a nonexistent reality whose existence depends solely upon your decisions and your actions. Observe that your present action (proceeding with your reading) is creating an imagined future (in which you have finished reading the book). That is the exact meaning of the future-today concept: we build the future, by acting in the present. Laércio Cosentino, CEO of Totvs, Latin America's largest software house, helps us explain this new concept of the future:

> Many people think that the vision of the future is what we see ahead in time; things that will happen. Here, in our company, we think in a different way. For us, the future is everything we, induce and make happen, whatever the way we do that. Thus, it is not only a matter of paying attention to tendencies, but one of determining a tendency, of modeling the future to our benefit.[1]

In practice, future-today management is anchored in the development of two essential capacities: the capacity for visualizing future realities, and the capacity for managing short-term pressure. These two capacities together help managers assume a strategic attitude that is balanced between today's needs and tomorrow's opportunities. This balance is a necessary condition for companies to overcome the predictive and pressing vision of the future and to start acting to anticipate it. This chapter examines how these two capacities, essential for future-today management, can be developed.

VISUALIZING FUTURE REALITIES

A fascination with the future has existed since time immemorial. People have always wanted to know what is hidden behind tomorrow's curtains, and the appeal of allegories of and speculations about the future still permeates human thoughts and actions (think of the recurring success of films and books that deal with apocalyptic predictions, or of astrology's millennial and perennial influence). The advent of futurology in the 1950s raised a methodological concern in the field of studies on the future, leading two decades later to the adoption of the now well-known scenario planning technique in the business field. From then on, the fortune-telling toolbox never ceased to increase its portfolio of techniques, offering companies many different ways to deal with tomorrow's uncertainties.[2]

We have noticed, however, that most companies still limit their analyses of the future to traditional prognostic techniques and methods. They analyze competitive forces, attempting to predict industry moves; track the potential market's opportunities and threats; conduct surveys to understand future consumers' preferences; and model demand through forecasting. Although all these actions are productive in stable environments that change slowly and predictably, they contribute only insignificantly in times when circumstances change haphazardly, such as now, because these techniques have a common characteristic: they start from what already exists to project what might be. Observe that even the scenario planning technique – a tool designed to improve anticipatory analysis of the future, making it more creative and experimental – has been limited by this predictive paradigm.[3]

The capacity for visualizing the future, as we conceive it, starts from a very different strategic posture. Instead of trying to predict the future, the company should try to detect signals that a future is emitting, or even imagine possible future events that could occur, and then consider what actions should be taken, today, to realize them. First we have to call your attention to a fundamental feature of this attitude: it is more a matter of changing mindsets than actually applying prognostic tools. It involves recognizing that, in matters related to market proactiveness, vision replaces prediction. Instead of trying to predict the future, the company tries to visualize it. The practical importance of this new vision of future is reinforced by CEOs such as Ricardo Pelegrini, president of IBM Brasil: "The more we acquire this forward-looking culture, the better we design, imagine and even develop future tendencies that lead us into new markets."[4] As we have seen, visualizing the future is not only a question of seeing beyond the present; it involves acting in the present to make this future real.

In our view, companies need to adopt two attitudes to be able to visualize future realities in the way we describe. These two attitudes are related exactly to the two types of future realities we presented in Chapter 2. Thus, a company will have to learn to detect the signals that every change emits before it actually materializes, tracking the undetermined reality in search of pulsating moments zero (MZs). It will also have to develop an ability to explore the uncertain reality, imagining potential MZs and working to transform imagination into reality. We will detail this process now.

Tracking the undetermined reality

In 1998, the Israeli Dov Moran was at a congress in New York, when he noticed two troubled executives trying to transfer information from one notebook PC to another minutes before the beginning of a presentation. Suddenly, an idea came to his head: "I thought: I have to create something that makes it easier." Two years later, his insight became reality: IBM started to sell in the United States a small device he had invented, the now ubiquitous USB flash drive (or pen drive). In 2006, following the flash drive's stupendous popularity, the US company SanDisk took over M-Systems, the company founded by Moran, paying US$1.6 billion.[5] This is just one piece of evidence that proactive actions based on signals detected in the market can yield outstanding results.

Signals of change appear everywhere: in newspapers and magazines, implicit in sales force presentations, in the information ocean that is the internet, in complaints posted on weblogs, in rumors about the sale of a main competitor, in conversations between friends in the check-in queue at the airport, in a list of bestsellers, in the attitudes of children at a party. Where should a company look for signals? Which signals should be taken into account? How do we tell relevant signals from worthless noise? Dazzled by such questions and avid to detect all kinds of signals, many companies behave like Funes the Memorious, a fictional character created by Argentinean writer Jorge Luis Borges. Being able to detect

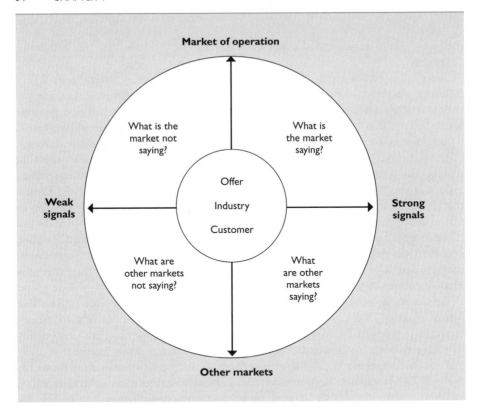

Figure 4.1 The pulsating moments zero radar

everything at the same time, he ended up not being able to classify the information he received any more; in other words, he was not able to perceive anything.[6] Companies that adopt this uncontrolled and unruly way of detecting signals wind up being buried by a landslide of information.

We designed an accessory tool to help prevent strategists from losing direction amidst this forest of signs: the pulsating MZs radar. As shown in Figure 4.1, this tool divides the undetermined reality in four distinct quadrants based on the origin and intensity of signals emitted by the market. Regarding the origin of signals, we understand that companies must track signals both within the limits of the market where they operate and in markets beyond their business focus. As for intensity, they must pay attention not only to strong signs from the market but also, and especially, to weak and sometimes imperceptible signals. At the center of the radar scanner are the three dimensions of market proactiveness we already know – offer, industry, and customer – toward which the company's tracking efforts must converge. Reducing the scanning area to these four quadrants, the radar simplifies the pulsating MZs tracking process and becomes an efficient tool that helps strategists keep their focus on early signals.

Let us start our analysis in the upper right quadrant of the scanner, which encompasses all the strong signals coming from the market in which the company operates. This area involves changes in the market in which the company competes, and the signals indicate clearly that the changes are about to occur. Exactly because of these characteristics, these signals are also accessible to most competitors. These almost explicit warnings are usually accessed by traditional diagnostic tools such as market surveys, structural analysis of the industry, and opportunity and threats analysis. When a company scans this quadrant it acts as if it is asking, "What is our market saying? What signals are evident that indicate an inexorable change in the offer, industry, and customer dimensions in the market in which we operate?"

Although proactive companies focus their attention on weak signals emitted by the market – precisely because they are still hidden and represent a powerful opportunity to anticipate the market – strong signs should never be neglected. Failure to recognize signals that have already become so intense that change is a certainty may blind the organization and prevent it from seeing a new incoming reality (think, for instance, of the reluctance of Brazilian textile companies to believe in the threat represented by Chinese manufacturers in the 1990s). Similarly, the recognition of evident signs may turn on the light of change, leading the company to rethink its procedures and business model. IBM's example in the beginning of the 2000s is well known and illustrative. After detecting evident signs of declining returns in the hardware production and sales market, the company revolutionized its business model and started providing information systems solutions.

While recognition of strong signs within a company's operating zone is necessary, a problem arises when it becomes the sole target of market intelligence actions. This is what happens, for instance, when a company guides its strategies exclusively by explicit information coming from its customers or movements made by its current and direct competitors. We have noticed that the vast majority of companies end up restricting their scanning efforts this way, drastically reducing the capture potential (observe that, in mathematical terms, they will be scanning only 25 percent of the area reached by the radar). This is the dilemma faced by companies that are excessively guided by their own market. They end up directing their radar's antenna only to strong signals within their sector of operation.

A simple redirection, however, may optimize the use of traditional diagnostic tools, unveiling strong signals that are being emitted beyond the limits of the market in which a company operates. In this case, strategists also aim their radar scanners at markets that they do not know (in the lower right quadrant) but that might influence change in the market where the company operates. What could the offer in other markets possibly signal with respect to the market in which a company operates? Which competitors in other markets could become entrants to the market in which the company operates? What opportunities exist in regard to customers in these markets?

Directing the radar to areas beyond the limits of their own markets, companies can hear what other markets are saying. They can, for instance, carry out surveys targeted at other industries' customers, analyze competition in markets that are apparently unimportant to them, or assess the impact of new offers in sectors far from their own. A company that produces furniture, for instance, might gain valuable insight through analyzing tendencies and behaviors in the civil construction market or in the (apparently) distant fashion market. Modu, a cellphone manufacturer, is placing a bet on the production of tiny, light devices that are compatible with accessory devices such as photographic cameras and MP3 players. This means a bet on simplicity, and goes against the multifunctional standard of smart phones. Signals that tend to confirm Modu's judgment are being detected in moves in different and fast-growing markets such as the new category of tablet computers. These signs show that tablets will increasingly absorb cellphone functions, reducing the need for a complex and multi-featured phone. This might seem a simple deduction, but it was only possible thanks to Modu's radar, which was fine-tuned to other markets.[7]

The effective search for signs of pulsating MZs starts, however, when a company uses its radar to scan the remaining 180 degrees of the business spectrum. This happens when it centers tracking on the market's weak signs. These are always more difficult to detect, and because of that, they tend to offer still undetected opportunities. Weak signals are coded warnings, and represent what the market does yet not state clearly. Recognizing them before the competition may bring substantial advantages to a company. But this is no trivial task. Today, signs may change from weak to strong at an astounding speed and in a very short time. Proactive companies must be able to recognize weak signals before they start to pulsate intensely and are perceived by all radars scanning the market. There is also an additional difficulty: weak signals are usually confusing and ambiguous, and may go undetected amidst background noise. The weaker a signal, the more difficult it is to tell it from noise (rather like trying to hear a whisper during a storm).

Weak signals are invisible to traditional survey tools and are only perceptible to the lenses of more accurate analytical instruments. Accordingly, several techniques are being developed to help companies detect weak signals in the market: emphatic design, metaphorical research, consumption observation, alternative approaches to the dynamics of competition, and even virtual scanning of the growing range of social media (these tools are addressed in Chapter 6, in the section on proactive research). It must be emphasized, however, that, no matter the technique adopted, it will be effective only if it is applied according to proactive premises and is open to new and challenging discoveries (something that does not happen often). It is useless to simply replace future-signals tracking tools if the company is not willing to deconstruct its prejudices and paradigms with regard to the offer, industry, and customer in the market in which it operates.

Like strong signals, weak signals must also be tracked both within and outside a company's range of operation. When tracking weak signals in its market (the upper left quadrant), a company will be trying to decipher the market's talk in search of hidden meanings, not clearly stated yet. These hidden meanings may include customers' latent needs and preferences, market regulations that are about to undergo drastic changes, concealed competitors' moves or emerging technologies that may support substantial modifications to current standard offers. Fiat Brasil, for instance, anticipated the competition's moves and created the concept of "Adventure'" after detecting hidden signs that pointed to a market segment of customers who did not want a four-wheel-drive vehicle but longed for freedom and contact with nature (the word "adventure" itself conveys this meaning). Though important, traditional surveys were not powerful enough to make such signs of change explicit. Most important was the company's capacity to observe customers' behavior and detect latent tendencies in the market in which it operates. (Fiat's proactive action is discussed in detail in Chapter 9.)

Finally, the use of the pulsating MZs radar is complete when a company starts to look for weak signals that come from outside its own market (the lower left quadrant) but could have some effect in its own context. Other industries' emerging technologies that may potentially combine with the technology adopted by the market, insight into customers in other markets that raise the possibility of new offers, and new indirect competitors appearing on the competitive horizon, are signals that can only be detected if the radar is pointed beyond the company's competitive realm. Looking for weak signals outside a company's range of operation is maybe the most complex part of the market signals detection process, because it blends difficulties inherent to the detection of weak signs with the challenge of trying to see clearly outside the company's familiarity zone. The rewards, however, are usually worth the effort.

We believe that the pulsating MZs radar is a valuable tool to use in a 360-degree perspective. Scanning for signs of different intensities in different markets drastically reduces the chances that a company will miss a vital sign, and helps identify those signals that are really relevant, an essential expertise in putting the capacity for visualizing the future into practice. But this capacity is even more productive when a company also develops the ability to explore uncertain reality, creating its own potential MZs. We discuss this next.

Exploring the uncertain reality

When examining an undetermined reality, like we have just described, a company tries to identify signs of change so it can anticipate its competitors. When exploring uncertain reality, though, a company is creating change on its own. This does not mean it will not hear signs of pulsating MZs. However, when exploring uncertain reality, a company also aims at inducing the future, creating potential MZs with their strategies and actions. Companies that act this way are twice as ambitious. An anticipated response to change is not enough to satisfy them; they also try to create change, and use it to guide the market. This is the difference between companies we call alert and those we call activators, which we introduced earlier in this book (see page 000 and Box 4.1). Companies that build change this way are never content with simply seeing beforehand: they want to see differently.

As we have seen, an uncertain reality represents a future state when no one knows for sure whether it will come true or not. It is *terra incognita* from where no signal comes out. Its exploration is therefore riskier, and it often scares less audacious strategists. We frequently see how ambiguity and doubts inherent to an uncertain future lead companies away from unknown (and many times promising) horizons. This fear is well-founded: exploration of an uncertain reality is, in part, a shot in the dark. However more closely its threats are assessed, some impossible-

---

Box 4.1 Two ways of visualizing the future

What is the difference between tracking and exploring the future? Tracking undetermined reality is like piecing together a puzzle: managers try to assemble pieces (signals) they find during the market scanning process. As the pieces are put together, the image of pulsating MZs (and so of latent changes) becomes clearer. The challenge is to be able to see the final image – and act anticipatively – with the least possible number of pieces, ideally before competitors also act.

The exploration of uncertain reality, on the other hand, is better represented by assembling Lego bricks: fitting different bricks together in different ways will create different images of the future. Here, the pieces, or bricks, are the questions themselves that companies raise about tomorrow. Companies will think of their potential MZs (changes that can be created) within this range of imagined realities. Observe that there is no hidden picture to be unveiled (as in a puzzle). The challenge here is to be able to imagine different possible combinations of questions to ask, and this requires managers to have a lot of creativity and an open viewpoint. If scanning of an undetermined reality demands attention, exploration of an uncertain reality is based on imagination. More important, however, than this difference, is the common objective of their actions: to visualize change and anticipate tomorrow.

---

to-assess uncertainty will always remain. This remaining dimension of uncertainty is the risk that represents what is not known about the future, no matter how intense efforts to apprehend it have been.[8] We believe, though, that this shot in the dark can be illuminated to reduce the risks that a company faces when exploring an uncertain reality. Let us see how we can do that.

Building images of the future

Our approach to the exploration of uncertain reality is based on the construction of what we call "images of the future." This process, in turn, is based on the scenario planning method, a well-known managerial model to help decision making in the face of uncertainty. The core idea underlying scenario planning is that analysis of the future must take into consideration a range of possible futures, relative to which a company will design its strategic options.[9] We tried to design a simple and immediately applicable method for managers that satisfied the demand for less expensive and time-consuming future visualization techniques, but the same time was capable of quickly and efficiently producing results.[10]

The process we conceived turns images of the future into a background for the creation of potential MZs. In other words, the company draws realities that do not exist (images) and speculates about MZs that would make sense in relation to the imagined realities. In materializing these potential MZs (that is, fixing on changes in the offer, industry, and customer dimensions), the company will in truth be starting to effect the realities imagined. Here we are back to the typical question posed by activator companies we highlighted in the beginning of this book. When they ask themselves "What do we want to happen?" these companies are really starting to create the conditions that will lead them to this desired reality. It is a reverse strategic process: possible futures are conceived and action is taken – in the present – to create them.[11]

To facilitate understanding of this process, we have represented the images of the future as a searchlight brightening an uncertain reality and illuminating the visual field that leads to the future in the offer, industry and customer dimensions (see Figure 4.2). Casting the beam of images on uncertain reality, the searchlight helps companies see potential MZs that make sense with regard to the images created. When they start to think of possible future realities, managers are, in truth, experimenting with imagined realities, and this power of simulation, which encompasses the strength of the images of the future, constitutes a proactive strategy tool. It may seem nonsense to ask strategists to forget the present reality and behave as if they are acting in an imagined reality. Such an uncommon request would certainly stir more mistrust than conviction. But this is exactly what happens when we watch a movie: we suspend our critical faculties for a while and believe that both the story and the characters are real. If the film entertains us – let us say, if the image was well constructed – we are absorbed by the narrative and forget completely that it is a simulation of reality. If we are able to do it before a TV set or in a theater, why not in a company?

It is important to emphasize that these images of the future are not predictive attempts. They are, above all, speculations about different possible futures, drafts of alternative futures that might or might not become real. We highlight this point because strategists are often betrayed by self-confidence, overestimate their power to imagine the future, and end up seduced by the images they themselves created. They frequently select a preferred image – usually because it confirms their unconscious expectations about the future – and this selected image fully guides the strategic decisions. This ultimately reduces drastically the perception

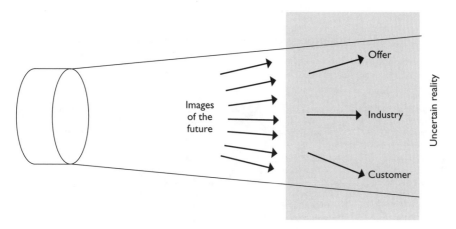

Figure 4.2 A searchlight of images of the future

of multiple possibilities for the future, and can bring unwanted consequences for the company. To avoid becoming a mere prediction, as described, the process of image construction must involve a delicate balance between imagination regarding the future and a sense of present reality, an ability we call "calibrated imagination." Calibrated imagination represents a balance between logics and intuition, between imagination and discipline. If, when exploring the future, managers must transcend the simple analytical examination of facts, they should not jump to the opposite extreme, bet on mere opinions about the future and cross their fingers that the one they choose will come true. As we say, "strategists do not play dice."

Thus, warned against the dangers of prediction and conscious that uncertainty may be exploited to the benefit of the company, strategists have a better chance of succeeding in the process of constructing images, which we will now start to describe.

THE CONSTRUCTION PROCESS

To put into practice the image construction process as we have conceived it, four fundamental actions are necessary (see Figure 4.3). First, we must define what we call instigating questions: that is, themes dealing with the future and about which the company is greatly interested in knowing more. When articulating the instigating questions, strategists are really posing the question, what should we know today about the future in order to create potential MZs in the offer, industry, and customer dimensions? Writing a list of issues that are meaningful and relevant to the company is the first step in an effective process of constructing images of the future.

After defining the instigating questions, the second action is to try to find answers to them. Managers do not have crystal balls and therefore they must analyze the factors that might influence these answers. When mapping these influential factors they begin to become aware of what they know – and what they do not know – about the future. In other words, strategists begin to identify the actual uncertainties they will have to face if they want to create relevant potential MZs.

After concluding this process of mapping the influential factors, managers are

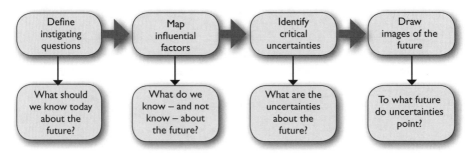

Figure 4.3 The image construction process

apt to identify which of them indicate highly predictable tendencies and which are remarkably ambiguous, so that it is difficult to evaluate their likelihood. In other words, they will be able to identify the critical uncertainties related to the future. Such critical uncertainties reveal events that cannot be neglected at all, and that will orient the final stage of the image construction process.

Finally, the image construction process is concluded by choosing, from among the identified critical uncertainties, those the group understands as having the highest impact on the company. Different images of the future are then constructed by combining the selected uncertainties. The images drawn are subsequently tested for their coherence and reasonableness. This creates a mosaic of possible futures, a true guide to the construction of potential MZs in the offer, industry, and customer dimensions.

We now look in more detail at the four actions of the image construction process.

Defining instigating questions

Objectively, instigating questions represent everything managers would like to know about future. They translate a company's anxieties and concerns about tomorrow. When well delineated, instigating questions help identify what areas of uncertain reality images of the future may help to illuminate. To attempt to construct images without previously defining these questions is like gathering a team and announcing, "Well, guys, let's draw the future!" Exploring uncertain reality this way would be like pointing the image searchlight in all directions in the night sky, instead of focusing it on specific areas of the firmament. Although open processes like this may lead to interesting speculations, it seems more logical to expect that they will result in constructions of dubious usefulness.

The definition of instigating questions must address all three dimensions of market proactiveness, and managers should articulate their questions about the future addressing the offer, industry, and customers of the market in which their company operates. This is sometimes no easy task. Executives often feel uncomfortable when suddenly called on to speculate about the future of the market. Having to interrupt their daily routine, they can feel confused and fearful of expressing their opinions, afraid of sounding foolish. A good way of easing the process – and relaxing the group – is to propose the following simulation to each manager involved in the construction of images: if you could talk to an infallible seer and pose two or three questions about the future, one for each market proactiveness dimension, what would you ask?[12]

This simulated challenge is likely to generate between 10 and 30 instigating questions for each dimension of market proactiveness, depending on the number of participants and on the level of good sense achieved. For smaller groups of less than ten participants, each member could be asked to formulate more than three questions for each dimension. If major difficulties come up, smaller groups of, say, three to four members can be created to balance managers' different levels of aptitude. In brief , what matters most is that the process creates favorable conditions that make strategists both believe in the strategic validity of the process and feel stimulated to participate, generating opportune and relevant questions.

It is important to agree on space and time limits for the images to be constructed before the instigating questions are defined. In other words, you should spell out the time span to be considered (six months, one year, five years?) and the market reach (local, national, or global?). Let us analyze the example of a winery whose executives are defining their instigating questions. The moderator might first ask the participants:

> What questions would you like to ask about the future, taking into account the offer, industry, and customer dimensions, and focusing on the fine wine internal market in the next three years?

This level of clarity and specificity is essential to fix the focus of the instigating questions and preventing them from differing too widely in scope.

A recurrent doubt at this point concerns the time spectrum that should be considered. That depends on the researched market's level of turbulence: the more intense the dynamics of changes, the shorter should be the time interval considered. The literature on scenario construction typically suggests a range of from one to three years for highly turbulent markets, such as web commerce, and 20 years or more for more slowly evolving industries. Traditional strategic planning has a typical one-year horizon. We suggest a range from two to five years, since a year is an excessively short period for dealing with more audacious visions of the future.

To continue our example, the winery's strategists draft 20 instigating questions for each market proactiveness dimension (some of them are presented in Table 4.1). These instigating questions ultimately represent areas of uncertainty that challenge the company in the offer, industry, and customer dimensions, and that, from there on, will guide the image construction process.

Once instigating questions are defined in the realms of offer, industry, and customer, the challenge shifts to the search for answers. As noted, there is no way of coming up with a definitive answer, because instigating questions deal with the future. It is possible, however, to evaluate events that might impact on the answers and try to understand the dynamics of them. Managers then jump to the second action in the process of constructing images, mapping influential factors.

Mapping influential factors

As we have already highlighted, influential factors represent events that could influence the answers to the instigating questions. We can start this process by looking at the instigating questions that are most interesting to the company, provided no instigating question is neglected or taken as less important than others (as we like to emphasize, instigating questions should not be swept under the rug). One way of organizing this process and ensuring equal treatment for all the questions is to start from the first instigating question and invite the group to analyze the factors that could impact on possible and pertinent answers. The group then continues to map influential factors relative to all instigating questions

Table 4.1 Instigating questions for a winery (internal market; fine wines; next three years)

Offer dimension	What products will be a substitution threat to wine consumption?
	Will new types of wine relevantly influence consumption habits?
	What complementary offers could be associated with the product?
	Will wine go on being regarded as elitist and exclusive to connoisseurs and initiates?
	What are the possible formats of the wine offer in a connected society?
Industry dimension	How will distributors (restaurants, supermarkets, specialized retail) influence wine consumption habits?
	What regulatory mechanisms could increase or reduce wine consumption?
	Will first-class wineries adopt the grape self-supply alternative?
	What are the alternative ways of distributing and retailing wine?
	What are the drivers of competition among old and new world wineries?
Customer dimension	What will consumers value in terms of product?
	Will wine consumption among women and young people experience considerable growth?
	How will wine, as a beverage, be seen by consumers in the future?
	What new consumer segments will exist?
	On what will consumers base their preferences and needs?

for all three market proactiveness dimensions. Returning to the winery example, the group might take the first question in Table 4.1, and formulate this mapping question:

> What factors could influence fine wine substitution for other products in the internal market during the next three years?

To answer this question, strategists should look for help to the MZs matrix presented in Chapter 2, and try to evaluate what changes that have impacted on the market in the past and present can teach us about future. They should think of past MZs and ask, what products in our industry have been abruptly replaced in the last five years? What blinded decision makers to the imminent substitution at the time? Are there any documented cases from other industries that could be helpful to our learning? They could use this question, going back in time roughly as far as the future mapping is going forward:

> What do we know now that we would like to have known three years ago?

It is important to highlight that this learning process which starts with past MZs should not be regarded as looking at the past in the hope that future will repeat it (this would be an attitude typical of a reactive company). Far from that: learning, in the sense presented here, is a way to better understand lessons learned by the industry and even by the company itself. The archive of past realities is a rich source of insights that should never be neglected. As we have said, past MZs can teach us a lot about the future.

Our strategists should also analyze what present MZs might have to say about the future. Some well-known managerial analysis tools are useful here, such as the PEST analysis of environmental variables (political, economic, social, and technological) and industry structural analysis (rivalry in the market, the threat of new entrants and substitute products, buyers' and suppliers' bargaining power), which are both widely applied in the analysis of current conditions of competition. An examination of the market's opportunities and threats may also improve a company's vision of the uncertainty area being scrutinized. Again, it is opportune to emphasize that the use of these tools should not be reactive. Thus, strategists must keep in mind that they are using them in an attempt to recognize uncertainties rather than as an elaboration of strategies to react to the present reality under analysis.

Once they have finished indicating all the factors that influence the instigating questions, managers will have a fairly dense framework of issues and events that could impact on answers about the future they are pursuing. Still with the winery case, this process might lead to the ideas set down in Table 4.2.

After listing the influential factors, strategists tend to distinguish between predictable tendencies – the near certainties – and the more ambiguous and less

Table 4.2 The main factors likely to influence the offer of fine wines in the internal market for the next three years

- New technologies that enable the creation of entirely innovative products
- Growth of emerging producing economies
- New market segments, such as women and young people, who value different attributes of wines
- Growth of demand for customized wines (with customers' active participation in the production process)
- Growth of the population's purchasing power
- Inspection and quality controls increasingly rigid
- Increase in price-sensitive demand.
- Offer increase due to growth of production capacity and arrival of new competitors
- Growth of brand image among consumers
- Increase in the production of currently little-used grape varieties
- Alternative packing formats

Note: these are examples only. Usually between 20 and 30 factors should be listed.

(if at all) predictable possibilities. In other words, they will be trying to identify the critical uncertainties, which are basic building blocks for the visualization of an uncertainty reality, and the focus of the third action phase in the process of image construction.

Identifying critical uncertainties

The identification of critical uncertainties challenges managers with a core question:

How do we measure the uncertainty level of a given influential factor?

This is no easy question because determining what is and what is not uncertain is always a matter open to discussion. Frequently, participants in image construction processes differ widely on the uncertainty level associated with a factor. A very simple solution to this disagreement is to analyze at what level managers agree – or disagree – over the behavior of the factor. The deeper the disagreement, the surer they can be that they are facing an uncertainty. Unanimous or almost unanimous agreements about the behavior under analysis usually indicate we are facing a tendency. Influential factors that raise intense discussions and doubts among work team members most often indicate relevant uncertainties, and it is these that should be carefully considered.[13]

The uncertainty level may be classified either as low, average, or high, or using a numerical Likert scale ranging from say 1 (low uncertainty) to 5 (high uncertainty). Participants may also express the level of uncertainty based on extreme situations such as "is happening" and "will never happen," with intermediate levels like "will take place shortly" and "improbable occurrence." Different positions along any of these scales will tell the group where the most relevant uncertainties are. Finally, it is also important to recognize what have traditionally been more predictable events, separating them out from the more ambiguous. For instance, events associated with demographic or technological dynamics usually reveal reasonably predictable tendencies, while factors such as competitors' future moves or consumers' attitudes often seem less clear. This helps strategists focus their efforts on those factors showing higher uncertainty, and stops them wasting time in analyzing tendencies that will obviously occur.[14]

As a last point, it is important to emphasize that determining uncertainty levels will always involve subjectivity to some extent. This is a process that sometimes proceeds slowly and therefore requires patience and determination from managers. It is necessary to keep in mind that uncertainty does not reveal itself abruptly. As Riobaldo poetically speculated in Guimarães Rosa's masterpiece *Grande Sertão: Veredas* (The Devil to Pay in the Backlands), darkness turns only very slowly into light.[15]

Our winery's strategists will now choose out of all the influential factors they have listed (as in Table 4.2) those they believe represent uncertainties about future. Next, they should pick the two most relevant uncertainties – which therefore become the critical uncertainties – which will be used to define four initial images of the future. Let us say the two selected critical uncertainties are related to the themes of new offers and new consumption segments. These two initial critical uncertainties will guide strategists in the process of designing images of the future, the main focus of the fourth and last action of the process we have devised.

Designing images of the future

The first step when designing images of the future is to cross the two selected critical uncertainties and build a two-vector structure like the one presented in Figure 4.4. Notice that each critical uncertainty is limited on its borders by two polarized behaviors. Those behaviors are nothing more than alternative hypotheses about the way each uncertainty might behave. The poles must be chosen as limits of what the group understands by extreme but still plausible behaviors (it is useless to build an image of the future based on a behavior that nobody expects to occur). Extreme situations ensure that the images developed will cover a very significant extension of the uncertainty area under analysis, so they will be genuinely different rather than subtle variations on the same theme. As we often say, the images must be pictures of different landscapes rather than different pictures of one and the same landscape.

Look particularly at the structure of Figure 4.4. The critical uncertainty "new offers" (horizontal axis) is limited to the left by the extreme "incremental innovation" – representing a future marked by few radical innovations, which is more inclined to maintain the current offer – while the right extreme, "radical

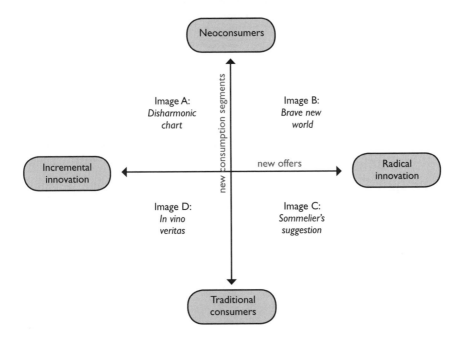

Figure 4.4 Four images of the future for the offer dimension

innovation," points to a future distinguished by remarkable and revolutionary changes. Along the vertical axis, the critical uncertainty "new consumption segments" has the extremes "traditional consumers" and "neoconsumers," respectively indicating a future with few changes in terms of new publics and demands, and another marked by the presence of new and unusual consumption segments. The intersection between these four extremes will result in four distinct images of the future offer in the wine industry.

Thus, image A (Disharmonic Chart) suggests a future scenario where new groups of consumers (perhaps women or young people) are not properly satisfied by an offer which is too slow to follow the path of a new reality. Image B (Brave New World) represents an uncertain reality where those new segments are supplied by new offers, so there are revolutionary changes in the industry. Image C (Sommelier's Suggestion) indicates a future where companies will strive to meet the changing preferences of traditional consumers, attempting to guide the market. Finally, image D (In Vino Veritas) suggests a reality characterized by the attempt to maintain the industry's status quo; few changes, and offer and demand stability. (Of course, this is a very brief summary. In practice, we recommend that a narrative text be prepared for each image constructed, detailing and linking its implications, effects, and interactions. What you will look for is a true and complete story about each image, capable of transmitting more clarity about the dynamics of the scenarios under consideration.)[16]

At this point you might ask, why four images and not, say, two or six? What should you do if, for instance, you have identified three or even four critical uncertainties? (They would require respectively 12 (3 x 4) and 24 (6 x 4) different images of the future.) Although there is no inflexible rule, we think four works best. Scenario planning practice allows us to state that, if the critical uncertainties are well delineated and the limits stretched to plausible extremes, four images of the future will be enough to cover a significant extension of the explored uncertainty area. A larger number would result in costs of analysis and construction higher than the benefits for visualization. A smaller number would be too few.

Finally, it is important to admit that the designed images of the future (no matter how many they are) will never be able to cover all possible uncertain realities. In fact, this is not their goal. There will always be unidentified critical uncertainties, and even those used in the construction of images may have had their limits under- or over-estimated, leaving possible realities out of the image searchlight's reach. You should not forget that an image of the future ultimately represents a simplified model of a reality that will always be more complex than any conceivable model.

That said, these images do give the winery's strategists a background on which to start projecting their potential MZs (in this particular case, in the offer dimension). How will they do that? We will finish our description of uncertain reality by addressing this question.

Generating potential moments zero

The extensive work of generating images has finished and managers now face the final objective in the process: to generate potential MZs from the designed images.

Images of the future are only valuable when they help strategists make anticipatory strategic decisions, otherwise they are mere plays of the imagination. Thus, now the time has come to think strategically, based on the designed images, and try to foresee the possibilities they offer for anticipation.

When starting this process, it is necessary to keep in mind that no designed image is better or worse than another: they are simply different. Therefore, we should not succumb to the temptation of calculating probabilities for a designed image, trying to establish which has greater chances of occurring, or even trying to justify the analysis of an image we think is more propitious. Here is important to reiterate that images are representations that deal with the limits of an uncertain reality, not prophecies.

The first step in this attempt consists of choosing one of the designed images and diving into the reality it suggests. In other words, strategists must momentarily turn off their sense of reality and literally dive into the story told by the image, as if they were certain it will become reality. Here, they ask themselves:

> If we were absolutely certain that image A (or B, or C) would come about, what anticipatory opportunities would it open for us?

This should prompt them to generate as many potential MZs as possible: for our example, changes in the offer the winery could create that would be meaningful in the context of the image under analysis.

Pursuing the example might make this clearer. Let's imagine the winery's strategists dive into the reality suggested by image A – Disharmonic Chart – and think as if they were actually living this reality. They would certainly articulate questions such as:

* What anticipatory spaces are there in a reality where new types of consumers are not being adequately satisfied by companies' offers?
* What products could we launch – or modify – to fill these gaps?
* What complements to our offer could be generated in this context?

Questions like these (and many others), generated in this true "suspended reality" exercise, sharpen strategists' reasoning and creativity. (At this point they are free from their daily worries and because of that, more open and inclined to generate challenging and fertile ideas.) You are recommended to speculate as broadly as possible, generating MZs that range from the realistic and certain to the imponderable. So you will certainly want to envision the potential MZs you think are feasible. These are usually the more logical, and come to mind as soon as the speculation process starts. But do not discard the unthinkable MZs: that is, changes that, though regarded as nonsensical today, might look like prodigious opportunities when stripped of their unusual nature. That is the distinctive art of "thinking the impossible."

The process ends when the strategists have evaluated the potential MZs relative to all four (or even more, when applicable) constructed images. The variety of potential MZs explored with regard to the different images will represent the many strategic paths the company could follow as far as the uncertain future is concerned. But, which is or are the most adequate way(s)? Which way(s) will generate most value to the company? In brief, which of the proposed MZs should actually be implemented?

If companies had unlimited resources and complete knowledge of the future, then every MZ that has been speculated on would head out of the planning office and into the real world. But reality is different, we know. The meager resources and the risks associated with projects force managers to make exclusive strategic choices. That is why the choice between all the imagined MZs is ultimately a very individual decision for each company. For instance, companies deal with risk in very different ways, as we will see in detail in the next chapter. It seems intuitively clear that those less inclined to accept business uncertainties will be more cautious when deciding what to do with conceived potential MZs.

To add objectively to the selection process, companies could test the potential MZs against different parameters. We usually call this evaluation process the "wind tunnel," because the performance of the MZs is checked under different conditions. The threats and opportunities related to a potential MZ are evaluated. This would cover, for example, acceptance by the market (how will consumers react to it?), competitors' reactions (what will our rivals do when they notice we are implementing this potential MZ?), and regulatory mechanisms (is our strategy sensitive to actions by governments or other relevant agencies?).

In addition to this external analysis, a decision on a potential MZ must – as for any strategy – undergo an accurate financial analysis, which clearly reveals the investment needed, the possible return, and inherent risks. This will help strategists evaluate how attractive – or unattractive – a potential MZ is in terms of profit generation. Numerous financial analysis tools may be used to that purpose, but their description is beyond the scope of this book.[17] Let us remind you too that the choice or recommendation of a potential MZ must also take into consideration issues that are not easily quantifiable, such as the strategic learning obtained from the proposed MZ and its long-term potential to generate value. The worth of a strategy cannot always be assessed using spreadsheets.

Finally, it is important to mention that, despite the analysis we have just described, a decision to implement any potential MZ will always contain its share of uncertainty. There is no perfect strategic choice; surprises and path changes will always be present. This is exactly why we believe that the exploration process presented is highly relevant. If they adopt it, strategists will be properly fitted to conduct the company through the haze of uncertain reality.

In brief, the capacity for visualizing the future we discussed so far presupposes the ability to transcend the vision of the future as beyond human control. Proactive companies must adopt a new vision of tomorrow, and start tracking pulsating futures and exploring potential futures in an organized and systematic way. But this will only happen if the company is able to deal with one of today's greatest managerial tensions: the balance between today's needs and tomorrow's opportunities.

We have now reached the second capacity in the scope of future-today management: that is, the capacity for managing short-term pressure.

MANAGING SHORT-TERM PRESSURE

One company went through this process and then abandoned its attempt to construct a proactive strategy. Why? Managers had a meeting to discuss the reasons. They put forward various explanations and debated the causes. Then one manager commented, "To be honest, we both want and don't want to be proactive. We agree that it's important for the company to anticipate the future, but we always end up tied to the present. We are all hostages to the short term."

No wonder this company's attempt at developing a proactive strategy failed even before a strategy could be put into practice. Although managers understood the benefits of adopting a forward vision, and had had these repeated to them endlessly, they were always derailed by the demand for quick results. At the least sign of any reduction in the profit margin, the red button of cost reduction was pressed, and down went spending on R&D, innovation, and marketing. Projects that were expected to show a slower return were pushed to the end of the line. "We have no time for the long term: our strategy is to get immediate results." This was the tacit mantra the company's decision makers worked to. (In truth, it is often not even tacit.) In other words, the company was trapped in what we call "short-term pressure."

The conflict between short-term and long-term requirements is one of the major causes of managerial tension today. It forces companies and managers to take difficult and contradictory decisions.[18] How can managers think about long-term initiatives when partners, shareholders, and investors are becoming greedier and greedier for immediate returns? How can they run the risk of more uncertain future investments when performance indicators continue to reward instant returns? How can they concentrate their thoughts on a reality that lies five or ten years ahead with quarterly goals deadlines close ahead? Increasingly pressed by "impatient capital," managers end up avoiding more audacious or longer-term-result strategies.[19] This forces most companies to shorten their strategic horizon, shrinking it to match the one-year period that usually guides traditional strategic plans. (See Box 4.2.) To find a way out of this dilemma and build proactive strategies, companies must learn to balance short and long-term demands, trying – as Peter Drucker said – to fine tune a harmony between current requirements and opportunities in the future.

We should make it clear that short-term pressure, as described here, does not mean short-term management. All organizations must decide and act swiftly on occasion to avoid jeopardizing their own survival. The long-term continuation of a company depends directly on what is done in the short term, no doubt: a poor decision today and maybe there will be no tomorrow! The point about short-time pressure is that it distorts the healthy process of short-term management, leading companies to focus exclusively on quick-return strategies, often to the detriment of future results. Thus, while short-term management refers to actions that are necessary now, in the present, short-time pressure refers to an over-emphasis on these same actions. In brief, when we talk of managing short-time pressure, it does not mean underrating present priorities, but rather finding room for long-term considerations in the strategic agenda. It is a matter of efficiently and pragmatically combining the short and long terms. João Castro Neves, CEO of AMBEV, a leader in the gigantic Brazilian beer market, brought an useful contribution to this debate: "For us, the long term is made up of many short terms. We know how important it is to think five, ten or fifteen years ahead and always attempt to bring this vision of the future to the average term, changing it into annual goals."[20]

Accordingly, we started to study attitudes and actions that could help managers overcome this challenge. We found that proactive companies balance the relative intensity with which they focus on short and long-term demands and their disparate routines and requirements, adopting a procedure we call "management balance." We also found that these companies create a genuine long-term culture supported by metrics and incentives that leave room for future-return strategies. This next part of the chapter addresses the questions of how these two objectives can be met.

Box 4.2 How long does short-term last?

Sand in the hourglass of change flows nowadays at an increasingly high speed, and it is not as easy to define short term as it was a decade ago. In volatile sectors, such as digital technology, the short term sometimes means two or three months, not more, while half a year might be seen as a rather distant horizon. Even in sectors such as the primary sector, traditionally considered more stable and where changes are less speedy, the short term has shrunk. Managerially speaking, however, the short term is still considered as a period up to 12 months that corresponds to a fiscal year. (It is no wonder that this time limit orients the vast majority of traditional strategic plans, which are almost exclusively aimed at present-day objectives and strategies.) Thus, for most organizations, short-term pressure ends up inducing a strategic vision that is restricted to the current year, something we call "365 vision." In other words, it is a perspective that tends to blind strategists to future opportunities, and a hindrance to companies wishing to anticipate change and create tomorrow.

Equipoise: the management balance

Business life – like our personal lives – is full of conflicting objectives: to grow and at the same time maintain profitability; to keep operating efficiently and also to innovate; to take care of present results and act with an eye to the future. The manager's greatest challenge is to cope simultaneously with these objectives without being paralyzed or swept away by them. We believe this dilemma is even bigger in the field of market proactiveness. Proactive strategies imply companies committed to the long term, accepting deferred returns, and the uncertainty

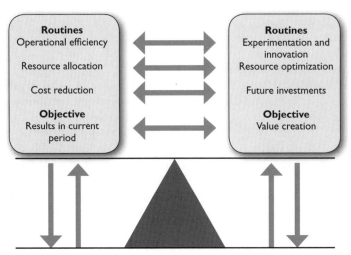

Figure 4.5 The management balance

and risks that surround actions which are intended to anticipate change. Often, unfortunately, the pressures of the moment weaken this commitment, directing strategists' eyes exclusively to current demands. So, to fertilize the soil for proactive actions, managers must have the capacity to see a picture of the future behind the veil of urgent requirements.

A first thing we can point out is that resolving this dilemma is not an issue of choosing between the short and long term choice (as you might think); it is one of complementarity. When we settle a conflict by opting for one of two opposing sides, we are, in truth, denying the existence of the conflict. Therefore, it is not a matter of prioritizing growth or profit, efficiency or innovation, today or tomorrow; it is a matter of simultaneously reconciling two apparently contradictory objectives. We need to find a way to provide A *and* B, instead A *or* B. We like to represent this subtle harmony as a set of scales, whose behavior depends on a careful distribution of weight between its weighing pans. In our management balance (Figure 4.5) the weights represent the short and long-term demands which managers have to face in their daily routine. Excessive weight in one pan will bring it clunking to the ground. This is what happens when short-term pressure blinds a company's view of future demands, tying it to the here and now; or perhaps less frequently, when an excessive focus on the future threatens its very survival in the present. Only a balance between the opposing demands will be able to keep the scales operating effectively.

Note that short and long-term demands follow entirely different routines and objectives. In the short term, the focus is on operational efficiency, which means a search for continuous improvement, an increase in productivity, and the ability to control processes. Resource allocation is always aligned with budgets in an attempt to preserve the planned outcome. An unflagging search for lower costs and waste reduction completes the requirements. All these demands are subject to a common objective: to achieve defined short-term results.

Long-term demands, on the other hand, are dramatically different. They involve experimentation and innovation, indispensable raw materials for market proactiveness. Resources – financial, material, and human – are managed in a more flexible way, in an effort to optimize rather than simply adjust them to budgets. There is more room for future long-term investment. Demands, in this case, are directed not to merely achieving results in the ongoing accounting period, but rather at creating long-term value for the company.

In practice, all demands of the type we have outlined require difficult decisions from managers. Should they engineer the production line to enable new product testing or keep production at full steam to achieve daily production goals? Allocate more resources to engineering in order to support an emerging innovative product or keep to the planned budget? Proceed with the current production pattern or change it (assuming this will mean an unavoidable loss of operating efficiency) to pursue a proactive strategy? Even when a company has enough resources to avoid having to make both explicit and tacit trade-offs (a rare case), internal demand for results (from shareholders and investors, for instance) will keep on challenging strategists' decisions. In the face of such a dilemma, what should you do to keep the management balance level?

Our contention is that managers, in order to successfully accomplish this task, must develop "ambidextrousness." In brief, ambidextrous companies have the ability to satisfactorily accommodate two contradictory demands: for instance, operating efficiency and flexibility, low-cost and differentiation strategies, and in our particular case, proactive (long-term) and reactive (short-term) strategies. These companies plan both for today and for tomorrow. They adopt a dual strategy, or in other words a double-horizon strategy, which accommodates short and long-term agendas and their corresponding demands. Studies are under way to try to discover and explain how this strategic ambidextrousness can be achieved.[21]

It is often said that an ambidextrous approach becomes more feasible when conflicting demands are managed by different units. This happens, for instance, when a company creates a new strategic unit aimed at innovation and experimentation, physically detached and entirely autonomous from the unit from which it stemmed. In this new unit, long-term objectives are free from short-term coercion and provide more room for risk and error (which are also crucial elements in the scope of proactive management, as we describe in the next chapter). The processes, routines, and metrics prevailing in this new unit are completely different. There is more flexibility, for instance to deal with new collection and payment terms, new suppliers and their different policies, and to assimilate long-reach indicators such as creation of value for the client and level of innovation. Within the scope of market proactiveness, we could say that this new unit, being somewhat protected from mother-unit repression, will end up creating a proactive culture, more akin to proactive management and adhering to the discourse of anticipation. This is what happens when a company acquires a smaller competitor that is known for its proactive mindset and makes it an autonomous unit aimed at experimenting with anticipatory strategies designed to produce later returns.

Companies can also deal with short and long-term contradictory demands in the same unit, as long as these are kept temporally separated. In this case, a company will alternate its strategic actions between short-term focus and long-term focus periods. As for our approach, this is what happens when a company acts proactively for a given period, focusing its efforts on launching a new product. During this "proactive phase," concessions are made and a more flexible management model is adopted than is used for present requirements. After the strategy is carried out and the product is launched, a focus on immediate demands and corresponding routines is reestablished – until a new proactive strategy is implemented and the focus is again shifted onto long-term initiatives.

Finally, a third alternative opens the possibility that a company might manage both sides of the management balance simultaneously within the same unit, counting on its employees' ability to synchronously manage short and long-term demands. This is the option usually taken by companies that lack the resources necessary to acquire a competing unit or to create a new unit within their own structure, and do not want to alternate between short and long-term strategies. This is maybe the configuration that poses the biggest threat to the weight distribution in the management scales, because managers must act as jugglers to properly accommodate conflicting demands and avoid privileging either side. A lack of ability to deal with this highly dynamic process may tip the scales one way or the other.

Which of these three approaches seems most promising to balance short and long-term demands? Studies in the field of new business models (a typically proactive logic strategy that usually generates conflicts between innovative and traditional models) have revealed, for instance, several successful and unsuccessful cases which have gone for either integration (two distinct models operated under the same structure) or separation (two distinct models operated from different strategic units).[22] The results have also demonstrated the difficulty of managing dual strategies, evidencing high levels of failure. The difficulties of responding simultaneously to both operational and experimental business requirements have been known for a long time (see Box 4.3). Hence, it is not so much opting for one of these models that matters, as acquiring the competence to deal with this intricate task and to take all the necessary actions to support the choice made.

A separation strategy, for instance, will be ineffectual if the new unit does not have real operating and financial autonomy, or if it is not free to develop its own culture and managerial systems. At the same time, the mother unit will have to offer its experience and knowledge and transfer, among other things, all brand advantages, market knowledge, and reputation to the new unit. As for integration, strategists will have to be able to deal with the conflicts of interest that develop when two distinct strategies cohabit. Frequently, long-term focused internal units end up being regarded as "living at the company's expense," and they are often suffocated by pressures exerted by opposing groups. In certain cases, managers who look for a less traumatic solution to the conflict eventually adjust long-term strategies to short-term demands. Then, proactive strategies end up being deformed to match a budget or operate at lower risk, typical requirements of a more short-sighted approach.

As we have seen, there is no optimum organizational way to bring the

Box 4.3 The difficult balance between exploring and exploiting

Two very similar words denote a crucial and significant difference in the context of market proactiveness: exploration and exploitation. Exploration evokes discovery, experimentation, risk, and innovation. Exploitation suggests a search for efficiency and productivity, permanent operation, and improvement. While the essence of exploration lies in experimenting with new alternatives, exploitation centers on the refinement of existing competences and technologies. To use an analogy, exploration may be compared to the search for new land to sow change, while exploitation is concerned about efficiently managing and cultivating known land.

In the realm of market strategies, exploitation actions have been so far related to more reactive attitudes, while exploration actions seem to be closer to anticipatory and proactive attitudes. Examples of exploitation are gains in experience and production volume that enable the company to operate a low-cost responsive strategy. Exploration strategies, on the other hand, may be found in typical proactive activity such as the construction of new market segments, launch of new offers, and design of new distribution channels. Exploitation strategies are more adaptive, oriented to serve existing markets and their explicit demands, while exploration strategies try to anticipate change and create markets.

The exploration–exploitation trade-off represents the central challenge for proactive companies. Exploration and exploitation strategies compete for resources and are usually regarded as antagonistic. While exploitation invests time and resources in less risky initiatives, exploration sets out to conquer new remote land, distant from the company's immediate objectives. Because of this, the literature on strategy has tended to neglect the possibility of setting off these two dimensions, assuming that companies that simultaneously contemplate both exploitation and exploration strategies will end up not satisfactorily carrying out any of them, entrapped in strategic indecision. More recent views, however, uphold the idea that complementarity between these poles is not only possible but beneficial.

This kind of complementarity can be observed, for example, when a company uses the deep knowledge and expertise gathered along its trajectory in the market (exploitation) to more accurately interpret signs of possible future changes in consumer habits, creating new products and services (exploration). This type of capability enabled Fiat to conceive the Adventure, a successful offer proactiveness initiative presented in this book. The balance between exploitation and exploration also shows up when a company proactively creates a new offer (exploration) and later adjusts this offer in response to the first impressions of early users, applying its production or engineering competence (exploitation). Here, an exploratory proactive action is improved based on a quick and intelligent reaction, supported by operating capabilities.

Note, in both examples, how harmony between exploration and exploitation requires the development of a more flexible vision, capable of perceiving these two possibilities as complementary rather than mutually exclusive. This calls for a multifocal vision capable of looking simultaneously in two different directions. This

> encompassing vision will help companies handle, at the same time, the present and future, today's requirements and tomorrow's opportunities (and threats). As a manager once appropriately said, "It's like keeping one eye on the goldfish and the other on the cat."[23]

management balance and its demands to equilibrium. Success – as in the examples we have mentioned – is contingent and highly dependent on a company's capacity for managing the selected model. In our point of view, however, another variable also influences this balance and may help companies deal more adequately with the dichotomy between the short and long terms. This variable is linked to a culture focused on the promotion of long-term decisions, on motivating and encouraging strategists to adopt a wider vision of the future.

Create a long-term culture

In his biography, commenting on the rise and fall of IBM, Louis Gerstner Jr. accurately described the importance of corporate culture: "culture is not merely an aspect of the game – it is the game."[24] It was a cultural change that saved IBM from collapse at the beginning of the 1990s. The statement made by IBM's former CEO – the tillerman who conducted this historical recovery – makes clear how relevant corporate culture is in the life of companies. This relevance is often described in relation to innovative strategies that involve uncertainty, where culture is deemed to play a fundamental role. We believe that creating a long-term culture is vital in establishing a better balance between the present and future in a company's strategic agenda, since it leaves more room for slower and sometimes uncertain return strategies in its list of priorities.[25] Octávio Florisbal, general director of Rede Globo, a leading Brazilian TV network and one of the world's most innovative companies in the segment, confirms the strategic convenience of this present–future balance:

> The day-to-day operation of a TV station is a lot more intense than in other businesses. Therefore, we operate strictly according to annual plans, month by month, tracking and measuring everything: tendencies, competitors, and the market as a whole. In the last few years, however, we have started to plan ahead and detected several strategic areas we should evaluate in detail and more proactively, such as changes in the behavior of media consumers.[26]

In brief, we can define organizational culture as a collection of beliefs, values, and norms that ultimately explains why a given company acts the way it does. Furthermore, culture influences what members of an organization expect from each other and what the organization, as a whole, expects from its relationship with other players in the external environment (clients, competitors, suppliers, distributors, shareholders, and other stakeholders).[27] We have therefore conceived a long-term culture whose principles promote a more balanced vision of both present and future, mobilizing all stakeholders in the search for that perspective.

Figure 4.6 The long-term culture

That culture will further an environment more susceptible to long-term focused actions, and help generate the required perceptions, attitudes, and behaviors. In order to create and foster a culture with these characteristics, however, it is necessary for the company to adopt and apply two distinct and complementary tools: a long-term indicators system and a long-term incentive policy (see Figure 4.6). The joint promotion of these two instruments will help companies develop a long-term vision, favoring the equalization of the opposing forces acting on the management balance. Let us see how it works.

Long-term indicators

Consider a company that is introducing market proactiveness in its strategic agenda but keeps using only short-term financial indicators (such as profitability and return on investment) to measure performance. It will not take long before incompatibility between the new and traditional metrics emerges. A situation will soon be reached where these antagonistic indicators can no longer be reconciled, exposing the short-term–long-term dichotomy and putting the strategies at risk. Thus, we would argue that that the first condition for a long-term culture is the use of long-term indicators.

The system of indicators a company adopts ultimately represents its strategic intent and expectations (even if these are subliminal). Hence, a table of indicators must be always constructed to help orient the strategy, rather than to be a mere control tool. Metaphorically speaking, an indicator system is like a car's accelerator, rather than its brake. Brought to our present context, this reasoning allows us to say that a company that adopts short-term indicators will barely think of the long term. The more short-term focused the chosen metric is, the higher will be the short-term pressure. Studies on the subject found that an emphasis on traditional financial performance metrics stimulates managers to adopt short-term strategies. Conversely, the use of non-financial indicators – such as those aimed at clients and innovation – is now regarded as a way of implementing long-term focused managerial attitudes.

There is strong evidence that the nature of a metric substantially influences managerial behavior. Indeed, agency theory – aimed at studying the relationship and conflicts of interest arising between a main party (for example, a company's partners or shareholders) and a contracted agent (for example, its managers and leaders) – reflects this understanding. Managers act to a great extent under the influence of external stimuli, albeit preserving their individual interests and professional survival. One conclusion we may draw from this reasoning is that performance metrics and related incentives end up guiding managerial actions, channeling managers' efforts to the achievement of what is being measured. A strategist will hardly pursue targets that do not show up in a company's dashboard.[28]

The concept of the balanced scorecard (BSC) – a powerful approach to performance measurement – may be very useful in the construction of a more balanced system of indicators that is capable of stimulating strategists to add the long term to their decisions. As is well known, the basic and underlying idea of the BSC is that a system of indicators essentially expresses the business model a company adopts. To add long-term concerns, a system must focus not only on financial indicators (which, ultimately, are simply pictures of past performance) but also on non-financial indicators in the dimensions of customers, internal processes, and innovation and knowledge management (the true agents of future performance). Proposing three complementary dimensions to the financial perspective, this structure helps companies overcome a historical deficiency of conventional metric systems: their inability to reconcile long-term with short-term indicators.[29]

According to the logic of the BSC, a metric system that fits with a long-term culture will measure not only immediate short-term performance but also the creation of future value in the spheres of customers, innovation, and internal processes. It is important that the system also caters for sustainable gains – that is, those showing some life expectancy – in all three dimensions of proactiveness. This is a fundamental issue because managers are often tempted to improve present-day results with gains that the future will show to be harmful. This is what happens, for instance, when slow-return investments are postponed or prices are lowered in response to competition.

Thus, the results on a company's scoreboard must include not only current unsustainable gains (often imposed by environmental contingencies or internal difficulties), but also future sustainable gains. The latter, despite the reduction in current profitability they initially cause due to the investment of time, people, and money, will certainly bring more significant, lasting and competition-resistant returns in the future.[30]

There is a familiar managerial saying that "whatever is measured, is done." In other words, when a company measures something, people automatically infer that it is important. On the contrary, things that are not measured tend to be ignored. In accordance with what we have been discussing so far, this means that a company's system of measurement will tend to influence its behavior and culture.[31] This helps us understand the importance of a balanced measurement system like the one we are describing. If a company privileges short-term financial indicators to the detriment of long-term variables, it conveys the message that its priority is on immediate results. The pressure, either internal (expressed by managers' concerns with budgets) or external (expressed by investors' demands), to achieve numerical targets will end up displacing slower return strategies and tying the company's focus to short-term events, consequently disturbing the management balance. A more harmonious measurement system will show managers that the company approves of and encourages long-term decisions. To be even more efficient, it is important that the system is in tune with an incentive policy that rewards future results. This is the second condition for the long-term culture we have conceived of.

Long-term incentives

Undoubtedly incentives are very important variables in determining individual behavior in organizations. Both in and outside companies, people usually act in response to what they expect to win or lose. Since bad quarterly results are liable to hinder their career, it is not illogical for managers to avoid uncertain and slower-return strategies. Short-term incentives encourage short-term attitudes, molding managers' behaviors accordingly. Therefore, a company's efforts to pursue long-term results may prove fruitless if decision makers feel discouraged from aiming at the future, simply because the organization's reward policy is not aligned with the nature of its non-immediate return strategies.

In order to stimulate a long-term focus, the incentive system itself must be based on the long term. In other words, the reward system should encourage slower-return strategies instead of discouraging them. Proactive strategies that show results only a year or two after implementation, or even longer, are incompatible with a reward system that privileges the short term. In such situations, it seems advisable to tie gains to long-term incentives, such as bonuses and share options. Research on reward systems aimed at favoring radical innovation – a typical long-term return initiative – has found that this type of incentive is perfectly appropriate to promote future-oriented postures. Hélio Rotenberg, president of Positivo Informática, the largest computer manufacturer in Latin America, agrees on the importance of rewarding innovation in incentive systems:

> A perfect incentive remuneration system for executives should contemplate, besides yearly results, rupture innovation. Even when the company's bottom line says it is doing well today, if rupture innovation is not an alternative, no one can say that the company will be doing fine in the future too. Thus, innovation must become a performance indicator for the higher executive levels of a company, stimulating them to pay attention to the long term.[32]

It is important to emphasize that the incentives need not necessarily be financial or monetary. Acknowledgement is also essential – and often even more fruitful – for the complex task of motivating strategic-decision participants and stakeholders to adopt a less short-term focused vision. Strategists must feel confident that the company supports their long-term decisions, acknowledges their audacity and resolve, and stimulates them to face risks. No company will ever learn to deal with the long term without motivating its strategists to take that step.

The US writer F. Scott Fitzgerald once described how valuable it is to hold two opposed ideas in your mind at the same time.[33] This is the kind of intelligence that needs to be applied when dealing with the short-term–long-term antagonism. We believe that a long-term incentive policy is a useful tool to promote this competence, especially when its operates with a long-term measurement system as discussed above. This will create a virtuous circle aimed at the long term: if managers' incentives are linked to non-financial long-term indicators too, the chances are good that they will look for long-term results. This will help strategists to cope with the dilemma of today's requirements versus tomorrow's opportunities. In other words, they will be able to develop a more flexible strategic capacity and to deal with this antagonism without collapsing.

There are many different incentive systems and corresponding types and methods of reward (an exhaustive description is outside the scope of this book). A company's reward structure must take into consideration aspects such as the standard level of recompense in the industry, how rewards are transferred (bonus, shares, promotions), the competences and the expertise associated with the work, and the personal abilities and characteristics of direct beneficiaries. It is also important to pay attention to the less tangible aspects of reward. Incentives refer to the extrinsic dimension of human motivation: that is, the proportion of someone's willingness to act that may be influenced – either negatively or positively – by factors extrinsic to the individual. But motivation has an intrinsic aspect too, in the sense of the disposition of individuals to take on challenges. This means that other factors – such as the exercise of autonomy and creativity, and the opportunity for self-realization – are also important in motivation. An excessive emphasis on external stimuli may undermine individuals' innate disposition to look for new challenges, a genuine interest considered fundamental to innovative cultures and characteristic of proactive companies that aim to change the market. While the lack of incentives may inhibit long-term decision making, its excess may generate an illusory and harmful engagement – a make-believe commitment – or even strategic sabotage. Finally, a good reward policy will be balanced and will contemplate these two facets of human motivation without carrying either to excess.[34]

In brief, managing short-term pressure, as we have described, means avoiding the pursuit of present-day goals to the detriment of the future, eroding tomorrow's competitive position. As mega-investor Warren Buffett once said, "If bad decisions are made in an attempt to achieve short-term goals, no later brilliant initiatives will be able to heal the harm inflicted."[35] In our opinion this saying could be used in the context of market proactiveness, where more audacious strategies are often abandoned in favor of more immediate return requirements. Proactive companies must orchestrate the short and long term harmoniously, whatever the context and situation in which a proactive market strategy is being executed. They must keep in mind that excessive attachment to today may become a disregard of tomorrow.

In this chapter we have explained how the capacities for visualizing future and managing the short term are essential to efficient future-today management. These are the two capacities that enable companies to manage future here and now. But, as we have seen, proactive management is supported by the development of three other managerial dimensions. One of these, uncertainty management, will be discussed next.

UNCERTAINTY MANAGEMENT

5 Learning How to Deal with Risk and Error

One of the reasons why companies are reactive is their defensive posture toward the unknown. Anticipating the future surely brings bigger risks and possibilities of failure; it is safer simply to respond to the market's demands, reproducing what everyone else (that is, each competitor) does. Proactive strategies – exactly because they deal with what does not exist yet – intensify this fear of what is indeterminate. In addition, because market proactiveness proposes drastic changes in the current managerial paradigm, it ends up increasing the fear of uncertainty inherent in every change process. All this constitutes a huge barrier to the establishment of market proactiveness. Proactive companies must learn to manage uncertainty.[1]

Two feelings automatically come to our minds when we face the unknown: the fear of taking risks and the fear of failing. Thus, managing uncertainty means dealing efficaciously with both risk and error. But we know that this is no easy task. The usual behavior pattern of a vast majority of organizations still consists – despite efforts to pretend otherwise – of aversion to making errors and taking risks.[2] We tried to understand why this happens and what practices may be implemented to overcome this paradigm. This is what we describe in this chapter.

DEALING WITH RISK

Just like people, companies do not respond to risk in the same way.[3] While some are better in assimilating the uncertainties that surround any strategic action, others are highly reluctant to confront the unknown. Proactive companies belong in the first group. Managers who favor market proactiveness know that risk is a potential element in the process of anticipating moments zero (MZs), and they therefore champion a culture in their companies that is not averse to this element. The reality we studied, however, does not reflect much occurrence of this; rather, it evidences most companies' reluctance to interact with the unknown and its inherent risks. This is a major hindrance to market proactiveness. It seems that the higher a company's risk aversion, the lower its possibility of acting proactively.[4]

The capacity for dealing with risk, as described here, represents the level to which an organization's managers do or do not take the risks associated with the execution of a proactive strategy.[5] The question here is, what determines the disposition – or aversion – to take risks? Why do some companies take strategic risks at higher levels and more efficaciously than others? How do their actions differ? In brief, what is their secret?

We found that companies that deal better with risk develop an analytical, rather than emotional, attitude to uncertainty. They take actions that are essential to avoid the development of a risk-aversion culture, but at the same time, their culture is conservative enough not to launch the company into ill-judged and uncontrolled risk taking. More specifically, we identified two basic attitudes usually taken by companies that deal better with risk. Let us discuss these attitudes and the necessary actions to put them into practice.[6]

Overcome the security fallacy

Toward the end of the 1990s, when digital music was on the rise, Sony made one of its biggest strategic mistakes ever. The MP3 format had just consolidated its position in the market and become a unique opportunity for the company to reinvigorate its greatest invention, the Walkman. However, if Sony participated in this market, there would be a risk of illegal copying of the music in which it held rights. Because of this risk and in an attempt to protect the company's market, its strategists decided not to include the MP3 feature in the new digital Walkman. The device could only play back music encoded in Sony's proprietary format (ATRAC). Consumers already acquainted with the MP3 standard did not like this idea, and the Japanese giant failed to capture this MZ. Attentive to signs of the revolution, in 2001 its rival Apple launched the now-ubiquitous iPod, a music player that was designed quite differently and was – most importantly – compatible with many different audio formats. We all know how this story ended: Apple now completely dominates the portable music market Sony created back in 1979 with its Walkman.[7]

This example illustrates well the meaning of the "security fallacy" as we understand it: a defensive attitude to risk that is adopted by companies concerned more with what they might lose than with what they might win. The fear of losing makes managers take "safer" and less audacious decisions. An unbalanced analysis of the likely gains and losses probably led Sony's strategists to discard the option of using the MP3 format in the Walkman. An excessive focus on the threat of loss made them neglect a promising opportunity. They did, in truth, embody the standard question every manager poses when facing a risk: What am I liable to lose if I take this action? It is necessary, however, for managers to learn a second and usually underestimated question: What am I liable to lose – or fail to win – if I do not take the action?

Research in the field of risk helps explain why strategists frequently favor the first question. The truth is that most of us value losses above gains, when facing uncertainty. Put plainly, the pain we associate with failure is greater than the pleasure we associate with an equivalent level of success (think of either winning or losing $1000). Thus, although losses and gains are always weighted when we deal with uncertainty, this weighting is most frequently accompanied with a value imbalance. This helps explain why managers, when facing risk, are usually and above all worried about what they might lose, neglecting what they might win. The sheer possibility of loss, no matter how small, prevents the company from betting on gains and contributes to keeping it inactive.[8]

Overcoming the security fallacy requires strategists to put some basic actions into practice (see Box 5.1). First, they must evaluate not only the potential losses related to a given strategy, but also what they will be missing if they decide not to execute it. Here, a fundamental paradigmatic change is necessary: a risk has more than just the negative facet that is so often emphasized. Every risk brings positive as well as negative possibilities. A stance that is exclusively focused on the negative side of risk and its minimization will unavoidably reduce the opportunity potential of taking a risk. Hence, instead of maximizing risk avoidance, strategists should understand the fact that every risk brings possibilities of gain (if that possibility did not exist, taking risks would be a meaningless adventure). Giving up this potential gain may be more harmful than the loss they try to avoid.[9]

To overcome the security fallacy, proactive strategists must also focus on the consequences of taking a given risk, instead of only on the probability of its occurrence. This is a mistake that paralyzes many managers: when dealing with uncertainty, they make such an effort to understand the probability of something going wrong that they forget to weigh the actual consequences of their actions. Decisions about potential events must be based more on the possible consequences (which is relatively accessible knowledge) than on attempts to predict their probabilities, a kind of usually incomputable and limited-access knowledge. Thus, it is more productive to invest resources in evaluating whether the consequences of a given risk will be serious or not. If they are likely to be serious, it is probably a good idea to avoid the risk, but if the expected losses are insignificant and the potential gains are appreciable, then it may be a good idea to take the risk.[10] It is advisable to keep in mind that an excessive focus on a risk's negative possibilities ends up inhibiting managers' actions, forcing them to assume defensive positions and preventing them from taking action.

A third and last issue related to the security fallacy involves managers' motivation over risk. Strategists – like most of us – are not immune to the aversion to loss we have already commented on. Thus, if decision makers are not stimulated to take the risks associated with proactive strategies, they will tend to avoid that responsibility. The creation of a risk-sharing culture and the development of balanced risk–reward structures are useful tools to stimulate strategists' appetite for risk taking. Sharing is built on the principle that risk aversion tends to decrease when risks are jointly and collaboratively taken, with the inherent fear of uncertainty also being shared. As was stated by Bernardo Hees, now head of North American Burger King and the former CEO of ALL Logística, a leader in logistics services in South America, "A 'partnership of opinions' is needed when we deal with risks. Joint decisions are much stronger."[11] Dealing with risk is both the task and the responsibility of everyone in the company, since no one is immune to its positive or negative effects.[12]

A balanced reward structure, in turn, prevents companies from adopting unbalanced attitudes to managers' gains and losses when they take risks. Often, strategists feel they have a lot to lose if the dangers associated with their decisions materialize, and little to win if the company profits. Fear of losing prestige or even their position in the company, together with a lack of financial interest in the gains resulting from a right decision, ends up demotivating managers and keeping them from choosing to take potential risks. No capacity for dealing with risk can survive this tacit mantra, something we usually call an "anti-reward" policy. Observe that companies that accept risks reverse this reasoning: instead of guiding their risk management by fear, they base it on encouragement.[13]

Box 5.1 Overcoming the "security fallacy"

- Focus on what the company might lose if a risk is not taken, instead of only on what it might lose if it does run a risk. Remember that not winning is also a way of losing.
- Risks represent both threats and opportunities. Focusing exclusively on the negative side of risk leads companies to avoid any risk at all and neglect inherent opportunities for gain.
- Face to face with risk, consider and evaluate the possible consequences if a loss or failure materializes, instead of only its probability of occurrence.
- Create a culture of shared risk, stimulating cooperation and sharing responsibilities. This will encourage people to take risks.
- Reward positive attitudes to risk. Remember that, if people are not motivated to take business risks, they will tend to remain inside the safety zone.

We will finish our description of the "security fallacy" with the words of the legendary Ayrton Senna, when explaining his success as a Formula 1 driver. He had just created one of the most extraordinary moments in the history of Formula 1. In 1993, driving on the Donington circuit in England, Senna's McLaren was squeezed right after the start and fell back to fifth place. Under heavy rain and equipped with slick tires – improper and risky under such conditions – Senna carried out a fantastic sequence of spectacular maneuvers, and needed only 40 seconds to overtake all the four drivers ahead of him. It seemed to him it was worth taking a gamble in these adverse conditions. After the race, he declared, "In conditions like these, it's gambling and it's taking chances that pays off. And I think we gambled good." Senna's achievement reflects a non-defensive posture toward risk, a stance aimed at breaking with the illusory safety in a "wait and see" attitude. This is exactly the characteristic attitude of proactive companies. They are not afraid of risky situations, and taking risks enables them to keep ahead of less audacious competitors.[14]

But having the guts to be so intrepid does not happen by chance. Just like in Formula 1, dealing with the risk of strategy requires preparation and attention. Companies must learn the various aspects of risk in anticipation and detail, recognizing its behavior and characteristics, lessening the chances of driving into a skid. To achieve that, they must acquire real expertise in business-related risks, a posture characteristic of the second attitude we identified: learning about risk.

Learning about risk

In the commonsense definition, risk is an undetermined, and thus unpredictable, element. After all, risk *is* risk exactly because of its random and accidental nature. In consequence, it is strongly believed that no knowledge can ever reduce risk-related uncertainty, and that learning about the causes, consequences and probabilities of possible outcomes is very difficult. This reasoning is misleading. It is now known that few risks are really unpredictable. Toyota's production of hybrid vehicles we mentioned in Chapter 1 is a good example. When US auto makers finally woke up to the new demand for smaller and more economic cars, halfway through the first decade of the new millennium, the Japanese company had already been generating knowledge and reducing its uncertainty over the risks inherent in the new technology for more than a decade. This previously acquired knowledge of the risks helped Toyota substantially in creating the Prius, a profitable MZ in the market. It is possible to reduce risk-inherent uncertainty as long as we have the necessary time and resources to learn about risk.[15]

What we call uncertainty, in brief, depends on the level of information we have about a given event. Thus, the more knowledge a company generates on the threats and opportunities related to a proactive market strategy, the more precisely it will be able to judge whether it is worth executing it. This will help companies distinguish between worthwhile strategic risks and those that only look likely to lead to losses, and thus encourage them to take the right action. One aspect, however, must be highlighted in this context. Often, an excess of information becomes a magnifying glass, amplifying the risks inherent in business. Much has been said about "analysis paralysis," a situation in which a company gathers so much information on business risks that it ends up inert, lost in a maze of variables and probabilities. This happens because there is only a positive relationship between the amount of information available and its usefulness for strategic decision making up to a given point: from then on, adding more information only glazes the strategists' lenses, instead of improving the decision quality. As Sofia Esteves, president of the DMRH Group, a leading company in the Brazilian competence recruiting market, told us, "If you focus too much on information, you end up becoming afraid. It's as if clarity confuses things instead of helping, because often you don't have all figures and information."[16] Thus, we can never repeat too often that learning about risk involves recognizing the line between useful and excessive information. Tons of data on the market and budgets crammed with graphs and spreadsheets are not always the best strategic advisers.

Learning about risk offers an additional benefit: it helps minimize excessive optimism and the illusion of control, psychological cognitive biases that often haunt decision makers dealing with uncertainty. This behavior frequently leads to the counterpart to risk aversion: daring exposure to the unknown, which is often an unwise and harmful attitude to take. It has been argued that this kind of exaggerated self-confidence can increase when difficult and relatively ambiguous decisions must be taken, which is exactly the case for proactive strategic decisions.[17] We believe that learning about risks allows decision makers to acquire a more realistic view of the threats inherent in a planned proactive strategy, which increasing their chances of assessing them properly. This attitude helps the company delineate its "boundary of risk": in other words, the limit beyond which the cost–benefit ratio of the risks of a given strategy is no longer favorable. As Luiza Trajano, president of Magazine Luiza, one of the largest retail networks in Brazil, once said, "a proactive company has to take risks, but at the same time, it must know how much it is willing to pay when it makes a decision."[18]

The actions we have listed help companies develop a learning posture with respect to risk (see Box 5.2). Together with those aimed at overcoming the security fallacy, they make a practical route for companies needing to improve their relationship with the risks involved in adopting a proactive market strategy. We already know that risk management is only half the way to an efficient management of uncertainty: it is also necessary to know how to deal with mistakes along the way. We often say that risk and error are two sides of the same coin: the way a company deals with error is intrinsically linked to the way it deals with risk, and vice versa. Thus, proactive companies must learn how to live with error, the second element of uncertainty we will now describe.

Box 5.2 Learning about risk

- Study the risk before you take it. Familiarize yourself with the risk and gain ground for future action.
- Remember that few risks are really unpredictable; risks give clues to what might happen.
- Study risks, but keep in mind that this knowledge may give you an illusory sense of control over uncertainty. Risks should never be underestimated: beware of excessive optimism and confidence.
- Do not overdo the search for information. Learning about risk also presupposes being able to filter what comes to a company's ears.

DEALING WITH ERROR

Let us be honest: we hate making mistakes. We live in a society where failure is an embarrassment, something to be hidden or forgotten. This is even worse in the corporate world, where an error may represent the loss of a bonus, a promotion, or even a job. At the same time, we endlessly hear management consultants claiming that mistakes generate knowledge and therefore should not be stigmatized. We live under the "paradox of error."

The proactive companies we visited have learned how to overcome this dichotomy. They regard mistakes made along the way not as causes for annoyance, but rather as growth potential. On the other hand, reactive companies are usually unwilling to run the risk of making mistakes; they prefer to "let our competitors do it wrong first," and give up opportunities as a result.[19] Just as with risk, improving the capacity for dealing with error requires more than the mere wish to change, it requires that companies continually practice two fundamental attitudes we identified.

Eliminate the boundary between success and failure

Few dichotomies are so disquieting to human action as the one that separates success from failure. The notion that these two states are opposite and incommunicable poles and that the existence of one presupposes the absence of the other seems indisputable. In this context, failure is regarded as an absolutely negative fact, a drawback to be feared and avoided. Studies in the field of error demonstrate that this misunderstanding is the root of a universal difficulty in dealing with failure in the course of action.[20]

The first action required to overcome this dichotomy is simply to consider the relativity inherent in the usual concepts of success and failure. We have to understand that a momentary failure might later on become an important element in a success. Conversely, we must keep in mind that current success might silently be paving the road to failure. This is what is called "danger of success."[21] Companies can be blinded by past victories, and become inexorably attached to strategies that are not capable of dealing with new market realities any more. Think of the IBM case we mentioned: the company remained bound to the success of mainframes while personal computers invaded the world. Or consider North American auto makers in the 1970s: dazzled by the success of a presumably immutable product – big and luxury cars – they did not become aware of a new market reality that demanded smaller and more economic cars, which as we have seen, was an MZ that ended up being anticipated by Japanese companies.

If success has its dangers, failure may bring benefits. This is illustrated by cases such as Jacuzzi. In the 1950s it made the mistake of positioning its new whirlpool bathtub as a therapeutic product, aimed at consumers suffering from arthritis – a market that proved to be both small and mostly composed of consumers that did not have enough money to buy the product. This "failure" led the company to realize the true potential of its innovation, which it repositioned as a luxury product targeted at high-income consumers. This strategic turnaround – propelled by a mistake – changed Jacuzzi bathtubs into a real icon in the market. This same ability to change mistakes into advantages led Sony to create what is still most purchased technological product in history, the Walkman (introduced in 1979, in 15 years it sold a fantastic 350 million units).[22] The Walkman became a reality only because Sony had the idea of reshaping an unsuccessful project (to develop a portable stereo recorder) and changing it into an offer that revolutionized the way people consumed music. That "failure" created what had previously been an unimagined market for portable music.[23] (Note that the Sony examples demonstrate that a company might – at different moments – be both efficient in one dimension of market proactiveness (here, dealing with error) and incapable in another (dealing with risk). This reinforces the importance of joint development and continuous practice of the capacities for market proactiveness we described in Chapter 3.)

Overcoming the success–failure dichotomy also means focusing more on objectives than on paths to follow. Harry Schmelzer Jr., CEO of electric motors manufacturer WEG, helps us explain this reasoning: "There is no right or wrong course; only your target exists."[24] It is exactly this vision that enables us to break the paradigm that separates success from failure. In this sense, failures along the way are seen as stages in the achievement of strategic objectives. Achieving objectives is more important than not making mistakes. Think of the not-so-rare occasions when the champion is not the team with the least number of defeats, but rather the one that was able to manage its bad results, learn from them and avoid making the same mistakes again. Frequently, what we call success is the sum of minor defeats and victories.

The attitudes we have described so far will help companies change their mindset concerning the success–failure dichotomy (see Box 5.3). Proactive companies must be aware that no path is exempt from misfortune, and that the best way to pursue success is to be open to facing mistakes along the way. In other words, they might as well nurture the "freedom to make mistakes" that is the second attitude to be put into practice when dealing with error.

Box 5.3 Eliminating the boundary between success and failure

- Remember that the distinction between success and failure is, above all, a convention; strategists must change their mindset and overcome this dichotomy.
- Remember those companies that were blinded by success and those that were able to see farther thanks to their "failures."
- Keep in mind that fleeing from failure also means fleeing from success, and that avoiding failure can lead the company to deviate from its objectives.
- Note that no company is excellent 100 percent of the time; great careers include misfortunes too.

Practice having the freedom to make mistakes

"Freedom to make mistakes" refers to an attitude to error that avoids recrimination, and is rooted in the perception that failures are opportunities to learn. Above all, we need to appreciate that the freedom to make mistakes does not mean that we can take the wrong path as often as we like, but rather that we need to take an analytical approach to errors. It does not mean tolerance of any and every kind of failure, or an absence of control and supervision. To be free to make mistakes means understanding that the possibility of going in the wrong direction is always present, and that failure may be a major source of new insights and findings.

As for any autonomous action, the freedom to make mistakes must have limits. In other words, companies must be able to identify the line beyond which the consequences of error are not worth the cost of learning about them. It is like a cost–benefit analysis of learning and error consequences. According to Natura's CEO Alessandro Carlucci, working at the limit of error "is like keeping error exactly the size you can cope with."[25] This true shaping of error helps companies avoid suicidal mistakes that could ultimately jeopardize the organization's health.

To put the freedom to make mistakes into practice, companies must also allow for the trial and error method. Leander Kahney – a reporter and editor who has been studying Apple for more than a decade – says that one of Steve Jobs' company's principles is trial and error. When working on a new product, Apple's designers and engineers conceive the highest possible number of solutions to each problem they encounter, and these are then tested to find the most effective. The iPod's innovative interface was created through a trial and error design process.[26] Thus, at the heart of the trial and error method is an understanding that what matters is to find the most adequate answer, regardless of how many wrong answers are considered along the way. Jairo Yamamoto, former CEO of Medley, a leading company operating in the Brazilian generic drug segment, stated it very well: "I would rather try ten times and make three mistakes than do only two things right."[27] How would your company deal with a 30 percent error rate?

Finally, a culture that promotes the freedom to make mistakes must also encourage outspoken debate about the mistakes that are made along the way. We like to say that proactive companies "look under the carpet." Instead of trying to hide their failures, treating them as top-secret subjects, these companies promote collective debates about mistakes. It is said that scientist Wernher von Braun (1912–1977), a jet propulsion pioneer, once presented an engineer on his team with a bottle of champagne because he assumed responsibility for the unsuccessful launch of a missile. The confession saved time and money for the project. Had this man not admitted where he had got it wrong, the project would almost certainly have been unnecessarily redesigned.[28] This is exactly what looking under the carpet means: do not pretend that mistakes were not made, but rather treat them as opportunities to learn.

A mistake that is advertised is less likely to happen again because reporting generates knowledge. Had 3M tried to hide its mistake, probably the Post-it – the result of using an inefficient adhesive – would not have become reality. The iPod would probably not exist if Apple's principles did not include a policy of open discussion about mistakes made along the way (think of the Walkman story). Companies must develop a memory for both mistakes and right decisions, and this is possible only through sharing. Some companies use a "lessons learned" system to jointly analyze both mistakes and right decisions. The system registers the reasons for past successes and failures. Reporting mistakes made in attempts to develop something new – and not only successes – means admitting that mistakes can generate knowledge so they must not be concealed or camouflaged.

But let us repeat, the freedom to make mistakes does not grant companies the license to err in any circumstances or make any kind of mistake. There are mistakes and mistakes: that is to say, both positive and constructive mistakes, and unjustifiable errors for which there can be no tolerance. In other words, there

---

Two incidents in the career of the great jazz pianist Thelonious Monk (1917–1982) provide useful examples of "right mistakes." The first happened during a solo jazz performance when he was recording "In walked Bud," a song included on *Misterioso* (1958). Monk inadvertently struck a wrong note, realized it, improvised a new melody, and literally transformed the recording by the way he responded. The musician's unique ability to deal with accidental mistakes meant that he made this one almost imperceptible. Monk's "right mistake" – because changed it into an opportunity – suggests the relevance of mistakes made to knowledge generation and new findings.

The second involves an answer given by Monk, when he was asked why he seemed low after an apparently successful performance. He said, "I made the wrong mistakes." Although it might appear contradictory, Monk's witty remark logically refers to the "right mistakes" we described; those that generate learning and, when understood and managed, may point to new horizons.[29]

Proactive strategists should learn from jazz musicians that errors are opportunities to improvize and find a new melody. In strategy, as well as in music, an error only becomes a "real" error when we don't know what to do with it. After all, as Alexandre Costa, the founder and president of Cacau Show, the world's largest fine chocolate franchise network, opportunely said, "What can you do with an error other than learning with it? You have already made the mistake, anyway!"[30]

---

are the right kind of mistakes and the wrong kind of mistakes. In the workshops and meetings we conduct on market proactiveness, we always mention the story of a manager who used to tell his team "I want new mistakes!" We tell this story because the notion of new mistakes reflects the idea of "the right mistakes" we are presenting. New mistakes come from taking a risk, and therefore they are justifiable and acceptable. These are mistakes that can lead to new perspectives on reality, something that is fundamental to market proactiveness. Sometimes, the right mistakes are even the result of simple error, but what makes the difference is that these are errors that can be turned into new opportunities (see Box 5.4).

As we have seen, practicing the freedom to make mistakes and its corresponding attitudes (see Box 5.5) helps companies stay open to faults, promoting a culture where mistakes are regarded as learning opportunities. In addition to being more open to acknowledging and discussing errors, it is also healthier if companies willing to act proactively create a "mistakes score" and try to evaluate whether mistakes have unearthed growth opportunities or are simply faults from which nothing positive can be drawn. When studying error management, we routinely ask managers what type of mistake their companies make. Most are faults that have nothing to contribute at all. And your own company? What type of mistake does it make?

The attitudes and actions presented in this chapter are fundamental to companies

Box 5.5 Practicing the freedom to make mistakes

- Remember that the freedom to make mistakes should not be taken as a license to err; a mistake-friendly culture does not mean tolerance of everything that goes wrong.
- Look under the carpet of errors: in other words, create a culture where mistakes are publicly shared so they can generate learning.
- Encourage people to use trial and error, and remember that companies that never make mistakes are perhaps not doing much.
- Distinguish the "right mistakes" from the "wrong mistakes." The right mistakes are new mistakes, created when searching for innovation; they are accidents that can often be turned into opportunities. The wrong mistakes are recurrent and unjustified mistakes from which nothing new can be drawn.
- Remember that chance discoveries only happen to companies that are willing to accept and analyze mistakes that are made.

willing to develop the ability to deal with risk and error, two essential capacities for the effective management of uncertainty. Together with the future-today management we have already presented, this is a basic prerequisite of proactive strategies. As we have seen, however, organizing a company to enable market proactiveness requires the development of two other managerial dimensions: proactive innovation management and personal proactiveness management. We finish the second part of this book by addressing these two subjects.

PROACTIVE INNOVATION MANAGEMENT

6 Innovating to Change the Market

Since Peter Drucker put innovation on the map of management, the capacity for innovating has been considered a key element of competitive success. Five decades have now passed since then, and no executive would today disagree on how essential innovation is to long-term growth and prosperity. But recognition of innovation's strategic relevance has also led to multiple – not always coherent – interpretations of the subject, to the extent that many think a substantial part of what has been thought and said about innovative processes is false.[1]

We believe that this misinterpretation has had two prominent side-effects. The first is the tendency – still strongly present – to reduce innovation to continuous improvement (process improvement, product adjustment, cost reduction, and quality enhancement). Although the managerial importance of such actions cannot be denied, this limited view neglects the true value of innovative processes: anticipation of change and finding ways to create new markets. As a result of this, incremental innovation – focused on improving what already exists – continues to be prevalent in most corporate innovation efforts. A second side-effect is subordination of innovation to market demands, with companies waiting for others to innovate in order to take advantage of a path that has been laid by competitors. Reactive innovation – as we discussed in the first part of this book – is one of the reasons why companies are usually so far from market proactiveness.

Proactive innovation management as we have conceived it points in exactly the opposite direction. More specifically, proactively innovating means shifting your focus onto radical innovations – those capable of impacting the competitive environment – instead of focusing solely on incremental improvements in services and products. To achieve that, innovation must be regarded as a process that is not based on market benchmarking or on reaction to competitors' moves or customer demands. Randal Zanetti, president of Odontoprev, confirms the importance of searching for new market parameters: "Benchmarking must only be a reference. Companies must focus their efforts on thinking something different from what is happening in the market. Discontent with benchmarks is a proactive behavior that may lead to innovation."[2]

We regard these two conditions as a virtuous circle in which they feed on each other (see Figure 6.1): focus on radical innovation will lead companies increasingly to transcend a simple response to the market. Simultaneously, this non-reactive posture will make strategists look more and more for radical innovation. This will

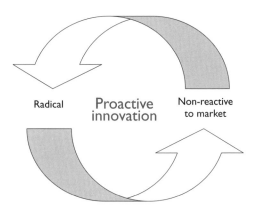

Figure 6.1 The mindset for proactive innovation

strengthen their mindset for proactive innovation, making sure innovative actions are more impactful and truly directed to the anticipation of moments zero (MZs) in the market. Finally, we would argue that this paradigmatic change requires a flexible and change-oriented managerial structure that opens up space for strategies and actions aimed at more ambitious innovation projects.

Thus, proactive innovation and flexible management are the two essential capacities for mastering proactive innovation management as we propose it. Let us see now how these two capacities can be developed, and what attitudes must be put into practice to activate them.

INNOVATING PROACTIVELY

In the realm of proactive innovation, managers face the challenge of cultivating a mindset that can result in radical rather than market-reactive innovations. Such a mindset must be driven by a true intention to look for superior results through innovation. This is clearly stated by Gustavo Valle, the former CEO of Danone Brasil who now heads the company in the United States: "How do we interpret innovation? If we keep on doing things the same way we have done so far, the results will be like those we have today. We should always try to refresh ourselves."[3] To achieve that, we have to identify barriers that hamper the development of truly anticipatory innovations by companies, and work to eliminate or neutralize them. The two attitudes we describe next show how to accomplish that.

Focus on radical innovation

We can objectively define radical innovation as focused on the development of something entirely new, as opposed to incremental innovation, which is aimed at improving what already exists. We may also understand radical innovation as a typical exploration process resulting from action directed at creation and discovery (this refers to a question raised in Chapter 4). A typical example of radical innovation is the launch of an entirely new product (or the creation of a new way of delivering it, or the creation of consumption preferences that had not previously existed). Incremental innovation, on the other hand, reflects an action of exploitation, focused on answering questions that had previously been asked. An example is the improvement of an existing product (or its distribution and delivery processes). In brief, radical innovation is the promotion of significant changes oriented toward discovery. Incremental innovation tries to improve and make small changes, usually aimed at solving previously detected problems. In brief, we may say that while radical innovation takes risks embedded in the process of creation, incremental innovation is more conservative and less inclined to accept discovery-related risks. Thus, the dimensions of radical innovation and incremental innovation exhibit striking differences that cannot be neglected, if we want to put the proactive innovation concept into practice (see Table 6.1).[4]

Proactive companies focus on radical innovation. We are not saying that they reject incrementalism. We know that, in practice, most companies apportion efforts and resources to both radical and incremental innovations. The balance is important, in that it inserts the whole company into the innovative process, something that does not happen often with radical innovative projects, which are usually restricted to spec ific groups at top management level. Besides balancing a company's investments with regard to the two innovation types we are discussing, it also contributes to strengthening and disseminating an innovative culture. Finally, there is no doubt that improvement innovations protect companies against competitors and meet market requirements (for instance, when a product's functionality is improved and this makes it more competitive). What we are saying is that proactive companies are not confined to incremental innovations in the offer, industry, and customer dimensions. Although they divide their investment between work on radical and incremental changes, these companies invest most of their resources in attempts to make something completely new. They know that an excessive or exclusive focus on incremental innovation can only make them good runners-up at best.

Overcoming an exclusive focus on incrementalism is not a simple task, though. Most companies, being used to improvement innovations, end up hindered by their own paradigms when they try to cross the border between incremental and radical innovative actions. In our view, these paradigms represent two major barriers we

Table 6.1 Incremental innovation and radical innovation

Incremental innovation	Radical innovation
Tries to improve what already exists	Tries to create what does not exist yet
Focused on exploitation	Focused on exploration
Promotes small changes	Promotes significant changes
Oriented to the solution of problems	Oriented to discovery
Conservative and risk averse	Ambitious and risk-tolerant

call "the two fears of radical innovation" (see Box 6.1). Thus, companies suffer from a fear of cannibalism – that is, the fear of destroying their own creations, eroding advantages they have already gained – and from a fear of rejection – the fear of seeing their radical innovations despised by the market. Overcoming these two fears is essential to more effectively generating radical innovations. (In saying this, we are certainly not neglecting the role of the innovative culture that develops when a company promotes and encourages innovation as the sheer essence of its business. In this context, the role of people and leadership is fundamental, demonstrating that innovation does not depend solely on the application of formal techniques and tools. In the next chapter, which addresses personal proactiveness management, we discuss the role of individuals in proactive management.[5])

The fear of cannibalism is regarded as a major obstacle to radical innovation.[6] The examples of Kodak and IBM given earlier in this book show this at work: at these points in their histories the companies acted reactively for fear of losing their existing advantage (in both cases, in the offer dimension). Fear of cannibalism ties companies to their past successes, making them to a certain extent dependent on their own strategies, and leaving little or no room for discontinuous innovations.[7] The antidote to this behavior is a change in the company's mindset regarding cannibalization, which leads it to treat cannibalization not as a dysfunction but rather as an opportunity to anticipate changes in the market. This can be described as proactive cannibalism.[8] This new mindset is anchored by a simple reasoning: destroy your advantage before others do it for you. As was said by Andy Grove, a decade-long CEO at the giant Intel, "You must be your own major competitor."[9]

Box 6.1 The two fears over radical innovation

- Fear of cannibalism: the company is afraid of destroying its own created advantages.
- Fear of rejection: the company is afraid of having its radical innovations despised by the market.

Offer proactive cannibalism occurs when a company decides to "sacrifice" and replace its products and services. Apple, Intel, Gillette, and HP are representative examples of proactive companies that constantly try to annihilate their own offers, often when they are still at the peak of their market popularity.[10] Industry proactive cannibalism happens when, for instance, a company creates an alternative way to distribute its offer, even if this new alternative competes with its traditional channels (as happened when bookstores launched virtual stores that captured a share of their own sales), or when a company expands its activities, creating a new brand name managed by a distinct business unit that may eventually compete with the mother unit or company (as can be observed in the automotive industry). Finally, customer proactive cannibalism occurs when a new product or new distribution channel destroys an existing preference or need in favor of a new preference or need that has been created by the company. Whether it is in the offer, industry, or customer dimension, one thing is clear: overcoming the fear of cannibalism by means of a more proactive attitude is a company's first step to becoming more open to radical innovation. As we often say about cannibalism, don't wait till your boat is hit by competitors' torpedoes, sink it beforehand and build a new one!

Fear of rejection also contributes to separating companies from radical innovation. This fear arises in both the offer and customer dimensions, when a company is afraid that a new offer or new attempt to mold customers' preferences or needs might not be accepted in the way it hopes for. We should emphasize that fear of rejection is usually not unfounded: radical innovations involve unfamiliar offers that usually require paradigm shifts or new abilities from users. Additionally, they may conflict with consumers' lifelong habits. This is the reason why there is often resistance to adopting them.[11] Thus, the strategy to fight the fear of rejection is to find ways to minimize the probability that the offer will not be accepted. To achieve that, companies must possess the ability to influence and prepare consumers, so they will understand and accept radical innovations to the existing standard and complementary offers, and changes in their own consumption preferences and needs. Danone's Activia yogurt (which we have already mentioned, and explore more fully in Part III of this book) is a prominent example of a company's capacity for modifying a consumption habit or need through learning. We call this expertise the ability to educate the market, and understand it from the perspective of three basic stages (Figure 6.2).[12]

Initially, the company is concerned with influencing the market with respect to recently launched innovations. Companies influence consumers via advertisements, merchandising and consultative sales (when a face-to-face person gives personalized advice); when they provide information on point-of-sale displays and product packaging; through channels like call centers and online support, and by instructing them in user's manuals. Other options include offering test drives for new vehicles, tasting sessions for new wine brands, and inviting customers to try the product free for a given period of time. As well as increasing positive interest in a product, companies need to reduce or neutralize any mistrust that customers show, for example by giving an extended warranty or promising no-quibble refunds. Finally, companies have another chance to influence markets by engaging with "opinion leaders" (that is, a product is linked to famous and influential people, or to specialists such as scientists and researchers) or with the special class of consumers

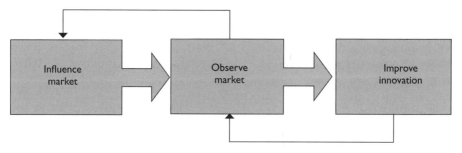

Figure 6.2 Educating the market

called early adopters (those who tend to be quick to adopt innovations and new technologies).[13] The idea here is that the opinion leaders and early adopters will become ambassadors for the innovation, and act as guides to the behavior of future consumers.

When influencing the market, the company will simultaneously observe customer behavior with regard to the new product or service, so it can discover any discrepancies between its innovation and what customers actually want. At this particular point, a company must be "smartly reactive": that is, quick to detect market requirements and to use them as inputs to improve the innovation. We are not talking here about testing the market before the innovation is launched, but rather about reaction after the launch (this reinforces the idea that proactive and reactive strategies can be complementary rather than mutually exclusive). Finally, companies can make use of field insights to improve launched innovations, again making them better match consumer demands. This process of adjustment is vital because radical innovations usually draw attention from competitors, who naturally see them as a threat. This may lead rival companies to promote changes to their own products and services, or even to launch campaigns to discourage consumers from trying out the new offer. If it does not respond to this activity, the company may see its radical innovation losing relevance or even being entirely replaced by a later introduction.

Note that the process of educating the market we have described is recurrent and therefore unceasing: as soon as an innovation is modified, there needs to be a new observation phase to see how it is received. Simultaneously, the company will work on its market-influencing activity.[14] We could say that the company educates and learns from the market at the same time. Educating the market helps companies overcome the fear of rejection which, together with the fear of cannibalism, is a serious obstacle to radical innovation. But efficiency in innovating proactively does not depend solely on radical innovation. Strategists must also learn to think innovation beyond both market benchmarks and responses to consumers' demands.

Do not make innovation subordinate to the market

A recurrent theme in this book is that innovation must comprise more than reaction to market stimuli.[15] A company will hardly be proactive if it subordinates its innovative actions to customer requirements or competitors' moves. It is important here to make clear that by not making innovation subordinate to the market, we do not mean that companies should be turning their back on consumers' demands, merely that these should be only one form of stimulus. This does not mean neglecting competitors' moves either; it does mean taking care to prevent innovation from becoming a simple photocopy of innovative actions by rivals.

It is in the offer and customer dimensions that the effects of market-subordinate innovations can be felt most strongly, because most companies end up blindly obeying the classical marketing rule "listen to consumers," believing that this can generate insights that favor the creation of radically innovative offers. The problem is that, when it comes to radical innovation, most consumers simply cannot imagine what might be offered to them. They may provide relevant information on existing offers, true, but they will probably have little to say when it comes to attempts to be proactive and reshape the product or its market. Companies must "listen differently," and be able to transcend what consumers say. Put differently, companies need to pick up on the needs that consumers are not able to articulate, their latent preferences and inclinations. To achieve that, the listening attitude must reach beyond tools such as traditional market surveys, because these are suitable only for identifying consumers' manifest wishes. In brief, companies must carry out what we call a proactive survey. In agreement with this line of reasoning, José Drummond Jr., president of Whirlpool Latin America, states emphatically, "It is an illusion, a fallacy, to believe that consumers are going to tell us clearly what they want. This does not exist. If you really survey differently and innovate, then you tell consumers what they are going to wish for."[16]

The matrix in Figure 6.3 illustrates the differences between proactive and traditional surveys. In traditional surveys, the focus is on explicit needs: that is, those consumers know about and are able to express. A simple example of an explicit need is a customer's complaint about an existing product or service, or a statement about their tastes and preferences. This kind of insight can be obtained from both customers and those who are not currently customers. In the vast majority of cases, companies tend to focus their research on the explicit needs of their own customers (the lower-right quadrant). The common customer satisfaction surveys are excellent examples of that. But even when the focus is expanded to other consumers (the lower-left quadrant) – for example, in a survey to find out why they are not currently customers – traditional surveys do not identify the things that consumers do not articulate clearly.

Proactive surveys, on the other hand, focus on *latent needs*: that is, needs that exist but remain hidden from the market because consumers themselves still do not perceive them. We could say that a latent need is "hibernating." Companies can explore the latent needs of both their customers (the upper-right quadrant) and non-customers (the upper-left quadrant), and an effective proactive survey will be targeted at whichever is more appropriate, or indeed at both. The aim might be

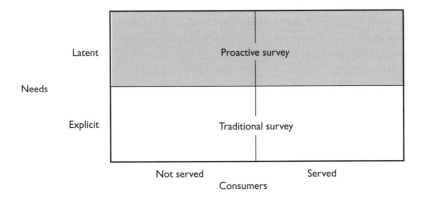

Figure 6.3 The proactive survey

to find out how customers interact with an existing product, and what innovations this suggests, or to understand why some people have no interest in the company's products and services, or prefer those of a rival. In both cases, traditional survey tools will contribute little because they cannot detect what consumers are not able to express. As Julio Ribeiro, president of Talent, one of the most creative advertising agencies operating in the Brazilian market, once told us, "Every time we conduct a survey to help plan an innovation we are surprised by people's incapacity for being aware of what they would like companies to offer."[17]

There are three basic causes for the shortcomings of traditional survey tools – such as polls, focus groups and in depth interviews – when dealing with latent needs:

- When asked, consumers usually restrict their preferences and needs to what is familiar to them.
- Consumers are usually not able to tell whether their demands are technically feasible.
- Consumers have difficulty in expressing clearly their increasingly complex and volatile wishes.[18]

It is as if traditional surveys were radio receptors capable of detecting only a limited range of wavelengths. This is why some techniques have been developed to ascertain consumers' latent needs (see Box 6.2). In brief, these tools try to read between the lines of the market's discourse, to grasp what consumers (whether or not they are customers) do not mention but often end up expressing through their actions and behaviors. Market surveys do not live by words alone.

Box 6.2 Well beyond questions

Some survey approaches have been developed to access what traditional surveys that use descriptive questionnaires, and even focus groups and in-depth interviews with consumers, cannot discover. Three of the most prominent among such approaches are:

- **Empathic design**: A technique based on the observation of people in their habitual environment. Specialists observe and document (photographing and filming) consumers' behavior and reactions (such as body language and facial expressions) when they are interacting routinely with given products (or services): for instance at home, at work, shopping, or parking their cars in shopping center parking lots. The logic behind empathic design is that information on motivations and ways of using products, how products fit into consumers' routines, the demand for add-ons, and the ways users themselves change products, may provide valuable insights for the generation of innovations. Note that observation is a necessary but not sufficient element of this technique. Above all, observation must take place beyond the walls of a research lab; this is the real difference that this technique offers. Think, for instance, of a company that is trying to identify latent needs related to notebook computers. The researchers could ask test subjects to use their notebooks in the artificial environment of the company's test laboratory, but they will learn much more by observing in real time consumers' spontaneous behavior in their natural habitat. This points up frustrations, mistakes, anxieties, creative use, and gives a sense of unverbalized needs. In this sense, the researchers put themselves in the shoes of the subject (hence the term "empathic"), trying to understand their wishes and demands. Empathic design figures large in the innovation methods of world-renowned design companies such as IDEO.[19]

- **The "innovative client" approach**: Under the expression "innovative client" we gather a variety of approaches based on consumer insertion into companies' innovation processes. The idea here is that consumers become active participants in the creation of innovations, instead of simply being presented with new products or services that have already been developed. The automotive industry, for instance, adopts this approach to generate new models and add-ons to their vehicles. The logic of *value co-creation* by companies and consumers for the generation of mutual firm–customer value is an approach we relate to the innovative client concept. It challenges traditional paradigms that restrict value generation – via products and services – to companies alone, and see consumers as passive and non-participating spectators. From the co-creation perspective, products and services are created based on interaction and exchange of experiences between consumers and companies. It is like regarding the market as an open forum where dialogue and exchanges of experience between companies and consumers result in the generation of singular innovations.

  Finally, the method for generating innovation focused on lead users can also be aligned with the innovative client approach. Briefly, lead users are a class of consumers with needs well ahead of normal market standards. Since their needs are not fulfilled by the current offers they frequently make their own modifications to products (as when a teenager is dissatisfied with a video game display and tries to change it, or when a keen cyclist changes the structure of a bike to make it lighter or improve its aerodynamics). Whether by inserting consumers into the production process, using their experience to jointly create value, or adopting product modifications made by consumers themselves, methods for inserting clients into the innovation process require a new approach to tracking latent needs.[20]

- **Metaphoric survey**: Briefly, metaphors and similes are figures of speech in which one thing (an object, an expression, a sensation) is used in place of another (a feeling about a product, for instance). By means of metaphors we are able to understand our experiences, through elements that are somewhat related to these experiences. Although verbalization is the most familiar way to express metaphors (think of the innumerable ordinary expressions we use such as "I'm hungry as a bear" or "She's as thin as a rail"), some people claim that visual images enable a much richer and deeper appreciation of their meaning. Thus, metaphoric surveys are based on the principle that human thought is supported by images more than words. We are, to a great extent, nonverbal beings.

In the realm of this reality, metaphors are regarded as representations of hidden thoughts, feelings, and perceptions that skip speech and, logically, traditional language-oriented marketing surveys. Techniques such as ZMETR, conceived by Harvard professor Gerald Zaltman, try to help managers elicit or bring out, by means of metaphors, latent feelings that guide consumers' behavior. Based on images picked by participants, on descriptions of how they relate to particular situations (for instance, the sensation brought about by a medicine), and later combination of these images, the technique tries to uncover conscious and unconscious feelings – and most importantly, the latent needs they point to – that may be behind the images and their representations. Metaphor-based surveys suggest that companies will do better if they try to "see" customers' voices rather than actually hear them![21]

The capacity for proactively innovating we have been discussing so far is an essential condition that companies must fulfill in order to properly manage proactive innovation. But as we have pinpointed, its execution demands a flexible managerial structure, capable of nurturing proactive and innovative practices and ideas. The capacity for flexible management is therefore the second necessary condition for effective proactive innovation management. We end this chapter by detailing how to develop this capacity.

FLEXIBLE MANAGEMENT

Proactive innovations do not happen by chance. As we have seen, companies must previously develop a mindset oriented to radical innovations that are not subordinated to the market. But this is not enough. Issues related to a company's structure and management also play a crucial role, and may facilitate or completely obstruct the generation of proactive innovations. Since some companies are much more innovative than others, there must be a reason.

The question here is, exactly what factors favor proactive innovation and how can they be nurtured? For some time now, it has been said that more malleable and open organizations provide fertile soil for the development of innovation, while more bureaucratic and closed administrations end up weakening audacious innovative models.[22] Luiza Trajano, from *Magazine Luiza*, confirms that: "If your assumptions are too strict, that is, limited as in a box or square, you usually do not develop innovation and do not find creative solutions to your problems."[23]

Thus, the concept of flexible management we adopted conveys this more elastic and change-friendly posture and yet does not neglect control and supervision, since these two activities are, of course, essential to the practice of management. This flexible management in turn depends very much on the company's architecture. In other words, companies we call "stiff" end up developing a more mechanistic style of management, while organizations with a more flexible structural design will allow managers to act more flexibly.

A number of basic characteristics separate stiff from flexible companies (Table 6.2).[24] First, flexible companies have decentralized structures and therefore let people act more freely. Freedom in this context means that managers have the prerogative to make decisions on what to do and how to do it on their own, without always having to ask for approval from their superiors. This is a different reality from that found in stiff companies, where centralized decision making ends up stifling people's creativity and innovative abilities. Decentralization, on the other hand, is apparent in more horizontal hierarchical relations: that is, relations are not regulated by the simple vertical reporting arrangements that are so typical of organization charts we all know. In this context, autonomy and cooperation among peers and partners is a lot more fruitful than the subordination and obedience that divide superiors and subordinates.

Flexible companies operate without excessive formalization of procedures and rules, leaving room for contingent actions that are "not in the script." This contingency-driven attitude is very important in the context of proactive innovation because it allows for healthy improvisation and quick decision making. In stiff companies, to the contrary, rigorous procedures and incontestable rules end up hindering learning and decision making. We are not saying that each and every process must be abolished: consistent procedures constitute the operational basis of every company. What we are saying is that these processes should not be regarded as ends themselves, in order to avoid suffocating people's flexibility. José Drummond Jr., president of Whirlpool Latin America, put this well:

> Every company needs solid processes, but people must be flexible. Have you ever seen someone firing a process, promoting a process? No, you haven't! You don't hire, promote, or dismiss a process. A process earns no bonus. Good talents remedy bad processes. Good processes cannot remedy bad talents.[25]

Finally, a relevant aspect of organizational stiffness is related to its own origins. Operational routines and habits of conduct become entrenched because they generate a specific type of knowledge that ends up being seen as the "best way" of doing things. Immersed in such a reality, the company develops a tacit (and often explicit) consensus on how its activities must be developed, rejecting other options, no matter how efficient they might be. The practice is reflected in a traditional statement: "Things have always been done this way here." It limits experimentation and creates barriers against the proposal of new innovative methods and tools. In a

Table 6.2 The stiff company and the flexible company

Stiff company	Flexible company
Centralized decisions	Decentralization of decision making
Subordination and obedience	Autonomy and cooperation
Formal procedures	Contingent procedures
Control and supervision	Empowerment and responsibility

certain sense, stiff companies fall in love with their own way of acting, and it is the managers' duty to wake them up from this egocentric dream.[26]

As we have seen, the adoption of flexible management practices requires a permanent rethinking of work methods and adopted behaviors by testing them against the present, restructuring them if necessary, and even replacing them by more adequate procedures. In this context, we believe that both control and cooperation are fundamental vectors. There is no managerial flexibility without a balance between control and cooperation on one side, and their opposites – empowerment and competition – on the other. The challenge consists in balancing these antagonistic poles, trying to achieve a position that is more harmonious and simultaneously fits the company's culture. Two attitudes must be put into practice to make this happen.

Overcome the "control versus empowerment" dilemma

Control is one of the most outstanding and approved managerial principles.[27] Abdicating control, many executives would say, is equivalent to renouncing management itself. At the same time, the very same executives know that excessive control produces side-effects that are not always healthy for innovative processes. Drowning in this dichotomy, managers encounter serious difficulties in finding a balance between control and empowerment. It is not a matter of abolishing control or of changing it into a managerial straitjacket: that is why this is a huge challenge. The resolution of the "control versus empowerment" dilemma is essential to the practice of flexible management. In our view, it can generate three distinct managerial positions (Figure 6.4).

Managers who are not able to renounce any share of control end up adopting

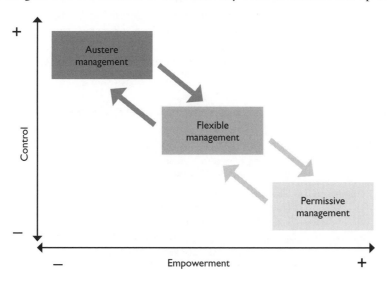

Figure 6.4 The "control versus empowerment" dilemma and the three managerial attitudes

what we call "austere management." Their conduct is characterized by extreme control and minimal empowerment. Austere managers are afraid ever to delegate or cede control. They see themselves as the conductors of a top orchestra, controlling each and every movement of their musicians.[28] Austere management assumes that everything must – and can – be permanently controlled by a formal authority.

On the opposite side, we have "permissive management." Here, empowerment is excessive, to the detriment of control. It is important to explain that this permissive posture is often not deliberate: it is what happens when managers delegate without understanding how to supervise. This unintentional stance often leads to devastating consequences. Those who are acquainted with managers who lack the ability to manage those to whom they delegate know what we are talking about.

Finally, there is the balanced alternative between these two extreme positions, which we call *flexible management*. Flexible managers know that while control is an inevitable component of their toolkit, this does not mean they must dictate everything. They understand that the aim is to find a style that involves minimal control but still enables things to function efficiently. The amount of power that is ceded is contingent. In certain situations, flexible managers will lean towards empowerment, loosening the reins, only to tighten them again when the situation requires it (represented by the pale grey arrows). At other times and in different circumstances, these managers will tend to control as a default, but provide their team with flexibility when it is convenient (represented by the darker arrows).

Thus, between the extreme limits that are characterized by formal obedience to authority and lack of accountability, flexible management will be guided by what we call "informal authority." That is, decision power is assigned to each individual according to their own competencies. Flexible management is regulated by a constant exchange of ideas and consultation among team members. A flexible posture may be pictured as a tug of war between control and empowerment. If you cut the rope, the tension is relieved, but you lose the game. Tension is vital to the game, as it is to harmonious management practices. Flexible management does not cut the tow-rope, but rather manages to tighten or loosen it as circumstances require.

Table 6.3 Competition and cooperation: advantages and disadvantages

Competition	Advantages	• Motivation to overcome challenges • Increased generation of innovative ideas and insights • Greater diversification and experimentation
	Disadvantages	• Segregation between losers and winners • Deterioration in learning and trusting relationships • Cost of developing simultaneous proposals
Cooperation	Advantages	• Generation of trusting relationships • Stronger interaction and knowledge generation • Cost savings
	Disadvantages	• Simulated cooperation • Concealment of individual inefficiencies • Lowering of personal initiative

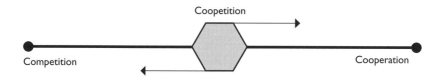

Figure 6.5 Competition, cooperation, and coopetition

So the aim is not to resolve the control–empowerment tension by choosing one over the other. Control is one of the key managerial tools, and it would be naïve to claim that a company can operate without monitoring. The challenge is to fine-tune the balance between necessary control and feasible empowerment. The same may be said about the second contrast we highlighted: the competition versus cooperation dilemma, which deals with the degree to which individuals and work teams should work together or compete against each other, and the implications of the chosen balance for innovative processes.

Overcome the "competition versus cooperation" dilemma

We know that innovation is very often related to internal competition. More specifically, we accept that rivalry between different work teams in the same company has a positive impact on innovative actions. In this scenario, teams are encouraged to compete with each other in the generation of innovations. This may involve, for instance, competition between those putting forward proposals to develop new products, services, and technologies. It is accepted that internal competition inspires individuals to overcome their limitations, and makes companies both ready to face market changes and able to defy the status quo.[29] Fomenting internal rivalry, however, can produce much less beneficial side-effects. Accordingly, the general agreement is that internal cooperation between work teams is the most beneficial and effective option.

In truth, extremes of both competition and cooperation have advantages and disadvantages (see Figure 6.5). While internal competition stimulates individuals to overcome challenges, leaves room for the generation of new insights and ideas, and promotes experimentation, over time it can create barriers that separate winners from losers, and ruin trusting relationships, mutual help, and the exchange of knowledge. The cost impact of developing simultaneous proposals must be also taken into account.[30] Similarly, while internal cooperation fosters trust-based relationships, increasing learning and interaction between teams – in addition to rationalizing innovation costs – it may also lead to simulated cooperation (that is, an appearance of cooperation resulting more from professional obligation than from any real willingness to cooperate), hide individual inefficiencies, and deaden initiative. Each company must decide on the relative intensities of competition and cooperation that best suit its culture and needs, trying to find both a balance between these conflicting extremes and a way to neutralize their side-effects.

The neologism *coopetition* has been used to describe the harmonious solution of the cooperation–competition tension within companies. In brief, there is coopetition when two companies cooperate on a given business (jointly purchasing to lower costs or sharing expertise, for instance) but keep on competing for market share. The idea behind the concept is that cooperation does not cancel competition, and vice versa.[31] We believe the logic behind this approach can also be applied to the internal context, in which case competition and cooperation between work teams may be regarded as parts of a continuum, rather than as static poles that do not communicate with each other (Figure 6.5).

The movement of arrows shows that coopetition will involve different degrees of cooperation and competition, leaning sometimes towards one, sometimes towards the other extreme, without ever completely abandoning either. How much competition or cooperation a company adopts depends ultimately on the circumstances and the company's culture. There are organizations, for example, where high levels of internal competition are readily assimilated by individuals, while for others the practice sits poorly with the prevailing values. Hence, the degree of competition and cooperation will depend on the company's organizational system, environment, competences, and last but not least, on the individual character of its professionals. The competition–cooperation interplay certainly generates greatly differing views, which are ultimately dependent on the mindset of managers themselves. This conclusion emerged clearly from our research: while some companies consider internal competition healthy and capable of generating knowledge, others regard it as a source of conflict, a waste of energy, and unsustainable in the long run. The research also identified a contingent side of the balance between competition and cooperation, which is subordinated to the specific conditions of each company, as we have already highlighted.

Flexible management, as we propose it, will therefore promote a balance between competition and cooperation strategies. Maybe the greatest challenge here is to avoid the division of employees into winners and losers, a difficult task when internal rivalries are pursued. Practices that can help here include the adoption of collective incentive and reward systems (although people or teams may also receive individual bonuses, there is a bonus that reflects the overall company results), and an emphasis on the benefits of learning (there are no losers, only winners, since everyone profits from the knowledge generated). Regardless of the way a company deals with this subject, it is always important to consider its inherent advantages and disadvantages, and to recognize that cooperation and competition are both necessary to leverage a proactive innovation process.

The capacities for proactive innovation and flexible management we have described so far are fundamental prerequisites to proactive innovation management, an important dimension in the process of organizing a company for market proactiveness. In the next chapter we address proactive behavior management, the fourth and last dimension of the proactive management model introduced in Chapter 3.

PROACTIVE BEHAVIOR MANAGEMENT

7 Developing Personal Proactiveness

People behave in different ways. Some are oriented to change, transcend their instructions, undertake initiatives, and search for new ways of taking action. Others, resigned and complacent, tie themselves to routine and passively wait for others to make changes happen. Proactive people belong to the first group. They are the ones who ultimately make the difference between proactive and other companies. Most companies, however, complain about the lack of proactive professionals among their employees. Proactive behaviors seem to be the exception – not the rule – in the world of corporations. This reflects, perhaps, the biggest challenge to proactive companies: to *manage people's proactive behavior*.

We define proactive behavior as a tendency of individuals to anticipate change. It is an attitude aimed at changing current conditions or at creating more favorable, entirely new conditions. When carrying out their daily professional activities, proactive people look for information and opportunities rather than simply wait to act after the information and opportunities reach them. Proactive behavior management, therefore, is every effort a company expends on the management of proactiveness at an individual level. Such management presupposes that personal proactiveness is not innate, and consequently poses the challenge of working to develop it.

We address proactive behaviors here from two fundamental angles. The first is related to leadership. Proactive managers – regardless of their hierarchical position or function – must be the initial agents of change. They will promote and facilitate people's proactive behavior. The second is related to how a company identifies and develops proactive talents and keeps them in-house. We adopt here the idea that proactive behaviors – like any behavior – can be deliberately managed. These two issues represent the two capacities that proactive behavior management deals with: the *capacity for leading proactively*, and the *capacity for identifying and developing proactive people*.[1]

THE CAPACITY FOR LEADING PROACTIVELY

If you search for the word "leadership" on the internet you will get countless different concepts and explanations. The importance of a leader is evoked in different fields from politics to religion, from education to military action. The same thing happens in the field of management. The function of a leader has for a long time been regarded as an essential condition for the practice of management, whatever the benefits or harm it may bring.[2] In addition, difficulties inherent in defining exactly what it is (art or science?) and where it comes from (nature or nurture?) demonstrate both the relevance and the reality of the subject in the context of companies. Its relevance is even greater in the specific realm of market proactiveness. The implementation of proactive strategies depends directly on leadership that is aware of the idea of anticipating the future and capable of making room for proactiveness to develop. Even when proactive companies are formed by proactive people (and here we are repeating what the many managers we interviewed told us), they can only effectively exert their proactiveness if the company's management is able to lead proactively. To achieve that, leaders must transcend the conventional way of leading (focused on task efficiency) and adopt an open, change-oriented attitude. They must also encourage what we call a proactive way of acting: in other words, an individual anticipation-oriented disposition to launch initiatives.

Lead proactively

We conceived proactive leadership as a leadership style oriented to promote and facilitate personal proactiveness. Proactive managers are *transformative* leaders, a leadership concept markedly distinct from the traditional way of leading.[3] More specifically, this means that proactive leaders adopt guiding mechanisms different from those of other leaders, although they also employ conventional leadership practices whenever necessary. In other words, managers who successfully practice proactive leadership are, in truth, able to harmoniously combine the best of both styles. Here is our first fundamental knowledge: proactive leadership does not reject reactive action, so necessary and present in day-to-day management (as, for instance, when a customer's complaint is successfully handled or a supplier-related problem is addressed); it only prevents it from occupying the center of management's attention.[4]

The practice of proactive leadership, from our viewpoint, is supported by four fundamental attitudes related to transformative leadership (Figure 7.1).[5] The first of them is associated with *inspiration*. Proactive leaders believe companies can anticipate change, and inspire other people to believe it too. They create and communicate the vision that a company can transcend responsive attitudes to the market, explain the meaning of this, promote confidence, and generate enthusiasm for proactiveness.

The second attitude involves *stimulation*, and is associated with intellectual stimuli to creativity, to inquiry, to new ways of regarding old problems, and to innovative thinking: all of them key elements of a proactive mindset we describe as *extended*. The third attitude, *recognition*, represents the leader's ability to value individualities: that is, the contributions each person makes to market proactiveness, indicating paths and fostering the development of each individual's proactive competences. Finally the fourth attitude, *charisma*, involves a leader's

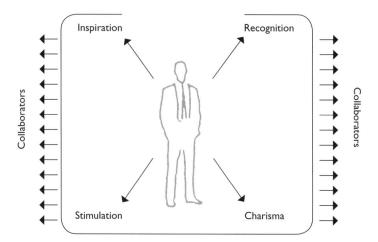

Figure 7.1 Attitudes of a proactive leader

personal ability to evoke admiration, respect, and confidence from people. Charisma changes proactive leaders into models, examples to be followed. It encourages people to adopt similar attitudes. Together, these four attitudes encourage proactive behavior, stimulating people to act autonomously and with anticipation. The role of leadership in the construction of a proactive mindset within companies is succinctly expressed by Fábio Hering, president of Hering: "The greatest challenge facing CEOs and leaders is how to give the whole team a proactive vision; how to give them the ability to see proactiveness as an element that helps perpetuate and develop the company."[6]

Transformative proactive leadership is considered vital to "vanguard" companies: that is, those operating at the edge of change.[7] In this sense, there is talk of a leadership based on values and principles, that inspires and motivates individuals to internalize the proposed objectives. In agreement with the flexible management practices we described in a previous chapter, this leadership style relies more on positive influences originated in responsible autonomy than on control and supervision mechanisms. Leaders who possess this quality additionally know how to deal with ambiguity and uncertainty, and are guided to action and oriented to change. And last but not least, they have a broad and sensible vision of the growing complexity of human relations at work.

Finally, it is important to avoid a very common misunderstanding over the subject of leadership. The extensive list of talents required from proactive leaders does not mean that they possess extraordinary gifts. Leadership is a social practice, a fact that leads us to two important conclusions. First: as a practice, the act of leading may be learned and developed. This means that the capacity for leading is not a gift that some few predestined people are born with, but rather something that can be developed. Proactive leaders are not superheroes; above all, they are people who have learned the worth of proactiveness for themselves, and therefore try to instigate and promote this behavior. This takes us to the second conclusion:

proactive leadership can only be built collectively. Proactive leadership will only thrive on cooperation and identification with market proactiveness. In other words, proactive leadership recognizes the value of the company as a whole as a support to market proactiveness. As Helio Rotenberg, president of Positivo Informática, said, what is important to proactiveness is "to have the right team! I do not see any bigger challenge than having the right team! If you have the right team, the construction of tomorrow is easy!"[8]

Encourage a proactive way of acting

A second important attitude in the realm of proactive leadership is related to what we call the proactive way of acting. More specifically, this means that a proactive leader also encourages people to look beyond their routine tasks, pushing them to anticipate change. In brief, they must launch initiatives instead of simply delivering what was asked of them. This is an important attitude because proactiveness will only be possible as an external strategy if the company is also internally proactive. This means that people and teams must transcend their expected performance, undertaking the initiatives that are necessary to solve problems and to create new solutions. In short, for leaders, it is not enough to be proactive; they must encourage and disseminate personal proactiveness among their subordinates.

We see proaction – or a proactive way of acting – as one of four generic attitudes to their assignments that people adopt, as a function of their personal level of initiative and their orientation to change (Figure 7.2). Thus, individuals akin to

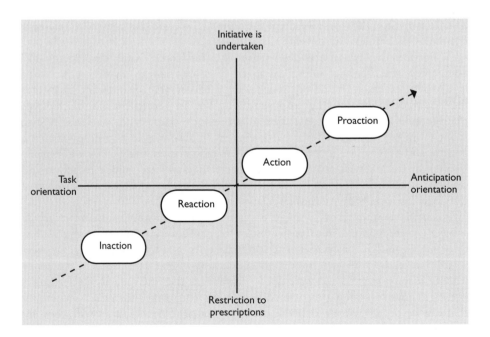

Figure 7.2 The proactive way of acting

inaction are strongly oriented to doing jobs they are ordered to do, and have little or no interest in taking decisions on their own. They are only worried about strictly fulfilling their obligations: that is, they do not swing into action (and are therefore inactive) over anything they are not ordered to do. Think of a machine operator who sees the job exclusively as carrying out a fixed sequence of operations, regardless of the operating conditions of the machine. Being confined to their own tasks, inactive people end up making little contribution to innovation and usually do not share their ideas and capacities with other people.

Professionals inclined to *reaction*, although these individuals also strictly follow instructions, take decisions to improve their own efficiency and do not remain absolutely limited by their obligations. In our example, this might mean that the operator keeps an eye on the equipment's operating status and call for preventive maintenance when necessary. Although these professionals are still reactive individuals, they see a little way beyond their fixed job instructions, and usually share their ideas with superiors and peers. In consequence, they contribute more to the generation of new points of view about problems, solutions, and changes.

Action-oriented people are the third generic type. They exhibit a higher degree of initiative, which goes beyond their fixed instructions and is oriented to anticipation rather than to simply meeting their obligations. This kind of operator would use their acquired experience and knowledge to call for preventive maintenance even before the machine develops a fault. People who take this attitude are not content with simply doing things right: they try to do the best. Active professionals are concerned not only with efficiency when performing their tasks, but also with delivering more than is asked of them. They are usually participative, share knowledge, and have an unquenchable thirst for new solutions.

Finally, people guided by *proaction* try to see what no one else has yet seen, and to anticipate changes. Note that they go even beyond that when it comes to taking the initiative. This is the operator who suggests and works to implement changes in the way a machine operates, to better protect it against wear and hence minimize maintenance costs. Proactive people are guided by anticipation and are innovative by nature. They always look for new ways of doing things. While people guided by action want to do their best, those guided by proaction want to do both their best and something new. Proactive people show an inclination to deal with challenges, and respond well to autonomy and freedom of ideas. They do not wait for things to happen; they make them happen.[9]

Considering these four types of behavior, the role of proactive leaders will be that of guiding people toward evolution to personal proactiveness (the dotted arrow in Figure 7.2). They must keep in mind that being inactive, reactive, active, or proactive is not a matter of genetics, but rather of attitude and how people see situations. A critical responsibility of proactive leaders is to help subordinates develop a more anticipatory stance. As a (relatively proactive) manager once commented, "I think everybody is proactive but some people's proactiveness seems to be dormant." He actually meant that people who are rarely proactive or not proactive at all might have their behavior changed by the action of leaders (exactly as people oriented to proaction might have their inclinations curtailed by leaders who do not support proactive behavior). Chieko Aoki, president of the Blue Tree hotel chain, summarizes the challenge of stimulating people's proactive behavior: "The questions I pose always stimulate people to be proactive: 'What different things are you doing?' or 'What are you doing beyond the expected?' I am sure people must be proactive by nature; I do not ask if they are proactive: I tell them to be proactive!"[10]

The famous Pygmalion effect may be evoked here. Much has been already said about the idea that people – regardless of their abilities or intelligence – are strongly influenced by expectations other people raise in them. Put simply, people from whom you do not expect much take in this negative attitude and end up delivering a mediocre performance. Contrariwise, people who sense that there are high expectations of them strive to achieve what others expect. The simple rationale underlying this approach is that the way people see reality – and themselves – is strongly influenced by other people's expectations.[11]

Thus, leaders who have positive expectations of their subordinates increase their motivation and self-confidence, and therefore take a first step towards seeing these expectations fulfilled. In the context of strategy, this means that people motivated by the positive vision of their superiors tend to adhere more firmly to objectives hidden behind their usual activities, and end up confirming the expectations about their intelligence and capacity. Ultimately, they display greater initiative and interest in contributing and in emotionally tying themselves to objectives: in short, they become more proactive.

But the opposite is also true, and neglecting this factor in leadership relationships may have negative consequences for people's performance and their motivation to act proactively. When a manager believes that a certain person has an action deficit and expresses that in words or actions – even unconsciously or involuntarily – this person will tend to respond with a lack of motivation. The person might disguise their lack of engagement with the company's objectives, but certainly will perform only to the point of avoiding criticism. In consequence, suggestions and ideas that could be used to improve the job will not be heard, reducing the group's efficiency and lowering the proactive level of both the company and the individual.

There is a relationship between the incentive people are given to act proactively and the belief that people can be proactive, and they must be given room for this ability to develop. This presupposes that personal proactiveness is like a muscle that must be exercised regularly to avoid its wasting away. This is perhaps the greatest challenge of proactiveness in the individual sphere: to identify proactive potential and develop it. That is the focus of the second capacity in the scope of proactive behavior management, which we discuss now.

THE CAPACITY FOR IDENTIFYING AND DEVELOPING PROACTIVE PEOPLE

Proactive leadership is undoubtedly the first condition required for managing proactiveness at an individual level. As we have seen, proactive leaders promote individual proactive behavior and guide people to be proactive. To activate this capacity, however, it is highly important that a company be a. the nature of personal proactiveness and how it becomes apparent. saying is that, even when proactive leaders play their parts well, this is no. companies themselves must be willing to identify and develop proacti. among their employees. Unfortunately, this does not happen very often. Althou₆ proactiveness is highly praised in the corporate world, the truth is that few companies know how to identify and develop this behavior. The word "proactiveness" itself is regarded as a managerial buzzword: that is, the sort of phrase that managers use regularly without much thought, and without really understanding its real meaning and implications. People say that professionals should be more proactive, that proactiveness is a quality that differentiates companies, that it is a rare and difficult-to-promote ability, and that it is innate in everyone, or can be taught and learned. However, debate on how proactive behavior can actually be identified and encouraged in a planned way is rare.

Thus, in order to prevent the whole idea of personal proactiveness from becoming nothing but hot air, it needs to be made operational. In other words, work must be carried out to promote it in practice. This points to some basic initial questions every manager interested in developing people's proactiveness will have to answer:

- What are the characteristics of a proactive professional?
- How do I recognize them when I am hiring someone?
- What aspects of our company may be favoring or inhibiting personal proactiveness?
- How can I develop people's proactive behavior?

Usually, directors and managers do not have clear answers to these questions. They give little thought to find out whether a person has a strong inclination to proactiveness, and what they can do to develop and improve individual proactive behavior. This is not an easy-to-solve problem. Research on proactive behavior at work shows that there is no simple definition of proactiveness. As with any other behavior, proactive attitudes are impacted by innumerable variables and circumstances. However, the research can help us draw some conclusions on the nature and characteristics of personal proactiveness, and understand the factors that influence it and how companies can address them.[12]

The studies show that proactive behavior – like any other behavior at work – results from a combination of personal inclination and aspects related to the professional environment (Figure 7.3). The evidence therefore suggests that people's personality makes them more or less inclined to act proactively. At the same time, factors related to the working environment also seem to influence the intensity of individual proactiveness. It is the company's duty to recognize the individual and environmental factors that influence people's proactiveness, and make them act more (or less) proactively, then take measures to intensify the positive factors and minimize the negative influences. This will help companies identify potential proactive talents among their existing personnel and when hiring

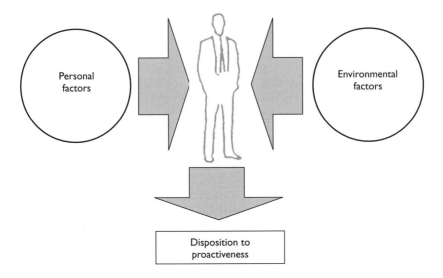

Figure 7.3 Proactive behavior at work

new personnel. It will also help companies develop systems and structures that favor proactive actions undertaken by people and work teams. Let us see how to accomplish that.[13]

Identifying personal proactiveness

The identification of personal proactiveness, as defined here, is a company's ability to recognize the disposition of individuals to act proactively. This applies to both potential and current employees. Above all, it is important not to lose sight of the fact that measuring proactive behaviors at work is in itself a multifaceted question, and therefore open to many different interpretations. As we have seen, research has provided different understandings of the nature and evaluation of personal proactiveness, but it has also indicated some common elements of this behavior and stimulated reflection on the characteristics associated with it. Only the examination of these characteristics will help decide how disposed someone is to act proactively.

Box 7.1 lists some characteristics frequently associated with proactive behavior at work.[14] It shows clearly that proactive professionals are oriented to change and act anticipatively in an attempt to impact the surrounding reality. Proactive individuals try to modify their circumstances or even intentionally create new situations. When a professional decides to act proactively, their intention is to change external conditions rather than adjust to them. Proactive professionals are also firmly guided by self-imposed objectives, showing perseverance and the resolve to overcome obstacles. In the terms we have used in this book, proactive people do not regard reality as predetermined and therefore unchangeable. To the contrary, they are what we call "voluntarists," because they believe in freedom of choice and the power to influence a context.[15]

> **Box 7.1 Characteristics of proactive professionals**
>
> - Change-oriented: they try to change circumstances and even intentionally create entirely new circumstances.
> - Not constrained by the situation or context they are in, they try to overcome obstacles.
> - Motivated by and systematically looking for opportunities.
> - Display initiative and determination to take action.
> - Inclined to persevere: difficulties do not dispirit them or prevent them from pursuing and reaching their objectives.
> - Anticipate changes and solve problems in anticipation.
> - Work today keeping an eye on the future: future-oriented.
> - Act with other people, and value partnerships and social networks.
> - Reach beyond what is formally required and try to do more than is expected of them.
> - Challenge the status quo and work paradigms.
> - Have strong self-belief.

This raises the issue of how to identify these characteristics in both existing and potential employees. Fortunately it is possible to analyze the individual disposition to proactiveness in a planned and methodical way,[16] using self-evaluation descriptive questionnaires and analysis of past data and experiences.

Only a few validated instruments currently exist to measure the personal inclination to proactive behavior. The Proactive Personality Scale developed by North American professors Thomas Bateman and Michael Crant is still the most commonly used.[17] The concept of a proactive personality mirrors the personal trait described there as change anticipation and modification of external conditions. On the whole, the scale is an attempt to evaluate at what level someone engages in anticipation and change-oriented actions, launching initiatives and searching for new opportunities. Questionnaires such as this can certainly be useful, but it is important to keep in mind their drawbacks and limitations, such as the ever-present bias towards giving the answers people believe are being looked for. It is best not to use them in isolation, but to combine them with other more qualitative approaches based on in-depth interviews. This will certainly broaden the perceptions gathered.[18]

The qualitative approach to proactive behavior may be based on the analysis of past data and experience. One technique is to question interviewees about their past behavior, for instance asking, "Tell us about a moment when an innovative idea came to mind. What was the idea? Were you able to put it into practice? What results did this idea produce for your company? Did you face resistance from your peers when trying to apply your idea? If so, how did you overcome the resistance?" The qualitative approach can also focus on an individual's level of initiative at work and how it helps people exceed expectations. Another useful question is "Have you in the past made any changes to your daily work activities? If so, was this your idea or did you collaborate with someone? Is change anticipation a habitual attitude of yours?" These questions are designed to discover how a person is guided by initiative and anticipation, instead of staying tied to tasks and prescribed functions.[19]

In brief, identification of personal proactiveness means trying to find the tendency to proactive action in individuals, helping companies recognize proactive employees and assess the potential for proactiveness of job applicants. In addition to the methods discussed above, a sense of observation and the feeling of managers and evaluators are also extremely important in the process. Often, a person's sheer physical posture or the subtleties of their speech reveal their inclination to proactiveness. Taking a sharp and selective look might suggest characteristics such as individual motivation and spirit in the face of change, attitudes to obstacles, and orientation to the future and new opportunities.

Finally, it is reassuring to know that proactive people, in general, have a sense of responsibility for change; a feeling that they must in some way contribute to improving their surroundings. They are attentive to the greater objectives of both the company and work groups. For a proactive professional, every job is their own job. In other words, proactive professionals pay attention to and try to collaborate to achieve established objectives, even when they do not feature among their personal targets.[20] The difference between being a sculpture and being a sculptor is analogous to that between being reactive and being proactive. Reactive people behave like sculptures in that they are shaped by contexts, by molds that impose limits. Ultimately, they become complacent and distant from the objectives of teams and companies. Proactive people, on the other hand, behave like sculptors. They do not strictly conform to (are not shaped by) assignments. They hold the reins of reality and opt for anticipation and action, instead of simply responding.[21]

Developing personal proactiveness

Just as personality deeply influences a person's disposition to proactiveness, context also exerts an influence. The environment inside organizations, including policies, rules, systems, and culture, is regarded as a major influence on the proactive behavior of individuals. Hence, the development of personal proactiveness – that is, a company's attitude to the promotion of proactive behavior – includes the analysis of organizational structures and norms that influence this type of behavior.

Dealing with context is important because otherwise those with proactive personalities might never actually put their ideas into practice. If a company's culture rejects proactiveness, proactive ideas and insights are much less likely to emerge or be implemented. Consequently, researchers have tried to gauge which environmental factors discourage people from proactive actions. We have classed them in four fundamental categories: autonomy, leaders' support, reciprocal confidence, and cost–benefit ratio.[22]

Autonomy

Autonomy at work is regarded as an important precondition for proactive behavior. People who enjoy freedom of action will be more inclined to act proactively in the search for new opportunities and solutions, while an environment dominated by limited autonomy will attenuate people's disposition to act proactively, stifling their change-anticipation initiatives. Autonomy stimulates people's self-confidence, encouraging them to propose new visions and ideas, essential attitudes in the context of personal proactiveness. People who have autonomy become more flexible professionals in that they act according to a broader perspective aimed at the company as a whole, an attitude that, as we have seen, is also related to proactive personality characteristics. Thus, in harmony with the flexible way of managing described earlier, companies developing personal proactiveness must provide an action-friendly environment. There must be freedom of decision – at least for a substantial part of the time – and people should be allowed to decide what to do, when, and how. This will show professionals that top management trusts their abilities, and encourages them to positively break rules and shift paradigms, to pick new ways of acting, and to act anticipatively to achieve strategic objectives.

Leaders' support

Support from leaders is in close harmony with issues we discussed earlier: the stimulus to proactive action must come from the top. This is sometimes described as "leading others so they can lead themselves": encouraging people to start actions, overcome their own limitations, and pursue their objectives.[23] It is also in tune with the issue of autonomy. Here, support from leaders will promote independent action and self-management, aspects that are in consonance with proactive attitudes. Leadership support exerts a strong impact on people's engagement with more proactive behaviors, in both the smaller context of work teams and the global context of companies. Such support is still more relevant when we take into consideration the fact that anticipatory actions and decisions usually result in higher risks and real possibilities of failure. The feeling that leaders are close to and trust subordinates is essential to encourage people not to give up their more ambitious plans and ideas.[24] The words of Luiz Eduardo Falco, former president of OI, offer an opportunity to reflect on this:

> Proactiveness is something that should be unlimited and, when stimulated to go in the right direction, it brings success to companies. Talents grow faster when free to move around in the company. Because a good leader is the one who develops people, and well developed people have to able to move around.[25]

Reciprocal confidence

It is said that when professionals feel their peers trust their abilities and competences, their self-confidence tends to grow, increasing the chance that they will put forward new ideas. Confidence among peers at work reduces risk and error aversion (as we have seen, two vital aspects of market proactiveness), promotes learning and exchange of experiences among teams, and makes people more open to change. Research in the field of service quality, for instance, shows that a mutually supportive and cooperative atmosphere among work teams tends to leverage proactive behaviors, for instance to anticipate problems that could come up when serving clients. This would clearly help to prevent future customer dissatisfaction and improve the level of service.[26]

Cost–benefit ratio

Obviously, people do not choose randomly what to do: we all evaluate the pros and cons of our actions. This is even more important in professional life, where we are all susceptible to success and failure, and where wrong decisions may cause substantial personal harm. People will think twice before acting anticipatively if they perceive that the risks to their careers exceed the potential benefits. If the social costs of a possible failure are high, most probably someone will choose not to risk it.

As we discussed earlier, this calls for policies that reward and recognize proactive actions, and do not punish failure in a carefully considered venture. This policy not only encourages the development of personal proactiveness, it also helps the company retain proactive talent. Professionals inclined to proactiveness will look to move on if they feel their proactive behavior is not being satisfactorily acknowledged, or if they suffer from a failure. Bonuses, rewards, promotions, and even informal acknowledgements play a twofold and important part in this context: they tend to stimulate people to act proactively, and they reduce the likelihood that expertise will be transferred to competitors. Alberto Saraiva, president of Habib, the world's largest Arab fast-food chain, helps wrap up our description and raises a very assertive question about stimulating proactive behavior: "Proactiveness is closely related to motivation. What level of motivation makes people act proactively: pecuniary or target-achievement motivations? Relationship or hierarchical position motivations?"[27]

In this chapter we have addressed the development of personal proactiveness, and concluded that it results from a proactive leadership and a company's capacity for identifying and developing proactive behavior. Proactive companies adopt strategies that enable leaders to favor the promotion of proactiveness in the organization. They also try to identify people's inclination to proactiveness and to hire professionals that possess this characteristic. In addition, they try to improve their capacity for evaluating the proactiveness of their own employees. Finally, proactive companies pay attention to the development of people's personal proactiveness, redesigning practices and cultures to make more room for anticipatory actions.

Proactive behavior management completes the cycle of proactive management introduced in Chapter 3 that provided the focus for the second part of our narrative. This managerial cycle is very important to support the adoption of proactive market strategies. It is also important to discuss how some companies have managed to implement their proactive strategies. We have now reached the third and last part of the book, which is essentially aimed at presenting the implementation of market proactiveness.

Part III
Executing Market Proactiveness

BUILDING A PROACTIVE MARKET STRATEGY

8 How to Put Market Proactiveness into Practice

In the field of strategy, the capacity for execution is fundamental. Without practical actions, a strategy is nothing more than an intention. In managerial terms, the line of reasoning that supports this argument is very simple: nothing actually happens when strategic aspirations do not go beyond mere talk, planning meetings and printing manuals and plans. In truth, as you say in English, we need to get on our bikes.

In order to realize a strategy, we just need to start acting. João Guilherme Brenner, CEO of Nutrimental, one of the largest Brazilian food-processing companies with a very innovative presence in the cereal bar market, assertively summarized this practical side of strategy: "You only have a strategy when you start spending money on it."[1] For us, nothing explains the execution of a strategy better than this statement. In other words, the budget is always a decisive indicator of a strategy's implementation.

In Chapter 3 we discussed the dilemma of strategy execution, a theme that is studied intensely nowadays by business school faculty and debated widely among executives. Strategy execution is very challenging, and requires steely determination from managers, especially when anticipation of market changes is involved.

To implement strategies, companies must have the capacities or abilities to, for example, assume risk, deal with mistakes, and be flexible when acting, as we have seen in previous chapters. In addition, after having talked to dozens of executives, we have become convinced that in order to make anticipation leave the realm of intention and become reality, a proactive mindset is absolutely necessary. This requires the creation of a proactiveness culture in the company. In this context, the old motto "Do the right thing right" is not enough, if changes are to be anticipated. In the world of proactiveness, our motto is rather "Do the right thing before things change."

After developing capacities, overcoming internal barriers, and above all, settling on the option for anticipation, it is time to act, to put the proactive market strategy (PMS) into practice. The moments-zero (MZs) matrix we have introduced is the guideline and main source of insights that help formulate a PMS. The matrix presents the timeline for MZs (changes in the market) across the past, present, and future realities, and the attitudes a company should adopt concerning such changes. These attitudes inspire and simultaneously structure the construction of a proactive strategy.

We already know that in every market there is a past reality, where MZs occurred, and some were extinguished, while others still reverberate through the present reality. The present reality, in turn, is also replete with changes that succeed each other according to the market dynamics and the external environment. Thus, the company must learn from past MZs, and be able to deeply analyze the present reality and understand all its changes.

The focus in constructing a PMS is the anticipation of moments zero that orbit future realities. Pulsating changes often start to become manifest well before we are able to determine precisely when the MZ will take place. The strategist needs to track the underdetermined reality, using the MZs radar. And there are also elements of a future reality that send no sign that they are about to happen, so it is therefore uncertain whether they will, although it is possible for this reality to be imagined or created by strategists with the aid of the future images searchlight.

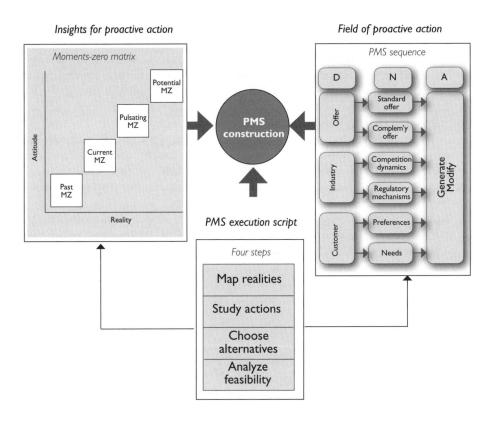

Figure 8.1 The proactive market strategy (PMS) construction process

Table 8.1 The four steps to formulate a proactive market strategy

First step
Map the four realities and their MZs
	• Analyze the four market realities for the offer, industry, and customer dimensions.
	   • Learn with past MZs.
	   • Analyze present MZs.
	   • Track pulsating MZs.
	   • Explore potential MZs.

Second step Analyze proactive actions at each level	• What might be generated or modified at each of the two levels of the offer, industry, and customer dimensions?
Third step Pick the promising alternatives	• What are the best options for proactive actions?
Fourth step Evaluate strategy feasibility	• Evaluate whether the company is in good condition to execute the devised strategy. • Identify internal and external barriers that could hinder execution of the strategy.

In Chapter 2 we presented different ways of formulating a PMS, and showed how it involves anticipating changes that happen in the dimensions of the offer (standard and complementary), industry (competition dynamics and regulatory mechanisms), and customer (preferences and needs). We also learned that anticipatory actions involve generating or modifying a level of each dimension. These actions are delineated in the generate–modify matrix.

This brief review of the concepts and tools we have presented allows us to introduce an overview of the PMS construction process (Figure 8.1). In practice, this process consists of:

• obtaining insights that may favor proactive action (through the application of the MZs matrix and its accessory tools)
• understanding the field of proactive action (possible sequences to formulate a PMS)
• following the four-step PMS execution script.

Observe that the PMS execution script represents a link between the MZs matrix (the source of insights for proactive action) and the DNA model. Thus, the strategy formulation process becomes more assertive, since the knowledge attitudes (learning, analyzing, tracking, and exploring) required to scan each of the four realities (past, current, undetermined, and uncertain) will be aimed at the three dimensions of proactive action (offer, industry, and customer) on each of their levels. In practice, the four steps which we now discuss in detail will guide strategists' actions in the execution of proactive strategies (Table 8.1). By following these four steps, strategists ensure that the PMS is executed.

THE FOUR STEPS OF A PMS

Map realities and market moments zero

Construction of a PMS starts by mapping the four market realities and their MZs. Here, strategists must sharpen their capacity for understanding the market's temporal aspect. The greater the capacity, the more refined the retrospective and prospective scanning of changes and the more fruitful their analysis and interpretation will be. We often say that more proactive strategists are lynx-eyed in visualizing past, present, and future market waves.

Let us see, for instance, how Apple's former chief Steve Jobs demonstrated this capacity for apprehending waves on the PC market. Apple's strategic inclination does not lead to reactive behavior toward its markets. On the contrary, through the years and through many innovative offers, the company has always driven changes in its segment. Its offers have been developed based on a remarkable capacity for analyzing the great moves taking place in the market, and above all, for detecting future realities. Apple's offer proactiveness in the segment of personal computers – even more vigorous after the introduction of the iPad – is stimulated, among other factors, by the anticipated vision of a "third golden wave in the use of personal computers," as was predicted by Jobs in 2001 at the MacWorld Conference, a yearly event promoted by the company.[2]

According to Apple's former CEO, three "golden waves" characterized the use of PCs in the 1980–2000 period. The first wave, from 1980 to 1994, was marked by electronic spreadsheets and other software applications that helped bring computers into people's daily lives. In the second wave, from 1995 to 2000, the World Wide Web connected millions of PCs and offered users a new and appealing convenience. In the third wave (starting in 2001), whose advent Apple proactively detected, PCs configured a reality Jobs called a "digital lifestyle," where the personal computer is a many-featured device capable of handling work, communications, and leisure tasks. Apple's ability enabled it to perceive that PCs would function as real "digital hubs," equipped with a large screen and complex applications to integrate them with other devices such as mobile phones, digital music players, cameras, and portable DVD players. Jobs was right, and the spectacular success of the iPad (a new standard offer in the PC category) confirms it.

Apple's experience raises a few interesting questions for companies going through this first step to PMS construction. Have you adequately characterized the strategic moves and market waves of the last three decades? How do these moves affect the present, and how might they influence the next market waves? What were the technological, economic, and social factors that determined MZs in the market in the period leading up to the present reality? What future images delineate the next market waves and their potential MZs?

Analyze proactive actions on each level

After mapping the market's four realities and their MZs, strategists proceed to study possible proactive actions. Here, PMS construction starts to become more practical. It is a matter of analyzing what might be generated or modified on each of the two levels of the offer, industry, and customer dimensions. To do this, strategists apply the generate–modify matrix, the tool that guides proactive actions.

The logic of this tool conveys a very simple idea: the generation of something that does not exist yet and/or the modification of something existing. When conceiving this tool, we were guided by the conviction that simplicity may be a significant help in the tortuous path of strategy implementation. We used to say that, in the ever more complex world of management, objectivity in action has great value. In this current step of PMS construction, the strategists' perception of what is relevant for clients is equally valuable. At the same time, possible proactive actions must be married to a company's financial interests, institutional image, and product positioning, among other issues. The logic here is very simple: strategists must practice what we call pendulum vision, alternating a view of the market (that is, customers) with a view of the company (that is, shareholders). When the pendulum dynamics are subverted, one of the sides will pay a price, to the detriment of the effectiveness of the proactive action.

We often say that understanding a customer is a lot more difficult than understanding product functionalities or operational and financial flows. This is true when constructing a PMS. Even better, in the case of anticipatory actions, we believe that the pendulum logic is tested in an more dynamic way *because* strategists are dealing with greater uncertainties.

Rogério Martins, product quality and development vice-president at Whirlpool Latin America, one of the world's most innovative companies and a leader in the Brazilian household appliances market, made a useful comment on this: "When engineers and marketers are guided exclusively by technology's appeal, they run the risk of not fulfilling consumers' needs, even when they offer something new."[3] He told us a story about industry innovation. A competitor decided to install television sets in the doors of refrigerators. It was something very innovative – in this case, a modification of the standard offer – but it turned out not to really appeal to customers. The irrelevance of this innovation was proved by the small sales volume, which forced the company to abandon production.

At Whirlpool, a deep and holistic understanding of consumers represents a crucial vector for the analysis of proactive action over new product offers. In addition, these actions must be tuned to a company's innovation strategy, and most importantly, they must generate the desired financial results, reinforcing the pendulum view. As was well stated by José Drummond Jr., Whirlpool's president for Latin America, "For us, innovative products must satisfy three basic requirements: be unique in their market, benefit consumers, and generate value for the shareholder."[4]

Pick promising alternatives

In a broad sense, the most promising alternatives for proactive action are those a company is able to execute successfully that have the potential to configure relevant MZ in the market (to recap, this relevance can be measured by changes in market range and impact). Let us return to Whirlpool's experience and try to better understand this step in PMS formulation.

Whirlpool strategists had an innovative idea: to produce the world's first single-door frost-free refrigerator. (Before then, the frost-free feature had only been available in two-door, necessarily more expensive refrigerators.) This was realized in the Consul Facilite model, introduced in 2008 to the Brazilian market. This best-selling product created a new market for the company, capturing thousands of consumers in social classes C and D who wanted frost-free fridges but could not afford the two-door models.

This proactive action was a great challenge to Whirlpool, and was motivated by the company's strategic aspiration to increase its leadership and capture more value in this huge market segment, which at one point accounted for 70 percent of all domestic refrigerators sold in Brazil. Over the previous few years the sales to this segment had dropped, and Whirlpool was interested in reversing this situation. José Drummond, Jr. explained, "We have always been very strong and profitable in the one-door segment, and falling sales in the product category did not strike us as interesting. We had already introduced energy-efficiency improvements but our products remained unattractive and lacked differentiating features in their category. Then we decided to take on the challenge of bringing the frost-free benefit to the lower-cost segments."[5]

This decision originated an extremely promising product that ended up changing the prevailing world standard offer of frost-free refrigerators. The promise lay in two relevant factors: a functional benefit that was not yet on offer in the category, and an attractive price. No other alternative for changing the functional attributes of one-door refrigerators was as promising as introducing the frost-free feature.

Evaluate the feasibility of the strategy

As we know, every competitive strategy must be feasible from the operational, financial, and market perspectives. To successfully lay the foundations, strategists must overcome internal and external barriers, an even greater challenge in the context of market proactiveness, because of their anticipatory nature and the consequent uncertainty.

As we saw in Chapter 3, proactiveness management requires the development of a bundle of capacities that are needed to help executives find opportunities for anticipating changes. If these capacities are not fully developed, internal barriers will naturally obstruct the PMS construction process. The barriers may be related to risk taking, for instance, forcing strategists to backpedal on certain aspects of a strategy, making it less aggressive or unusual. The barriers may also be related to a difficult or short-sighted interpretation of market signs, or to fear of making mistakes during execution and compromising the results. Thus, the analysis and removal of internal barriers is a crucial step in ensuring a strategy's feasibility.

From the external perspective, every anticipatory action may face all kinds of barriers in the offer, industry, and customer dimensions. Imagine, for instance, that a very innovative and differentiated product is introduced to the market. In the offer dimension, the first challenge or barrier that strategists will face is correctly positioning the product in the target market and conveying its advantages. What is the best and most intelligent way of communicating the new product's differentiated benefits? In the industry dimension there may be major barriers in the domains of suppliers (that could find it difficult to integrate with the new processes required by the strategy), distribution channels (that often show lack of understanding or loose adherence to new functions or roles), and regulatory agents (if the legal framework is insufficient to support anticipatory action). Finally, in the customer dimension, the most common barrier is difficulty in accepting or assimilating change, a characteristic that means companies need the capacity to educate the market, changing or generating preferences and needs.

Whirlpool, for instance, had to overcome technological and financial challenges in the process of developing its Consul Facilite refrigerator in order to make possible the creation of this MZ in the market. Technologically speaking, successful execution of this proactive action was ensured by encouraging all the company's suppliers to make a strategic commitment to the development project. From the financial viewpoint, it is important to keep development costs at a level that allow the product to be sold at a price accessible to the target customer segment (in this case, one with relatively low purchasing power) and still provide the required return.

Externally, the main obstacle the company's strategists faced was finding a way to communicate what was new and important about the model. The frost-free feature was a real benefit to those who wanted to avoid the chore of manually defrosting their fridge, but at the same time this was a chore this market segment tended to take for granted. As Mario Fioretti, Whirlpool design and innovation director, said:

> The consumer did not ask for frost-free refrigerators because she simply could not verbalize that. That is, she could not express in clear words that she would like to be spared the unpleasant task of defrosting a fridge, because this feature was only offered in more expensive products she was not sure she could afford.[6]

From that situation emerged the challenge of clearly and convincingly stating the product's major functional benefit. Patrícia Garrido, Whirlpool's research manager, detailed how the company tackled this challenge: "The problem was describing the benefit without naming it 'frost-free.' We decided to say it was 'the only refrigerator that did not build up ice in the freezer compartment.' This sentence had to appear in all the advertising material."[7]

All the technological, financial, and market positioning challenges of the new product were overcome by Whirlpool, and it managed to increase its leadership in the single-door refrigerator market. This was an MZ: relevant to the market and very rewarding for the company.

When it comes to MPS construction, we have a lot to learn from Steve Jobs's sharp anticipative vision of market waves, an essential skill that enables us to deal with the future and conceive anticipatory actions. Similarly, Whirlpool's experience tells us that correct execution of proactive market strategies requires the internal leadership to model behaviors that favor innovation, competence for the execution of technical requirements, and above all, the ability to tune in to the customer's world. In brief, as we have seen, everything starts with a vision and a firm strategic will, but nothing happens if there is no willingness to act and capacity to overcome barriers.

In the remaining chapters we address the construction of proactive strategies, focusing specifically on the offer, industry, and customer dimensions, and also present other successful experiences of companies that have adopted the motto of market proactiveness: "Believing is seeing."

OFFER PROACTIVENESS

9 Creating a Moment Zero for an Offering

In the offer dimension, companies have promising opportunities to act proactively and innovate. When it works properly, the anticipation of offer moments zero (MZs) increases a company's competitive power and generates big profits. Let us examine Apple's product trilogy – represented by the innovative iPod, iPhone, and iPad – which significantly leveraged the company's financial results in the last eight years, amazing customers and making shareholders extremely happy. The iPad, for instance, the most recent of the three, delivered a fantastic performance in the market: in only nine months, the product's first generation nearly hit the mark of 15 million devices sold in 2010, exceeding the expectations of analysts and the company itself. At the time this chapter was being written (March 2011), Apple was expecting to produce US$20 billion in revenue from the sale of 30 million iPad 2 tablets, thinner, lighter, and faster than their predecessor,[1] a successful recipe that proves the ability of offer proactiveness to increase sales and profitability.

In our frequent conversations with executives in different situations, and also in classes, lectures, and workshops, we have always emphasized the idea of marketing's necessary commitment to a ceaseless search for differentiation, as an inspiring strategic orientation. We tend to say that, in scenarios of growing competition, marketing actions that are taken without this commitment show a tendency to be unsustainable in the long term. Thus, differentiation is the rule of the game strategists must follow to create relevant value proposals and to attract ever more demanding consumers, who are continually exposed to a flood of offers.

We know that differentiation efforts may be applied to marketing in many different fields: in the definition of distribution channels and policies (think of the revolutionary door-to-door distribution Avon created in 1886), in pricing strategies (as seen in retail's price battles and different payment schemes), in marketing communication (we all remember the publicity campaign developed by the Italian clothing retailer Benetton), or above all, in the dimension of products and services, which is the main subject of this chapter. Undoubtedly, this last dimension has become a promising avenue for proactive innovations that generate market-impacting MZs.

Let us get back in time to illustrate the impact of an unusual offer on the market. Travel back with us to the year 1877. We are now in a peaceful North American consumer society. Someone wanting to take pictures would have to spend around $50 to purchase all necessary gadgets, a kit clumsy enough to discourage any beginner: "heavy camera, tripod, plates, paper, boxes to keep negatives, tent to be used as darkroom, small chemistry laboratory … funnel, hard-bristled brush, balances, weights and washing bowls."[2] And, to carry on with their photographic adventure, beginners would also have to pay for private lessons to learn how to use the equipment and handle the chemical compounds. These circumstances ultimately exemplify what we ironically call a "disheartening offer of inconveniences."

A decade later, in 1888, the same amateur photographer-to-be might see an advertisement offering a small camera with a built-in 100-picture film roll for only $25. The Kodak camera had arrived on the market, a genuine offer replete with never-before-imagined functional conveniences. In addition, buyers could count on a picture development service for $10. All the photographer had to do was to send the camera to the manufacturer's laboratory and wait ten days to get back both their pictures and the reloaded camera. These facilities – which were then extremely surprising to consumers – were masterfully condensed to create the ad's title: "You press the button, we do the rest." A modest illustration of a camera in the palm of a hand proclaimed its ease of use and the convenient services that were being introduced to the 19th century's complex world of photography.[3] This represented enough of an incentive to develop a consumer market and attract thousands of buyers. Kodak's successful history was beginning. It was a high-intensity and high-amplitude MZ that lasted for many years, up to the disruptive advent of digital photography, a new technology that shook the very foundations of the successful company around its centenary (see Chapter 1).

Kodak's example, like many others in different industries and times, demonstrates the endless possibilities of change anticipation in the offer dimension. Offers are an essential way of delivering benefits to clients. The more unusual these benefits – as in the case of Kodak's camera, launched decades ago, or the vigorous iPad introduction to the market in 2010 – the more attractive the offer will be to consumers.

The Kodak camera's success confirmed the impact of proactive innovations in the realm of the standard offer, creating a new consumer market in the world of photography. Observe that the launch also included a complementary offer, since the package included picture development services. We will now look at favorable opportunities that combine these two offer levels.

THE STANDARD OFFER AND COMPLEMENTARY OFFER: SYNERGIES AND OPPORTUNITIES

We already know that standard offers involve a product's core benefits and attributes, whereas complementary offers add extended benefits to clients. In the case of Apple, the unusual functional benefits added to the iPod, iPhone, and iPad are market MZs at the level of the standard offer. The thousands of songs and applications available at iTunes and the App Store are complementary benefits or conveniences that make the standard offer even more attractive.

Apple's successful trajectory, by the way, shows the company's great capacity for acting proactively and synergistically at both offer levels. This increases its firepower compared with opponents in the market, and they end up imitating its innovations. Undoubtedly, the 65,000 low-priced applications available at the App Store (hundreds of which may be downloaded for free) leverage iPhone and iPad sales by providing an astounding range of possibilities for their use. Thus, if we regard the marketplace as a desert, the synergy between these two offer levels is an oasis where everyone would like to be: millions of consumers in search of new consumption experiences, companies eager to provide them with products and services, and countless application developers trying to take part in this market game created by Apple.

Still talking of synergism, let us examine the case of the young Dutch company TomTom. Founded in 1991, it is now a world leader in the segment of portable GPS navigation equipment, after developing a series of innovative and advanced technological systems that enabled it to offer complementary services to millions of users all over the world. The convenience menu of complementary offers includes systems such as TomTom Map Share (costless sharing of cartographic changes between users), TomTom HD Traffic (traffic information updated every three minutes), TomTom IQ Routes (a database containing more than 800 million speed profiles to help people choose quicker routes any time and anywhere), TomTom Hotel Reservation (users can book accommodation en route directly from the equipment) and the TomTom Weather Report (local daily and five-day weather forecasts). This wide range of very convenient complementary services enabled the company to surpass the industry's offer pattern – GPS navigation – and to quickly reach leadership in a hotly disputed market.[4]

These examples show that competitive differentials in both standard and complementary offers are determined by a company's capacity for innovation and access to new technologies that are increasingly available to the market. These technologies also end up absorbing most of the available benefits into the standard offer, constantly creating new challenges to find ways to differentiate an offer. In this context, many offer patterns that seem inviolable now might be subverted in the near future (see Box 9.1). Proactiveness will then result from a company's differentiated look at the ongoing conditions of the offer, in search of unusual alternatives that could overturn the rules of the game. This is no easy task. We often hear executives say things like "Our sector has always operated this way and will keep on operating this way," or "Our customers will not accept radical changes to products and services." These beliefs reinforce market reactiveness and make companies hostage to changes in the offer dimension that they cannot anticipate. This kind of chronic myopia is typical of "adjusted" organizations that, as we have seen, end up acting *after* MZs have occurred in the market.[5]

As we have seen, the synergy between proactive actions at the two levels of offer increases companies' ability to conquer markets. We have also addressed the fact that challenges inherent in product and service differentiation, the core part of any market strategy, are increasing. However, only companies that strategically opt to break with the attitude that they need only make small adjustments to their offer will be in a position to grasp the opportunities for proactive innovation opened

---

| Box 9.1 Standard offer? No thanks! |

The market is gradually becoming less and less tolerant of standard offers. This creates many opportunities for companies to embrace offer proactiveness. Think of the hotel industry. Checking out at noon is the norm in this industry, regardless of when guests arrive. But why should a guest who arrives at 11 pm pay the same as another who has been using the hotel services since 2 pm? If the car rental segment can deal with customers who use its services for a fraction of a day, why can't the hotel industry do the same?

Think now of DVD rental. In 1999, the Californian company Netflix put an end to the frustrating experience of paying a daily hire charge (and being charged extra if you fail to get the DVD back in time) by creating an innovative DVD rental system which operated through the mail, where customers are charged a monthly fixed amount regardless of how many discs they hire. This was a successful MZ in the sector, clearly differentiated from the existing standard offer. Customers were able to use the company website to list between one to eight films they wanted to hire each time. The company then mailed them one of the DVDs (depending on what was available for hire at that moment), including an pre-paid envelope for returning it. Clients could order another film as soon as they sent back the previous DVD. This was a highly convenient system that, in three years, attracted millions of customers. But the technology has moved on in this field too, and now the company is successfully providing video on demand over the internet, using streaming-video technology. Subscribers can watch the movies on computer screens without having to save files to their hard disks, let alone have a disc mailed to them.

In some retail areas, like the drugstore segment, for instance, the standard offer characteristics are changing almost continuously. The changes include the product range – we used to say that, in a drugstore, customers could find everything they needed *including* medicines – and service delivery, with new convenient options such as the "drive thru" alternative so that is familiar from fast-food restaurants. There is always an opportunity to shift the paradigm of a market's standard offer.

---

up by these challenges. As we now go on to see, these companies, which we have called alert companies and activators, generate MZs in the offer dimension, acting to give an anticipated response at the very first signs of change, or even deliberately creating change.

RESPONSIVE ANTICIPATION AND CREATIVE ANTICIPATION IN THE OFFER DIMENSION

We live in markets that are flooded with offers. Companies fight to meet consumers' preferences, offering countless products with different functional features or showing an appealing and differentiated image. Think of a product category and you will soon be able to think of several brands and purchase options. We tend to say that we live in a general store full of novelties, where consumers reign absolutely and plainly exercise their power of choice. In this context, immersed in a profusion of products, companies are the main generators of MZs in the offer dimension. As we saw in Chapter 4, an MZ may result either from responsive anticipation (the detection of signs of change) or from creative anticipation (constructing images of the future). Either way, companies regard the future and ask: how can we anticipate changes in our sector's offer?

Responsive anticipation

Everywhere in the market there are signs of change in current offers. Signs may be detected in the turbulence caused by technological advances that leverage innovation processes, but they are also to be found in the behavior dynamics of users of the standard and complementary offers in the sector. Signs also show up outside the market's borders: in the offer arena of other product categories, in the actions of companies competing in other markets, and finally, in the purchasing behavior of users of innumerable other products.

Let us see the responsive anticipation perspective in practice, taking the successful example of the introduction of H2OH!® to the Brazilian market. This was an MZ created in 2006 by Pepsico, which ended up generating a new soda pop standard. The drink was a lot lighter than most existing soft drinks, and had a healthy appeal (Figure 9.1). The new product soon captured thousands of consumers, attracted by the name and the market positioning of the offer, which set it apart from the traditional category of nonalcoholic beverages. The offer positioning was reinforced the ingredients: a predominance of water, a low concentration of lemon juice, and some gas to give it a subtle fizz. Launched initially in the Argentinean and Mexican markets, H2OH!® soon became a best-seller in Brazil, taking a share from other participants in the highly competitive light soft drinks market. H2OH!®'s leadership in this new category (of low-calorie carbonated soft drinks)[6] has remained untouched for five years now, although its competitors include Coca-Cola's Aquarius Fresh.

To generate this new standard offer, Pepsico detected strong signs in the

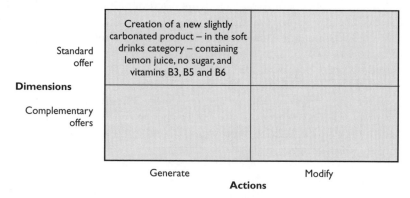

Figure 9.1 The generate–modify matrix for H2OH!®

Brazilian nonalcoholic beverage market itself that pointed to a faster growth of noncarbonated beverages (water, juices, and isotonic and soy-based beverages, among others). The participation of noncarbonated beverages in the nonalcoholic drinks market had jumped from 30.5 percent in 2001 to 36.2 percent in 2005. And between 2005 and 2006, the diet or light soft drink market had also grown.[7]

At the level of the behavior of soft drink consumers, the company's strategists also detected distinct signs indicating barriers to the category's growth, such as consumers' fear of obesity and dislike of too much gas in products. Outside the borders of its own market, the company detected habits and behaviors that pointed to people's increasing concern with a healthier lifestyle: a high importance attached to the body and to exercises to improve fitness, a lower consumption of sugar, fat, and food overall, and the increasing consumption of vitamins and other food supplements. The media's reporting on the global obesity crisis contributed to reinforcing these tendencies.

Pepsico's proactiveness becomes evident from the company's strategic perception, which led it to anticipate the interpretation of these latent market signs. Pepsico strategists saw that they pointed to a demand from consumers who were sensitive to the healthy appeal of water and juices, but still valued the casual and tasty side of soft fizzy drinks. Thus, the proactive question the company posed in order to anticipate the market's demands was, "How do we reconcile these two apparently antagonistic consumption trends?"

The answer materialized in H2OH!®, a product that capitalized on the best of two worlds, from both functional and emotional perspectives. The attributes "no sugar" and "lightly carbonated" suggest both the healthy balance of the water world and the delights of the soft drinks universe, providing a pleasurable but guiltless treat, a user-valued indulgence. With regard to this combination of factors, H2OH!® represents an anticipatory action because Pepsico was able to detect and interpret signs that led to the generation of a new standard offer in the soft drink category. So far, no competitor in the market had been able to reconcile the "lightness" and "well-being" aspects with "fun and flavor" so well, a combination that offers an innovative value proposition in the congested soft drink market.

The results of Pepsico's proactive market strategy are clear to see. Six months after its launch, in the period ranging from October 2006 to March 2007, H2OH!® became the leader brand in the segment of diet/light soft drinks in the São Paulo Metropolitan Area market, reaching a 29.8 percent market share, compared with Coca-Cola Light's 25.4 percent share. Relative to the same period of the preceding year (October 2005 to March 2006), the segment increased 31.4 percent, with H2OH!® accounting for 58.7 percent of this increase in sales in the geographic area under analysis (which represents 20 percent of the Brazilian market as a whole). This proves the positive impact of the H2OH!® MZ on the market, through Pepsico's anticipation which inaugurated a new concept in the segment of sugarless drinks.

H2OH!® has continued to lead the new category of lightly carbonated soft drinks. In 2007, competing with Coca-Cola's Aquarius, it held a 83 percent market share. In 2008 a new brand, Guarah, entered the market, but H2OH!® continued to lead with a 69.7 percent share. In 2009 and 2010 H2OH!® was still leader with an average participation of 70.4 percent in the market, followed by Aquarius with 27 percent, and Guarah (a brand Ambev withdraw from the market in 2010) with 2.6 percent. The offer proactiveness that materialized in the introduction of H2OH!® to the market represented a major increase in competitive power for Pepsico's operation in Brazil.

The challenges of sustaining a proactive strategy and maintaining H2OH!®'s success in the market are described by Andréa Álvares, president of Pepsico Brasil's beverages division:

> With H2OH!®, we were able to deliver several benefits that corresponded to the latent wishes of consumers and created a new concept in beverages. It is a precursory product that was created to offer differentiated features. It is not a fad, but rather an alternative beverage in whose growth we will continue to invest. We have here the permanent challenge of expanding this segment within the beverage market, so that more people can choose this alternative. To achieve that, we have to keep innovating to make H2OH!® increase its participation in consumers' daily life.[8]

H2OH!®'s history clearly displays the benefits that result from responsive anticipation of market signs: a proactive company is able to detect and interpret them effectively. Let us now address creative anticipation, another promising perspective to help the construction of a proactive market strategy.

Creative anticipation

We already know that when a company adopts the creative anticipation perspective it builds images of the future and acts according to creative insights in an attempt to forge change. In the realm of the offer dimension, we have witnessed many relevant service and product innovations brought about by this "endogenous creative movement."

Google's successful trajectory is a perfect example of this. Google became one of the highest-valued and most significant companies in the world by finding an unique way of activating creative anticipation in the offer dimension. Google was not the first search engine conceived for the internet, but it overwhelmingly defeated pioneer competitors Alta Vista and Yahoo! after developing a powerful web data classification system. In this particular case, the third major player to enter the market was able to generate the most intense and encompassing MZ: it changed the rules of the game to become the leading player in the web search business. This case demonstrates the supremacy of a proactive vision over a pioneer vision.

Google's revolutionary search engine was the fruit of a critical uncertainty that was obstinately worked on by one of the founders, Larry Page. Young and ambitious, Page conceived an uncertain reality: "to download the whole web into his computer" (see Figure 9.2). This possibility seemed almost unreal, unachievable by a human being, except when the human being is as visionary and

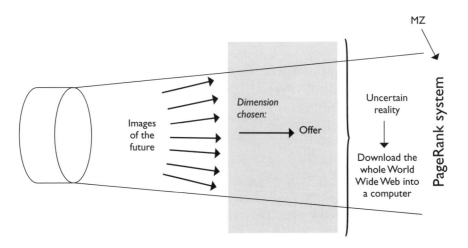

Figure 9.2 A future images searchlight: Google's search engine

proactive as Page proved to be. His capacity for analysis led him to meticulously research how internet links functioned. Based on that investigation – carried out in partnership with his colleague and Google co-founder Sergey Brin, under the academic supervision of Professor Terry Winograd – Page created a system that was capable of classifying websites according to their relative importance, using a simple algorithm to define relative importance: the higher the number of links pointing to a given website, the greater its importance. This enables search engines to rank the relevance of results, an invaluable help to users.

So was born the PageRank system, with is now the state of the art for internet search engines: it created a new standard offer that soon became hegemonic in its market segment and a daily habit for millions of internet surfers across the world.[9]

At the complementary offer level, Google also demonstrates extraordinary competence for anticipation, and has developed countless additional services. The complements to web-search services include electronic mail services (Gmail), geographical localization and mapping services (Google Maps and Google Earth), a shared online agenda service (Google Calendar), an economic and financial information service (Google Finance), a quick search and hard disk storage application (Google Desktop Search), a task manager integrated with email service user accounts (Google Agenda), and many others.

Google's relevance on the web comes particularly from its competence in creating attractive offers, anticipating the expectations of millions of users. Consequently, the Google homepage is the world's most visited website. Its brand is among the world's five most valued trademarks. In 2011, it ranked first in the world's top companies reputation index.[10]

As we have seen in these examples, offer proactiveness helps leverage business performance, generating both sales increase and value capture. We end this chapter by looking at a successful Brazilian case of change in the offer dimension, whose results are evidenced in both these perspectives.

HOW DID FIAT ANTICIPATE A CHANGE IN OFFER, IN INTRODUCING ITS NEW LIGHT-OFF-ROAD CAR CONCEPT TO THE BRAZILIAN MARKET?

The automotive market has always been a changing one, with share going quickly to newly developed products, so it can be regarded as a "microcosm of industrial competition."[11] From the advent of the legendary Ford Model T in 1908 to the launch of modern industry icons, cars have been a captivating – and even thrilling! – product for millions of consumers all over the world.

We can classify the complex appeal of cars on two dimensions. First, a car is an engineering artifact that integrates thousands of components and several different systems, and its development requires complex manufacturing processes. Second, face to face with an automobile, users respond in a complex way that melds objective, logical, and emotional elements.[12] Thus, when it is introduced to the market, a car must have a strong brand appeal: it must embody strong functional and aspirational attributes that appeal to consumers. In a sense, these attributes are orbiting in the universe of car buyers, waiting to be embodied in a specific model.

We will now see how Fiat Brasil anticipated change in the market and developed the Adventure concept, which it later adopted in some of its models. Acting in response to strong and weak signs its analysts detected both in and outside the auto market, Fiat modified the industry's standard offer in certain car segments, smartly reconciling functional and aspirational aspects (see Figure 9.3). This successful proactive market strategy created new sales opportunities and brought attractive results for the company.

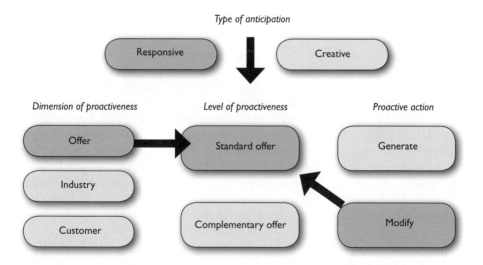

Figure 9.3 The sequence of proactive actions leading to the introduction of the Fiat Adventure

Interpreting the environment and detecting signs

The Adventure concept originated from Fiat Brasil's capacity for analyzing the overall market environment and interpreting signs coming from users of certain car categories. In addition, Fiat's strategists were inspired by the observation of both social consumption tendencies and signs of change in the lifestyle of people who live in big cities, where the car plays many different roles in the day-to-day lives of millions of consumers.

As the name itself implies, the Adventure concept directs our attention to the universe of off-road four-wheel-drive automobiles, very convenient vehicles both in the urban context of big cities and out in the country, on mountains and rural trails. The proactive vision of Fiat's strategists was able to see beyond the "off the shelf" concept of the four-wheel drive. These vehicles, usually large and robust, had attracted a growing share of car buyers. From 1994 to 1997, sales in the off-road segment of the Brazilian automotive market – comprised of average-sized pickup trucks, jeeps, and sport utility vehicles (SUVs) – jumped from 16,000 to 37,000 units, despite the fact that these vehicles were imported and therefore more expensive than locally made cars.[13]

Fiat recognized the possibility of innovatively modifying these functional attributes and attaching a differentiated aspirational appeal to its Palio Weekend station wagon model, forging the "light-off-road" concept. This was a car inspired by features that appealed in the off-road models, such as style, height, and robustness; that would be good-looking and roomy enough to accommodate plenty of luggage; and that would sell at a very attractive price compared with imported vehicles in the same category. Fiat developed this concept by detecting market signs and analyzing information gathered by means of structured surveys and proactive observation of tendencies in consumer behavior.

The analysis of past reality may help us understand the beginning of Fiat's journey through the conceptual construction of the Adventure range, which was introduced to the market in 1999. Four years before, the car manufacturer had made its first incursion into the still-unexplored "light-off-road" universe, launching the Pick-Up Trekking, which was based on its Uno platform. This special version of the Uno was equipped with mixed-use tires and also offered the differential of a higher ground clearance. The introduction of the Pick-Up Trekking to the market, combined with attentive observation of tendencies in the use of four-wheel-drive vehicles, provided Fiat with interesting lessons that helped the conceptual development of the Adventure. Fiat Brasil's export and product director, Carlos Eugênio Dutra, confirms this: "We learned that the market could be worked in a different way; that is to say, we started to understand that there was room for a more encompassing development of the light-off-road concept, especially with regard to the functional and aspirational aspects."[14]

In 1997 and 1998, competition in the Brazilian station wagon market was fierce. Market players included Volkswagen, whose Parati model topped the segment, Fiat, with its Palio Weekend, Ford, with the Escort SW, and GM, with the Corsa SW. The biggest challenge was the to create attractive differentials in the car's functional dimension, beyond the standard features of style and space, which had become a part of the segment's existing core offer. The category also lacked attractiveness in the aspirational dimension; in other words, all these models were short of excitement.

The concept of Adventure was born, therefore, as an attempt to bring a value differential into this highly competitive environment. In its research to find new attributes it could introduce into the SW category, Fiat detected signs of potential change, as shown in Figure 9.4. Smart interpretation of these signs and the capacity to develop interactive analyses of research data and to sense the mood of the market gradually disclosed an opportunity to anticipate an MZ. Edson Mazucato, Fiat's marketing director, said, "We are used to relying a lot on numbers and comparing everything. Numbers always tell us something interesting and excite our market feeling."[15]

Signs in the market itself included the sales growth in both average-sized pickups and other four-wheeled vehicles, both of which are regularly used in urban environments. Fiat also identified some interesting aspects of owners' behavior. Most owners loved their vehicles but did not make any use of a substantial part of their features. Many did not even know how to turn on the four-wheel drive. Fiat's strategists deduced that "style" was a decisive aspirational factor for cars in this category. The research also indicated that certain functional attributes had a strong appeal: for example, the high ground clearance gave urban users a feeling of security.

Outside the car market, Fiat analysts detected strong behavioral tendencies in big-city dwellers: a desire for freedom and to escape the stress of metropolitan life, an increased importance attached to environmental protection and contact with nature, an aspiration towards well-being, and a wish to achieve a good balance between work and leisure.

Fiat's proactive initiative became manifest when the company interactively analyzed this huge flood of strong and weak signs and got a sense of a product category that would better meet market needs. The latent factors – both rational and aspirational – pointed to a station wagon, but one that had the attributes of a light-off-road vehicle. The company was also encouraged because it looked as if this concept could be realized at a price that would be more attractive than traditional off-road cars, and yet higher than the original version, the Palio Weekend.

Developing the new off-road-light concept

This led to Fiat's proactive strategy: the introduction of a new and esthetically appealing light-off-road car at an affordable price and with strong aspirational appeal. Functional attributes such as higher suspension, mixed-use tires, external protection, and light-metal alloy footboard and wheels, all characteristic of light-off-road vehicles, made the car look sportive and appealing. The Adventure concept's aspirational appeal was boosted by a set of equipment that included air conditioning, electrically operated windows, hydraulic power steering, and auxiliary headlights.

With respect to engineering, the development of the Adventure as a concept demanded structural modifications to the original model. Thus, to functionally sustain a value proposal based on the light-off-road concept, Fiat's engineers

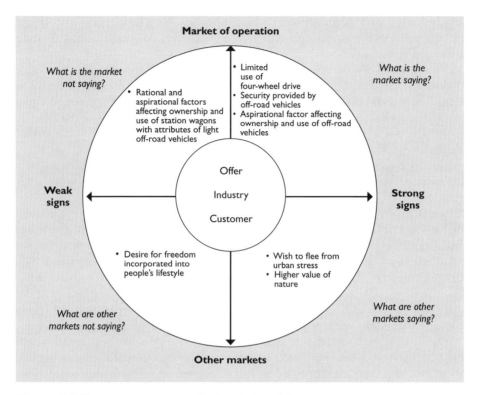

Figure 9.4 The moments zero radar for the Fiat Adventure

carried out a series of adaptations, including adoption of the Pick-up Strada's adjusted front suspension, a 40 mm increase in both the wheelbase and ground clearance, and reinforced back spring and dumper supports. One of the main concerns of the product design and engineering teams was to ensure there was both esthetic and functional integrity in the light-off-road concept. They wanted to avoid any suggestion that this was a station wagon that had simply been given a visual makeover to make it resemble an off-road vehicle, since that would weaken the Adventure concept.

Sustaining the proactive market strategy

We know that a market strategy is only consistent when companies are able to sustain it for some time and to reinvigorate their value proposal by responding to changes in the competitive environment. The excellent reception given to the Palio Adventure in September 1999 led Fiat to increase its proactive bet on the concept. In the following year, the Palio Adventure was incrementally improved to reinforce its good image in the market, but Fiat wanted to go farther. According to a proactive reasoning aimed at guiding the market and maximizing returns from the newly created asset of the Adventure concept, Fiat concluded that the concept could be extended to other models and categories.

So the company continued to invest in this new offer opportunity. In August 2001, the Pick-up Strada Adventure was launched, inspired by the Palio Adventure's successful DNA. Changes in functionality and esthetics made the new pickup more attractive, and reconciled the Adventure's versatility with the practicality of the extended crew cab, creating a best-seller. Next was the Dobló Adventure, in October 2003. The Dobló range was already well accepted in the multivan market niche developed by Fiat, and this new model expanded the user base of this category, which had initially been designed for commercial use. The Dobló Adventure has also performed well in sales terms, evidence that the new concept positively reinforced the car's differentiated style.

Still in 2003, the second generation of Palio Weekends and Strada Weekends entered the market, featuring stylistic and functional improvements. Also in 2003, Ford launched its very successful Ecosport model, a new car in the SUV segment. The Ecosport's success confirmed the market appeal of light-off-road vehicles. We should emphasize that this innovation by Ford cannot be considered as a standard offer modification strategy like Fiat's. The Adventure concept was implemented by adapting existing models, but the Ecosport was a completely new car, a new-generation standard offer. Fiat's strategists read the successful introduction of the Ford range as a strong market sign: that there was plenty of room to expand the Adventure concept.

Finally, in 2004, further evolution of the Adventure concept produced a third generation of Palio Weekend and Strada Weekend models, consolidating their leadership in the station wagon and small pickup categories respectively. In September 2006 the Idea minivan was rebuilt using the Adventure concept. From 2005, the minivan category grew in importance to the market, and several competitors, including Fiat, struggled to win over consumers in search of internal room, versatility, and economy: all features provided by these single-volume "small big" cars. Offering attractive differentiating features such as bars on the roof, external lateral footboards and protection, a compass, and lateral and longitudinal inclinometers, the Idea Adventure generated high sales, a performance that was sustained during the following years.

The competition's reactiveness

The competition's reactive strategies to the Adventure concept started in the station wagon category in 2003, when Volkswagen introduced the Parati CrossOver model. In 2005, Volkswagen applied the light-off-road concept to its successful single-volume Fox, and launched the CrossFox, an esthetically attractive model which sold well. Between 2005 and 2007 several other models joined the light-off-road category, such as VW Saveiro Crossover, Peugeot 206 SW Escapade, VW Parati Track&Field, Citroen C3 XTR, and Ford Fiesta Trail. This intense competition is evidence of the change in the market Fiat had anticipated in 1999, when it created the MZ that the Palio Weekend Adventure model represented.

In 2008 Fiat's market strategists had to face the challenge of sustaining the Adventure's value proposal and keeping its leverage. Their strategic agenda was shaped by the emerging issues for this category. What could they do to optimize the aspirational and functional factors of the light-off-road category and yet find a new differential for the Adventure concept? Was there still space to build on the style and visual appeal: would developments here be strong enough to reinforce the aspirational factor that was so important to the Adventure's DNA? What new functional attributes could provide a relevant differential for the Adventure models? The answer pointed to the development of a feature that Fiat called the "locker." This relatively simple – yet very relevant – technological innovation was incorporated into all the models in the Adventure family.

The locker is a "system that blocks the differential gear and eases car conduction in adverse driving conditions."[16] When it is activated by the driver, the system operates up to a maximum speed of 20 kph, and is automatically turned off when this limit is exceeded. This operating logic proved to be a useful convenience rather than a limitation in light-off-road cars.

The development of this original differential gear blocking system for 4 x 2 automobiles challenged both Fiat's in-house engineering teams and its technical suppliers. The prototypes were produced and initial tests were carried out by the auto maker's own team. They managed to deal with the performance issues that arose in the first prototypes and achieve enough flexibility to make the locker work as was intended. The integration between the product design and engineering teams throughout the project was marked by flexible management.

The story of the locker feature's development confirms the importance of keeping a sharp eye on the offer dimension, and proved the company's capacity to sustain its proactive market strategy. This newly developed functional attribute enabled the company to surf the light-off-road category's wave of maturity. It also helped increase the value capture prospect – that is, it allowed for higher margins.

Using capacities to anticipate change

A capacity for dealing with error and the ability to manage flexibly were determining factors in the development of the locker system. From an all-embracing perspective, the design and implementation of the Adventure concept was only possible due to a synergistic combination of the capabilities necessary to successfully carry out proactive market strategies (see Table 9.1).

Starting with the capacity for innovating proactively, we can notice that the Adventure concept does not represent the incremental improvement of a product. Rather, it was a modification of the offer that impacted on and changed the market, shifting demand towards a new light-off-road segment derived from saloon cars. We can see too that the latent preference for cars with these attributes emerged because of Fiat's capacity for seeing beyond the kinds of data gathered by traditional market surveys. As Fiat Latin America's president C. Belini said, "No customer has come to ask for an Adventure car or for a locker system. We had to anticipate in order to exceed the market's expectations."[17]

Other capacities have been equally important in leveraging Fiat's proactive strategy. The development of the Adventure project involved the work of different teams in areas including product concept, marketing, engineering, and production.

Table 9.1 The Fiat Adventure concept – capacities applied to PMSs

Capacities	Contexts
Capacity for leading proactively	Proactive commitment of directors and functional leaders to creating an esprit de corps favorable to the development of the Adventure concept, leveling off expectations and shifting paradigms.
Capacity for identifying and developing proactive people	As the Adventure concept evolved, delegation of power to people of different functional ranks involved in the project increased.
Capacity for dealing with risk	Even though there was no intention of developing a completely new car, the Adventure concept involved both financial and marketing risks.
Capacity for dealing with risk	Knowledge and creative insight garnered in the development of the locker feature. Initial frustrations concerning the planned operation were overcome.
Capacity for visualizing future realities	Fiat bet on the light off-road category based on interpretation of market signs and interactive analysis of information.
Capacity for managing short-term pressure	Observing the market from a long-term perspective, Fiat believed there was a new offer opportunity. Time was essential to help mature the concept, both internally and in the market.
Capacity for innovating proactively	Creation of the Adventure concept without any specific demand from the market: that is, based on the exploration of latent preferences of a given customer segment.
Capacity for flexible management	Flexibility in managing the functional relationship between different work teams ensured a precise execution of the Adventure concept.

In this multifunctional environment, populated by people with widely differing views and technical backgrounds, the capacity for leading proactively as well as that for developing proactive people decisively helped achieve the project's objectives. This relates not only to the schedule and budget, but also – and especially – to the faithful execution of the new concept. People's effective involvement in the project was a critical contributory factor to the success. Windson Paz, Fiat's quality director, emphasized this point:

When we think of the Adventure, we must work according to a different mindset. Everyone involved in the project must be able to feel they are working on something different from what we are acquainted with. This differentiated involvement and perception was crucial for the project.[18]

The key success factors also include a capacity for dealing with risk and a capacity for managing short-term pressure. As for risk, besides those customarily related to a project's financial return, Fiat's market strategists had to deal with the uncertainty associated with the reception of the Adventure concept by potential users, since this unusual value proposition had changed the attributes of the standard offer. Regarding the capacity for managing short-term pressure, it is important to highlight the fact that Fiat has been betting on the Adventure concept since 1999, and to date has managed to maintain a long-term strategic vision. Comparing the first and current generations of Adventure cars, we can clearly perceive the concept's esthetic and functional evolution, a gradual achievement that helped consolidate the value proposition. In addition, Fiat, like no other auto maker, extended the Adventure concept across its line of products, demonstrating its faith in a long-term bet on the light-off-road category.

Finally, the capacity for visualizing future realities is fundamental to help understand this successful anticipation of a market change. Skillfully adopting the MZs matrix, Fiat's strategists were able to track the pulsating reality of light-off-road cars, and to detect and proactively interpret its signs. Without combining this capacity with others (Table 9.1), the pioneer Adventure concept would never have been so successfully conceived and introduced to the market.

Reaping the fruits of anticipation

Throughout the last 11 years, Fiat's proactive market strategy, as it materialized in the Adventure concept, has produced excellent results for the company. The Adventure shows strength in all stages of its evolution, when we measure the strategy's achievement in terms of sales. The range of cars with some kind of functional or esthetic modification like those introduced by the light-off-road concept currently comprises 17 models. Fiat produces four models: the Palio Adventure, Idea Adventure, Dobló Adventure, and Strada Adventure; Volkswagen has four models: the CrossFox, Gol Titan Rally, Parati Crossover/Trackfield, and Saveiro Crossover/Titan; Peugeot also has four models: the 206 Escapade, 207 Escapade, Hoggar Escapade, and Partner Escapade; Citroën has two models, the C3 XTR and C3 Aircross; and Ford (Fiesta Trail), Renault (Sandero Stepway), and Nissan (Livina Xgear) complete the list. In 2010, 87,801 vehicles were sold in this market, 49,228 of which were produced by Fiat, giving it a substantial market share (56 percent).

The success of the proactive market strategy Fiat started to develop in 1999 and sustained over the last decade can be measured by the growth in sales and profitability. The Adventure line effectively contributed to increase market share in some car segments and proved itself important in generating financial results for the company in Brazil.

As we have seen so far, the offer is fertile soil in which to sow proactive market strategies. The examples and cases mentioned in this chapter illustrate how companies can capture higher value in the market when they anticipate changes in offer.

In the next chapter we address industry proactiveness, and present other successful stories of market change anticipation, this time focusing on proactive actions taken in the realm of the value chain, changing the competitive dynamics of a sector.

INDUSTRY PROACTIVENESS

10 Creating Moments Zero in a Competitive Environments

The headlines of the world's major economy and business newspapers always disclose facts that help us understand competitive environments. We often read news about mergers and acquisitions of companies, alliances between competitors, new regulations, differentiated ways of distributing products, agreements signed by companies and suppliers; in brief, a varied menu of events that, in some way, indicate dramatic changes in industries.

At just the time we were writing these lines, for instance, *Valor Econômico*, the most important Brazilian business periodical, published an article entitled "Retail increases pressure on suppliers."[1] It looks at the Brazilian furniture and electronic equipment retail sectors, focusing specifically on challenges and difficulties in the commercial relationship between suppliers and the three gigantic retail networks operating in the sectors. Suppliers feel pressurized by the bargaining power of their megaclients, which are always demanding more benefits such as bonuses and volume discounts. The bargaining power of the three giants derives from the rapid process of consolidation in the sector, which left these companies with about 30 percent of the market (in 2010, electronic and home appliances sold 246 million units in the Brazilian market, generating R$89 billion in revenue).[2] This context of market concentration, as well as the current competitive dynamics, may be interpreted via the classic model of industry structural analysis, which takes into consideration the forces that guide competition in a sector.[3] There is a clear concentration of power in the hands of buyers – the mega retail networks – to the detriment of the bargaining power of all the suppliers. From the point of view of large retail networks, competitive rivalry in the industry is strongly influenced, among other aspects, by a search for competitive advantages based on low price, geographic reach, and intensive promotional activity.

Note that the competitive dynamics established in the industry end up intensifying suppliers' reactive actions, in their attempts to protect themselves from the large retailers. In fact, when a supplier, competitor, or distributor limits itself to reacting, this player is only confirming the established market reality and its rules. Only proactive behavior can modify the status quo and alter the current competition pattern. That is exactly what Dell Computers did, for instance, when in the middle of the 1980s it implemented an innovative and direct system to sell its computers. (The strategy has since been revised, but at the time it represented a moment zero (MZ) for the industry.)

An area in which reaction is typical, but striking proactive actions can also be observed, is sustainability. It is known that many stakeholders demand strict conformity with environmental legislation along the value chain, and are increasingly pressing companies to ensure they provide it. This reactiveness brings benefits, but limits companies to adaptation or response to the legal requirements for their sector, narrowing the search for new businesses and relationship opportunities in the sphere of sustainability. On the other hand, companies like Walmart, on a global level, and Banco Santander, in the Brazilian market, are successfully adopting proactive strategies in this field, meeting the challenge of changing structures and the behavior of players in the commodity chain. These attitudes create direct impacts on both the competitive dynamics and the way business is conducted in the segments in which they operate (see Box 10.1).

When they interfere with a segment's competitive dynamics, proactive companies can create advantages that yield new possibilities for capturing value. Let us observe AMBEV, the biggest brewing business in South America: when the company advanced into the chain and assumed direct control over sales and distribution operations in several local markets – incorporating functions previously carried out by dozens of distributors all over the country – this brought it productivity gains, and directly impacted on the business's financial margins. In this case and in many others where changes in competitive arrangements were anticipated, industry proactiveness is an alternative way to look for profitable and sustainable growth.

As we saw in Chapter 2, anticipation of change in the industry dimension may happen on the level of competition dynamics, involving the structure and behavior of suppliers, competitors, and distributors, as well as on the level of a sector's regulatory system, involving obstacles and opportunities for the industry's players to act along the commodity chain. We also know that proactive market strategies may be built either to respond to the first signs of change, tracking an undetermined reality, or if a company deliberately opts for creating change, based on images of the future, as we illustrate in this chapter.

Box 10.1 Market proactiveness to promote business and value chain sustainability

The corporate world is continuously changing. In the last few decades, the increasing speed, intensity, and extent of these changes has posed huge managerial challenges to organizations. In addition, questions relating to management, ecology, and the environment are emerging in this complex scenario.[4] These themes offer many opportunities in the field of market proactiveness. A company may choose strategies to conduct changes that promote sustainability in the commodity chain. A strategic path like this only opens up and is paved when a proactive mindset replaces the idea that, in terms of sustainability, operating in conformity with legal rules and regulations is enough (a clearly reactive posture).

Building the future of retail today

Walmart, a world giant retailer, has already felt the sour taste of stakeholders' criticism over matters related to environmental protection. Since 2005, the company has been forging a new domestic strategy to deal proactively with the subject. In the same year, former world CEO Lee Scott defined three ambitious goals to improve the sustainability of Walmart's operations:

- use 100 percent of energy from renewable sources
- eradicate waste
- sell products that are sustainable with regard to both the company's resources and the environment.[5]

Incorporating sustainable business deeply into its strategic guidelines, the company started to intervene strongly in its supply chain, carrying out several programs on a single global sustainability platform that now involves thousands of suppliers and business partners in many parts of the world. In 2008, when promoting a meeting with Chinese authorities and businesspeople to discuss sustainability, the company firmly stated, "We regard the relationship with our suppliers as a way of surpassing conformity. In 2012, our goal will be that suppliers whose production we buy 95 percent of achieve the highest possible scores in the audits of social practices and environmental control we perform."[6]

The effective involvement of all players in the value chain of the segment is a very necessary condition for Walmart to achieve its global sustainability objectives. The evidence supports this claim: 92 percent of retail's environmental impact is indirect. In other words, only 8 percent derives directly from the retail company's own operations.[7] In this context, change anticipation to favor sustainability is based on interdependence: the company's proactiveness must induce proactive actions in its commercial partners. In the last few years, Walmart has quickly brought about synergistic changes in the behavior of the players in its commodity chains. Because of its huge size and bargaining power, Walmart's proactive engagement in the construction of a sustainable business is shaping new operational arrangements in the retail segment in many markets around the world.

Walmart's Brazilian operation is playing an outstanding role in this strategy. In June 2009, Walmart Brasil formalized its strategic commitment to sustainability and promoted the emblematic event "Pact for Sustainability," which gathered more than 1000 people in São Paulo, including government authorities, suppliers, NGO representatives, and academics. Some of the goals attest to the audacity of the proactive targets it has set related to the supply chain:

- a 70 percent reduction in the phosphate content of soaps and laundry detergents by 2013
- offer at least one organic product for each food category by 2012
- offer laundry products that are at least twice as concentrated by 2012
- reduce packaging by 5 percent throughout the supply chain by 2013.

Among many initiatives undertaken in Brazil as part of its "End-to-End Sustainability" project, the company, in partnership with a group of suppliers, carried out an extensive analysis of the lifecycle – from raw materials to disposal – of leading products, to develop improvements and reduce environmental impacts. This proactive action involved the following products and companies: Pepsico's chocolate-flavored Organic Toddy, Nestlé's Pureza Vital line of bottled waters; Unilever's Concentrated Comfort fabric softener; Johnson & Johnson's Band-Aid; Colgate-Palmolive's Pinho Sol disinfectant; 3M's Ponjita Naturals Curauá bath sponge; Procter & Gamble's Pampers Total Comfort diapers; Coca-Cola Brasil's Organic Matte Leão; Cargill Liza's line of vegetal oils, and Walmart Brasil's soap produced from recycled cooking oil. In January 2010, 18 months after the project was launched, impressive results had been achieved on several sustainability fronts: significant reduction in water, energy, and raw material consumption; a decrease in the emission of greenhouse-effect gases (GEG); cost reductions; reductions in packaging; and general improvements in products and productive processes.[8]

International recognition for the several initiatives and advances achieved by Walmart Brasil in the promotion of sustainability in its supply chain came in 2010 with the C.K. Prahalad Global Sustainability Leadership Award, bestowed by the Corporate Eco Forum, an organization created in 2008 by the leaders of world-class companies to promote debate and exchanges of insights about sustainable innovations. The main purpose of the award is "to acknowledge exceptional and globally relevant actions carried out by the private sector to demonstrate a fundamental connection between sustainability, innovation and successful businesses in the long run."[9] That is exactly what Walmart has been proactively pursuing over the last few years.

Creating a new way of doing business in the financial sector

Ten years ago, when president Fábio Barbosa invited Santander's current sustainable development executive director, Maria Luiza Pinto, to assume a "new function in a new area to be created" in the former Real-ABN Bank, he told her something thoughtful and provoking:"I think we should bring something new to our business strategy. How can we transcend the obviousness of the financial system and generate more value for the public? We need to incorporate something that does that into the bank's culture."[10]

Since then, the bank has undertaken a remarkable journey in search of sustainable practices. The word "journey" was very appropriately employed by the company itself to describe the many behavioral changes and practical transformations both within the company and in the sector's value chain. The decision to include sustainability in the business strategy comes from the belief that sustainability can result in better performance, challenging the false dilemma that is still, unfortunately, brought up in many discussions on the subject:"You can either look for profit or do business the right way. You can't do both at the same time."[11]

According to the viewpoint of the bank (which merged with the Spanish Santander in 2008), the paradigm shift starts with changes in the behavior of individuals. In other words, it is a matter of constructing change from the inside out. This is one of five "essential features" of the company's trajectory in search of sustainability.[12] In this sense, proactive leadership played a fundamental role in consistently incorporating sustainability into the company's culture. The greatest inspiration comes from the president, who posed a seminal question: "What is the cause our bank is fighting for?" Fábio Barbosa explains the question in a very precise way:

> It is important to look ahead and notice that the world is changing and asking for a new way of doing business, in harmony with society. We need to resolve this false dilemma that you are either successful or do things right. It is possible to be successful the right way, doing the right thing. That does not mean neglecting economic aspects but rather integrating the social and environmental dimensions into decisions and thinking systemically.[13]

To inoculate all levels of the organization with the virus of sustainability, an intensive and systematic internal awareness program has being implemented by the bank over the last few years. Significant results have been achieved concerning employee awareness and, most importantly, their adoption of new sustainable practices.

Sustainability needs employee awareness to advance, but will only gain muscle when the company is able to incorporate the subject into its operational processes. That is, it needs to be inserted into the core of its business. This is how the bank describes another of the essential features of its trajectory. This level of insertion means, among other things, innovation in the development of social and environmental products and services, and the creation of new investment alternatives and credit options that encourage sustainable practices. The challenges of promoting this are confirmed by Maria Luiza Pinto:

> Sorting out recyclable materials is not complicated. It is a lot more complicated to pay attention to the credit policy and promote changes in favor of sustainability. We have to change the essentials; otherwise, we could argue that we were socially responsible, but we couldn't say that we work for sustainability.[14]

In the field of investments, in 2001 the bank launched an Ethical Fund, the first Latin American socially responsible investment fund. It is a variable return investment fund exclusively composed of shares of companies that excel in both their social and environmental conduct and their corporate governance. In the period from November 2001 to November 2009, the Ethical Fund's accumulated profit reached 531.65 percent, well above the Bovespa index (445.45 percent). In the credit field, in 2002 the bank developed an innovative method to analyze the social and environmental risks of financing corporate clients. In addition, these clients were encouraged to adopt sustainable practices, which is now a routine procedure in such operations. In the field of microcredit, Santander has already helped more than 200,000 people with loans totaling more than R$1 billion, becoming the largest Brazilian private bank for this type of loan.[15] Still talking about loans, the bank is proactively acting upon the value chain of some sectors, such as construction, granting loans to enable sustainability-driven projects.

The company's proactive action in the field of sustainability has earned both national and international recognition. In 2010, Santander was named as a 'Model Company' by Exame's *Sustainability Guide*, a prestigious reference on corporate responsibility in Brazil. Also in 2010, the bank was included in BM&F BOVESPA's (that is, the São Paulo Stock Exchange's) Corporate Sustainability Index, composed of shares of 38 companies known for their commitment to sustainability and social responsibility. At the international level, among the bank's many awards is the *Financial Times* Sustainable Banking Award. In 2008, it won in three different categories: "Sustainable Bank of the Year," "Sustainable Bank of the Year in Emerging Markets," and "Sustainable Bank of the Year in Latin American Emerging Markets."[16]

Putting sustainability into Santander Brasil's strategy has achieved two very favorable results: it has both boosted the bank's reputation and brought outstanding financial performance. Santander's unique ability to reconcile financial results with social responsibility has given it "company of the future status," in the words of Harvard professor Rosabeth Moss Kanter. Her research left no doubt about new tendencies in the way business is conducted. The future will belong to companies that are more proactive and sensitive to major causes: "Transformational companies that are in the frontline define new directions to business in the future: they enjoy success and prosperity and, at the same time, benefit their communities and the world as a whole."[17]

RESPONSIVE ANTICIPATION AND CREATIVE ANTICIPATION IN THE INDUSTRY DIMENSION

Anticipation of changes in an industry's complex web of interfaces is not an easy task. In fact the opposite is true: when a company decides to interfere with a segment's competitive dynamics or regulatory standards, it faces a grueling journey to change structures or behaviors, as we have seen for the Walmart and Santander Brasil strategies. It is always a game with many moves, that provides possibilities for both tactical and strategic arrangement.

We now discuss cases where proactive strategies in the industry dimension had a two-way impact: besides transforming the competitive scenario in their segment, they brought significant results to the companies that anticipated change.

Responsive anticipation

There are several pulsating signs in any market's competitive dynamics. Whether it is in mature or emerging markets, in more or less competitive sectors, or in more or less regulated segments, signs of change are intermittent. To scan these signs means encompassing different contexts in the industry dimension, sweeping the whole spectrum from future price and changes in financial margins, to consolidation tendencies in the sector or even the emergence of new business models. Few companies are able to overcome the challenge of both anticipatively responding to changes and transforming the market. Most of them follow the rules of reaction, adapting to conditions imposed by the competitive dynamics.

Take the IBM case, for example. As we saw in Chapter 1, this company made a reactive move that is now widely known when, in the 1980s, it neglected the growth in the personal computer (PC) market and left room for companies such as Microsoft, Intel, and HP, which proactively surfed the oncoming PC wave. IBM's reaction was late, and this cost it big money. Fifteen years later, contrary to old adage that history repeats itself, IBM started to make significant changes to its business model. Since then the company has been piloting a radar that is well tuned to pulsating changes in the segment, as well as always regarding the future as offering tempting opportunities. It started acting proactively on the market, impacting the value chain of the information technology (IT) industry. IBM's proactive moves (see Table 10.1) reflect the company's refined capacity for detecting and interpreting signs of change in the market and for anticipatorily responding to them with innovative business strategies that changed the computer industry's competitive scenario.

The mission to transform IBM started when new CEO Louis Gerstner arrived in April 1993. The business that had successfully supported IBM for many years was by then clearly weakening: sales of mainframe computers were going down. In the period between 1990 and 1993, the revenue from mainframe computer sales plunged, from US$13 billion to US$7 billion.[18] In addition, financial margins were being squeezed by an increased competition that offered more attractive products and prices. This rather disheartening combination demanded vigorous strategic action from the newly arrived CEO.

In the short term, Big Blue's recovery plan followed the classic method of pursuing financial stability by controlling the "cash hemorrhage," a priority established by Gerstner to rescue profits. From the viewpoints of market orientation and customer relationship, this had merit, though it was an essentially reactive strategy. As Gerstner himself declared, the company needed to "implement a basic strategy toward clients … convincing them that all the company's efforts were targeted at satisfying their interests, rather than at forcing them to buy 'iron' [mainframes]

Table 10.1 IBM's proactive moves in the computer industry

Proactive move	Signs of change in the market
Creation of a new business model based on services (1994)	Demand for solutions integrating different information technologies
E-business strategy (1996)	New business models in customer companies, supported by network computing, handling transactions over virtual layers
On-demand business strategy (2002)	After the ebusiness era (with a convergence between technology and businesses), generated demand for advanced consultancy IT services to leverage overall business performance
Smarter Planet strategy (2008)	Demand for "smarter computing" services in an instrumented, interconnected and smart world

to ease immediate financial pressures."[19] It is clear that the company was looking for a mechanism to adjust to the market, trying to satisfy customers' requirements coherently. Despite its reactive character, this more customer-sensitive approach was the "basic" – to use Gerstner's own word – factor that led the company to understand the need to design a new business model, which would later enable it to anticipate several changes in the market and to intervene in its competitive dynamics.

In 1994, two years before the outbreak of the internet revolution – which deeply changed the computer industry – IBM detected signs of change in the market that urged it to design a new business model: to become a service provider, capable of offering integrated solutions. The fruit of proactive thought, IBM's decision ran against the received wisdom, which dictated that PCs – then hegemonic in the world of individual users – would become dominant in business computing too, wiping out the market shares of IBM and other mainframe manufacturers. Hence, the signs detected by the company helped it anticipate two significant changes.

The first change pointed to a business context where the computer industry would be increasingly driven by a demand for services, with clients avid for solutions that could integrate technologies from several different suppliers while enabling them to keep their internal processes unchanged. The second big change that was detected in advance (in 1994) on IBM's radar was the advent of the new model of network computing, a real shift in the paradigm of stand-alone computing, which had until then been characteristic of the PC world. The new model was designed around the internet, especially after it penetrated the market more intensively from 1996 onward. In the world of networks, a PC was nothing more than another connected device, just like TV sets, mobile phones, and the like. In the corporate world, PC functions could just as well be carried out by other broadband-networked systems.[20]

These signs of change led the company to strengthen its services and network operations unit, ISSC (Integrated Systems Solutions Corporation). In 1996 this area became an autonomous services division known as IBM Global Services (IGS), which now accounts for 56 percent of the company's revenues worldwide. At that time, besides being a huge cultural change in the company, IBM's proactive move ended up impacting the whole value chain of the segment, since the services unit could not only recommend products manufactured by competitors such as Microsoft, HP, and Sun Microsystems, but also provide technical assistance and maintenance services on all these products. The competitive dynamics was clearly changed in that IBM, now offering integrated solutions, started to establish alliances and partnerships which had previously been unthinkable.

The advance of the world wide web of computers – the now ubiquitous internet – led IBM to deploy a second proactive move. In October 1995, IBM's preview of the world wide web appeared as a *Business Week* cover story with the headline "Gerstner growth plan: yes, the CEO really has a vision. Its name is network computing."[21] Thus, driven by the beliefs that the internet would become a hegemonic platform for many business transactions and that it was something of much wider reach than simple access to digital information or electronic commerce,

IBM introduced a vigorous and well-advertised e-business strategy in 1996. The new business strategy started to focus on the company's service portfolio. The prospects for increased revenue were excellent. In essence, IBM conceived a new high-connectivity business model where companies, their suppliers, and customers would be linked, and would carry out countless virtual transactions. As a consequence of this revolutionary reality, companies should review in-depth their operating processes and marketing strategies. To achieve that, they needed to improve their IT resources.

Following its e-business strategy, IBM prepared to anticipate new demands and to expand its ability to serve its customers, who now had countless novel possibilities for completing transactions in the virtual world. In the context of e-business, business architectures gained unprecedented flexibility. In consequence, companies increasingly demanded "reliable servers, secure databases, large storage capacities, processing power, more sophisticated management processes and service integration systems."[22] IBM acted proactively and extracted the best from the new managerial reality that was emerging in companies. Its strategic moves reverberated throughout the sector's value chain. Once it had decided to focus exclusively on the business-to-business (B2B) market and to strengthen its corporate software portfolio, IBM acquired companies such as Lotus Development (responsible for the development of Lotus Notes, a corporate cooperative network software that runs on many different platforms and operating systems). At the same time, to concentrate energy on the B2B market and privilege businesses offering larger financial margins, IBM sold its network services unit (that is, its internet service provider) to AT&T.[23] All these proactive moves in the value chain resulted in the optimization of IBM's capacity for acting as a provider of integrated IT solutions, reinforcing the company's shift into services.

In March 2002, after consolidating his successful ebusiness strategy, Louis Gerstner handed over control of IBM to Sam Palmisano, then a top operational executive with the company. The newly promoted CEO announced IBM's third proactive move: an on-demand business strategy. The new concept is related to the idea of "a company whose business processes – end-to-end integrated both within the organization and with key partners, suppliers and customers – are able to quickly respond to any customer demand, business opportunity or external threat."[24] This new business strategy significantly enlarged IBM's range of action toward customers, and once again impacted the sector's value chain.

What signs of change in the IT industry did IBM's radar anticipate that led it to opt for the on-demand business strategy? The signs emerged from the adoption of the e-business concept and its dissemination to managers. The ripening of internet-based technologies allowed companies to connect directly with their customers, suppliers, distributors, and other business partners, rendering traditional business processes more efficient, and generating productivity gains and economies of scale. However, the power of the internet and the operational convenience of e-business were not enough to guarantee success in the face of increasing market competition, growing financial pressure, and constant external threats.[25]

Consequently, companies had to develop new managerial abilities and become able to anticipate and respond to complex market demands in real time. To achieve that, they needed to invest in IT resources to transform their business processes, involving supply chain management, design of services, human resources management, and client services. A new market was then opened up to IBM; the company itself named it business performance transformation services. In 2002, preparing to grow into this new market, IBM acquired Pricewaterhouse Coopers Consulting and created a business area called IBM Business Consulting Services.[26]

The on-demand business move was proactive because it anticipated the convergence of technology and businesses. The change impacted the competitive dynamics in the computing industry, and created the need for consultancy services aimed at leveraging the performance of businesses.

Finally, from 2008 on, IBM started on another proactive move which ended up significantly expanding its range of action and its portfolio of customers and commercial partners, once again impacting the sector's value chain. The name it gave to its new strategy – smarter planet – invites us to reflect on the scope and range of this new vision of business, conceived by IBM itself and based on the idea that innovation must "make a difference for the company and for the world."[27] That vision supports IBM's anticipation strategy, in that it detects signs of the emergence of smarter computing, a technology capable of providing advanced solutions to complex problems that arise in an increasingly more "instrumented, interconnected and smarter" world.[28] The words of Ricardo Pelegrini, president of IBM Brasil, confirm the relevant purposes of the company's new move:

> We are designing and sharing with the market our vision of a world where one trillion things are interconnected, and they are not only computers on the internet. All this is available as latent smartness and is still unused. All this information may be processed to the benefit of companies and society.[29]

The smarter planet value proposition is attracting countless new businesses to IBM, in many different areas, including solutions for companies, governments, and cities (IBM focuses particularly on offering smarter computing solutions to traffic and security problems, which are very common in big cities). Never before in the history of the computer industry has a company so dramatically expanded its range of action, establishing new business paradigms for the segment. The new era of smarter computing brought huge challenges that IBM anticipated, as we can tell from the emblematic words of Naveen Lamba, IBM global industry leader for intelligent transportation, when referring to the complexity of solutions to make traffic management in large cities smarter: "For traffic, real-time information is too late."[30]

Several successful solutions developed by IBM in the context of the smarter planet strategy prove that the company is overcoming the challenges of this new computing era. Focusing its recent proactive market strategy on the smarter planet concept, IBM strengthened its value proposition and differentiated it from the competition. This confirms the company's resolve to anticipate changes and guide the competitive dynamics in the IT industry.

Creative anticipation

Besides detecting the first signs of change in the market, as IBM did, companies may also interfere with an industry's competitive dynamics by deliberately acting to promote change. A deliberate change strategy is usually powered by endogenous factors such as a new offer with a differential advantage, whose introduction to the market causes changes in the competitive dynamics (changes in the supply chain structure or in the behavior of players), or when a company conceives a new business model that causes changes in the rules of the competition game.

Observe the example of Tetra Pak. Any competitor would like to gain the estimated 90 percent market share the company holds in the Brazilian long-life food packaging market. The "long-life" tag conveys the technical concept of an aseptic package, developed to "keep food and its original flavors safe and fresh for at least six months without refrigeration or preservative additives."[31] The aseptic process protects food and packaging materials from harmful bacteria. To achieve that, production processes must be completely sterile, including the food itself, packaging materials, production machines, and the environment in which the packaging occurs.

Tetra Pak started commercializing its long-life package in the Brazilian market in 1972, although it had had a presence in the country since 1957, six years after the company's foundation in Sweden. The company now offers more than 150 different package models and sizes, serving more than 150 client companies that produce and sell different types of food product such as milk, juices, teas, coconut water, mayonnaise, and tomato sauce. Tetra Pak's solutions go beyond simple packages. The company provides complete and integrated lines to process, package, and distribute products, and automation services, including personnel training and equipment maintenance planning. Transcending simple package production, Tetra Pak solutions alter its customers' value chains, in that it influences inputs, production and distribution processes. It could not have reached this commanding position without a proactive and deliberate strategy to change the behavior of players in the commodity chain.

Tetra Pak's trajectory in Brazil started in the 1970s, when the company detected opportunities to expand its business in the segment of milk processing and distribution. It detected a future reality whose impacting MZ would result in leadership in the niche of long-life milk, what had not existed in the liquid milk market until then (see Figure 10.1). Tetra Pak's vision of the future would cause a rupture in the dairy market, which had been structured in three large segments: cheeses, pasteurized milk, and industrialized products (such as condensed milk and powder milk). The rupture happened in the pasteurized milk processing and distribution chain, and led to a remarkable transformation. Milk that underwent the HTST (high temperature short time) thermal treatment process required efficient cold processing to keep it in good condition, and had usually to be consumed on the day it was prepared. Tetra Pak developed an UHT (ultra high temperature) process which meant the product could be preserved in its packaging for up to six months.[32]

Although it used a technological innovation that brought convenience to end users, the strategy for introducing long-life milk to the market would never have

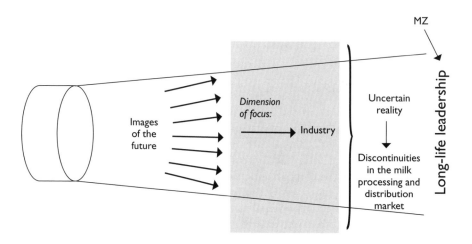

Figure 10.1 The future images searchlight for long-life milk

succeeded without the commitment of players in the processing and distribution chain. It was not enough to educate end users on the benefits of longer preservation, hygiene, and ease of storage, even when they were suffering from high inflation and keen to economize. The behavior of players such as dairy companies and bakeries (then the major distribution points), that had an interest in keeping the status quo of a pasteurized milk market that was regionalized and had only a few players, had to be changed proactively.

In the first few years only a few companies invested in the new product, hampering its expansion in the market, mostly because of the small installed capacity. Following a reactive style of reasoning, dairy companies were actually more interested in keeping the pasteurized milk market than in offering new products to clients. Hence, they usually priced the new product higher than pasteurized milk. At the point of sale, too, bakeries opted to set higher margins for long-life milk, for fear of losing their traditional pasteurized milk consumer base. The expansion of the long-life milk sector faced another strong barrier when in 1983 it was made subject to the Brazilian value-added tax while conventional pasteurized milk was not. For about a decade, all these difficulties clogged the course of introducing the new product to the liquid milk market.

Keeping its eyes on the long term and in an attempt to realize its vision of the future, Tetra Pak changed its strategy toward players in the production chain, and started offering aseptic packaging and milk processing lines to companies that traditionally did not operate with pasteurized milk, shifting the focus away from the regionalized companies. In doing so, the company changed the competition dynamics in the sector, attracting newcomers to the long-life milk processing and distribution business. These newcomers were able to take advantage of the longer life of products – in both transportation and storage – and operate from locations far from consumer markets. This helped their costings and their access to markets.

From 1994 on, the product gradually gained importance and increased its share in the liquid milk market, mainly because of Tetra Pak's market penetration strategy and the new players it had attracted to the distribution sector. At that time, supermarkets, in a market that was already mature and that represented a new and powerful sales channel, helped leverage long-life milk penetration in the overall liquid milk market. The product's ascent is clearly confirmed by the numbers: between 1990 and 2000, the long-life share jumped from 4.4 percent to 68.8 percent of the overall milk market. Since 2000, processed volumes of long-life milk have been growing at rates well above those of pasteurized milk, and in 2009 they reached an impressive 74.6 percent share in the overall liquid milk market.[33]

Paulo Nigro, Tetra Pak's CEO in Brazil, confirms the wisdom of conceiving and implementing this valuable strategy, based on how the company regarded the future and aimed at transforming the Brazilian milk processing and distribution market:

> Twenty years ago we had to make a choice and decided to reinvent our assortment of processing and packaging systems for pasteurized products (cooled distribution) and create a new line of systems aimed at products that could be distributed at ambient temperature (long-life products). We observed what consumers lacked, and imagined how we could increase milk availability and make it present in all Brazilian homes. Armed with a vision of the future and the capacity to materialize it in the long term, we were able to change the value chain of the liquid milk market in Brazil.[34]

Tetra Pak's proactive strategy certainly changed and expanded the Brazilian milk market. Consumption doubled in the 1993–2006 period, jumping from 5 billion to more than 10 billion liters. This impressive growth was due, among other macroeconomic reasons, to the introduction of long-life milk to Brazilian consumers. Over the last 15 years, the category has grown by 15 percent annually on average.[35] Exploiting the growth in the long-life milk market, Tetra Pak leveraged its offer of aseptic packages into other markets such as juices, soy beverages, flavored milks, cooking products, sauces, tomato products, and even solid food, following the introduction of aseptic cardboard packages to this market.

The examples we have discussed so far help us understand the relevance of the industry as a stage on which companies can take highly profitable proactive action. This chapter ends with another successful case of industry proactiveness that corroborates the promising possibilities of anticipation in this particular dimension.

HOW INDUSTRY PROACTIVENESS BOOSTED THE GROWTH AND PROFITABILITY OF LOCALIZA RENT A CAR

"Nobody wakes up dying to buy an used car from a car rental company."[36] These few words from Eugênio Mattar, Localiza Rent a Car's chief operations officer, vividly convey the challenges his company faced in working to create an MZ that ended up impacting both the Brazilian car rental industry and a fragmented user-

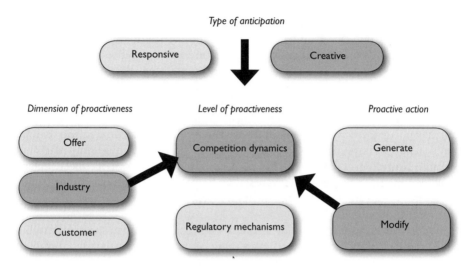

Figure 10.2 Proactive action diagram for the Seminovos Localiza case

car market, where thousands of retailers fought to gain the favor of millions of purchasers. Localiza's strategic decision to advance into the value chain and create its own network – named Seminovos Localiza (Semi new Localiza) – to sell cars that had been used in the rental business modified the segment's competitive dynamics (see Figure 10.2). Localiza's vision of the future led it to believe in a potential market reality that would enable it to innovatively sell its used cars (fixed assets of the company) on a scale compatible with continuous fleet renewal. Localiza's deliberate strategy altered the market structure and made the company's organic growth possible, leveraging the profitability of its car rental business.

Eugênio Mattar's remark points to the idea that Localiza's proactive strategy was built within the *customer* dimension. In other words, the company generated a purchasing preference for formerly rented cars by eliminating the stigma that was attached to them because of their perceived poor quality. Undoubtedly at a secondary level, Localiza's proactive strategy had to include educating customers about the quality and competitive price of its offer, or would not have been able to sell its ex-rental cars at market prices. However, note that the strategy had its roots in the *industry* dimension – Localiza advanced into the value chain – and grew in importance when the company changed the rules of the game other rental car agencies played when disposing of their used cars. These cars were usually sold at auction, or in bulk to authorized dealers and other reselling companies.

Over the next few pages we will discuss how Localiza's strategists set about this proactive action which materialized a seemingly improbable reality in the Brazilian car rental market.

Analyzing growth alternatives

In 1990, 17 years after its creation, Localiza Rent a Car owned a fleet of about 3600 cars and was a leader in the Brazilian car rental market. It had achieved leadership in number of outlets well before this time, following a process of initial expansion in 1981, which involved the acquisition of competing companies, especially in northeastern Brazil. By 1983 Localiza was present in all Brazilian state capitals, but growth continued, and an efficient brand licensing strategy spread the company's reach into hundreds of upcountry cities. Towards the beginning of the 1990s, however, despite its uncontested leadership, Localiza suffered from a weakness: it had to take a big writedown when it sold its used cars at auction or via authorized dealers. The high depreciation costs strongly affected the business's results. The company's future growth plans were in danger, threatened by the operational and financial limitations to the car sale process.

The company's executives explored the experiences of the large car rental networks operating in the huge North American market, such as Hertz, Avis, and Enterprise, making benchmarking visits in an attempt to understand their processes. In the business model that had for a long time been prevalent in the North American market, auto makers like Ford and GM owned hire companies (Hertz and Avis respectively), and practiced a buy-back system. Under this system the automaker sold its cars to the rental company, which used the fleet for one year then sold the vehicles back to the manufacturer, at a 25 to 30 percent discount off the original cost.

But Localiza had learned from past experiences, and this contributed to the decision to advance through the sector's value chain and create an MZ in the market by establishing Seminovos Localiza, its own car sales network. The company had often suffered from the negative impact of selling its cars to independent retailers or authorized dealers because they had a practice of bringing down prices in periods of low demand for rentals. All the technical and operational details of car purchase and sale processes were carefully analyzed and experienced by Localiza. Having owned an authorized dealer for a brief period, Localiza had already acquired a clear understanding of the commercialization process.

In Brazil, Localiza too had to accept a high writedown when a car was sold, but it did not have the privilege of having an automatic buyer for its used cars. It had

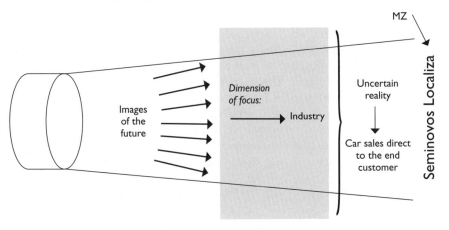

Figure 10.3 Future images searchlight – Seminovos Localiza

to negotiate with dealers, and the prices it could get varied, not least under the impact of macroeconomic variables such as interest and inflation rates. In 1990, for instance, the government's economic stabilization and inflation control plan caused a sharp downturn in business activities in the country, drastically reducing used car prices, a not very stimulating context for Localiza.

The company had a strong strategic intention to grow further, not just to increase its leadership in the market, but because it believed economies of scale would enable it to reach new levels of profitability. In 1990, based on knowledge gathered from its own past experience, from this active research, and on deep analysis of the dynamics prevailing in the market, Localiza proactively visualized a future reality and decided to create a new model: it would retail its used cars directly to end consumers at market prices (see Figure 10.3). In spite of the fact that this was an uncertain reality, the company believed it would systematically optimize its quality standards and be a deciding element for sustainable growth of the car rental business.

Advancing into the car sales chain

Localiza's first experience of selling cars directly to end consumers took place in July 1991, when it opened a showroom in Belo Horizonte, displaying a banner, "Localiza sells its used cars." It offered cars that had had 24 to 26 months of prior use, of a quality not much different from other cars available in the used car market. It had not yet created the concept of "seminovo" (semi-new). The average age of the cars it offered did not correspond to a value proposition of little-used cars: buyers knew the vehicles had had heavy usage. This showroom did not represent an MZ of high intensity and amplitude, but it helped Localiza learn and get ready for bigger leaps.

But changes were needed. Localiza's internal practices, its staff's mental attitudes regarding car conservation, and its fleet renovation cycles were not compatible with making an attractive value proposition to used car buyers. In addition, Localiza's strategists knew that the faster car fleets are turned over, the more leveraged are the quality standards of the rental operations. Thus, the performance achieved by the point of sale in its first year of operation was modest: only 15 per cent of the cars were sold to end users. In other words, wholesalers were still the most effective channel for disposing of used cars. This test run made it clear that changes were needed to the business model. This frustrated the company's strategic decision of advancing toward end consumers and capturing better prices. An intensive internal program to develop people's sensitivity and to change processes was implemented in the company. In a historic meeting with its leaders, president Salim Mattar formally asked for support and intense engagement in the implementation of all necessary measures. People at the top management level were aware of the long and arduous journey they would have to undertake when conducting the strategic change.

Adopting long-term vision and flexible management practices, the company changed several internal processes, and the quality of both sold and rented cars clearly improved. At the same time, Localiza started to shorten its fleet renewal cycle, and it opened its second point of sale, in Rio de Janeiro. The experience gained from these two showrooms taught Localiza about operational details such as how to handle customers at the point of sale, and how to offer service packages such as special financing plans and car-exchange systems.

Localiza was now processing its past experiences and preparing a strategic leap that would result in a new value proposition for the sale of used cars and expand the geographic reach of its own network. In another decisive meeting with his managers, Salim Mattar urged the company to shape a new value proposition for the car sale activity: "From now on, we will offer a new car sales value proposition to the market, and we will call it Seminovos Localiza."[37] That was the start of a new stage for Localiza's car sales operation, an initiative bound to create a huge impact on the Brazilian car rental industry.

In 1993, the Seminovos Localiza brand was launched and the company intensified its market efforts to leverage the car sales operation. Until that point it had operated sales showrooms from locations next to its car rental shops, but now, both to help in expanding the activities and to develop the personality of the car sale business, the company decided to physically separate the points of sale. Marco Antônio Guimarães, director of the Seminovos Localiza Division, explained the new phase of the operation: "Car sales and car rental are two very different things, and we realized we needed to create a separate identity for Seminovos Localiza, with a specific logotype and colors. We have in fact started a turnaround in the car sales division."[38] The process of expanding via "independent" points of sale contributed effectively to a growth in sales. In 2002, the Seminovos Localiza network included 14 showrooms from which 13,331 cars were sold to consumers after being withdrawn from the rental operation.[39] These eloquent figures proved the worth of the *seminovos* concept that had been proactively forged by the company. At the same time, they demonstrated that Localiza had judged well in its efforts to eradicate the stigma of poor quality that had attached itself to former rental cars, and attract a growing number of buyers.

The Seminovos Localiza operation was now sufficiently large and mature to justify new investments in marketing, in human resources, and in information technology. These in turn helped to support a new stage of growth and refinement in the operation, especially in matters related to customer services. The strategic goal was to provide customers with an experience that was positively differentiated from the usual standards in the sector. Process improvements were implemented in the sales process, and Seminovos Localiza's sales operation was now regarded as setting the standard for excellence in the used car sales business.

These strategic refinements gained the company both loyalty and recognition from customers. Post-sales surveys carried out in the last few years indicated that 93 percent of customers, on average, would buy again or suggest the company to a friend. Around 30 percent of all customers had already bought a third, fourth, or even fifth car from Seminovos Localiza. In 2008, despite the downturn caused by the world economic crisis, the company continued to invest in its car sales operation, pursuing improvement and growth plans. In 2010, the Seminovos Localiza platform accounted for the sale of 75 percent of all cars withdrawn from the car rental operation to end consumers, a total of 35,500 cars. The network

Table 10.2 Seminovos Localiza – capacities applied to the proactive strategy

Capacity	Context
Capacity for leading proactively	The internal culture of semi-new cars developed by the company was supported by a proactive leadership that shaped managerial behaviors and facilitated implementation of new processes to prepare used cars for sale. Top management's proactive adherence and commitment was essential to enable car sales to end consumers.
Capacity for identifying and developing proactive people	Strategy development required the creation of a highly proactive managerial team capable of anticipating and facing operational obstacles during the car sales implementation and consolidation processes. The team was also important to strengthen an internal culture favorable to the Seminovos Localiza operation.
Capacity for dealing with risk	The "at risk" model adopted by Localiza to sell its cars demonstrates the company's capacity for developing a proactive strategy. In addition to depreciation risks, the company also assumed all remaining investment risks involved in expanding its own sales network.
Capacity for dealing with error	During the construction of its proactive market strategy, the company made several errors, such as for instance, financing car buyers using its own financial resources. The mistakes taught it valuable lessons. The internal and external consolidation of Seminovos Localiza required a lot of experimentation in both the operational and marketing areas.
Capacity for visualizing future realities	The "Seminovos Localiza" concept was forged based on the company's sharp vision of the future, driven by the imperative to promote profitable growth in the car rental business at a high quality level.
Capacity for managing short-term pressure	Localiza bet on the long-term success of its car sales operation: the rate of 80 percent of all cars sold to end customers was only reached after 15 years of operation. Market education activities and the guideline that cars should only be sold at market prices demanded from top executives a great capacity for managing the short-term pressure for return on investments.
Capacity for innovating proactively	The proactive strategy required innovations such as the pioneer creation of the "Seminovos" concept, but also demanded the shaping of operational processes and services differentiated from prevailing standards in the used car sales sector.
Capacity for flexible management	Flexibility in management was tested during strategy construction, being exercised in operational fronts such as car maintenance and preparation for sale, as well as in the definition of new car purchase policies, in an attempt to find a mix that could favor sales from Seminovos Localiza showrooms.

now had 55 points of sale spread over the main Brazilian cities. These numbers demonstrate that the uncertain reality the company illuminated with its proactive searchlight, back in 1991, had been made real. Referring to the successful trajectory of the Seminovos Localiza operation, Eugênio Mattar highlighted some decisive capacities for the conduction of the strategy: "We assumed all risks related to the operation we have created based on our long-term vision. We invested heavily to turn our vision into reality."

Using capacities to create changes

The challenge of advancing into the value chain and of developing a car sales operation capable of supporting the growth in the rental business required the development of several capacities, without which Localiza would not have been able to bring to reality its vision of the future. Powered by the seminal question that moves activator companies – "What do we want to happen?" – Localiza's strategists started to articulate several actions aimed at implementing the ideal model of a future car sales operation that would enable the company to compete effectively in the market. Table 10.2 outlines the capacities put to work by the company as well as the managerial context in which the proactive market strategy was constructed.

Leveraging business profitability

The proactive strategy to create and consolidate the Seminovos Localiza operation was decisive for the growth and quality improvement of the car rental business (the Localiza Rent a Car operation ended 2010 with 61,445 cars in operation and 234 agencies). Additionally, it settled the integration process with two other business divisions of the group: Localiza Franchising (which operates a system composed of 242 franchisee agencies spread all over Brazil and seven other Latin American countries) and Total Fleet (a corporate fleet management business that accounted, in 2010, for a fleet of 26,615 cars). In the last five years, company growth was above 23 percent in all business divisions. The synergistic management of these areas enabled it to introduce cross-selling strategies with low operating costs, and leveraged overall profitability.[40]

The deliberate strategy of betting on large-scale car sales to end consumers changed the segment's competitive dynamics and enabled Localiza's profitable growth. CEO Salim Mattar emphasizes the proactive behavior that guided the vision of the future and the establishment of the company's daring objective:

> Twenty years ago we intended to sell thousands of cars to end consumers, although we could not see this reality very clearly. There was only one certainty left: we neither wanted nor could bear the high costs of depreciation involved in selling our cars at auction or to wholesalers. This iron will has tremendously helped the construction of the Seminovos Localiza operation. It brought growth and higher profitability to the business as a whole.[41]

As is demonstrated by all the case studies presented in this chapter, industry proactiveness is a promising alternative to capture value in the market, to impact on competitive dynamics, and to favor companies capable of anticipating changes.

The next chapter addresses the execution of strategies in the field of customer proactiveness, focusing on stories of companies that anticipated consumers' preferences or behavioral changes.

CUSTOMER PROACTIVENESS

11 Creating Moments Zero in Customer Behavior

The anticipation of changes in customer behavior is a challenging task that demands special abilities from companies. These abilities include an attentive regard for the many nuances that determine customers' present consumption preferences and needs. When screening the future in an attempt to change consumption behavior, strategists must be equipped with the ability to develop what we call an empathic and persuasive relationship with customers. Otherwise, they will not be able to create relevant moments zero (MZs) and stimulate the positive involvement of customers, who are always bombarded by numerous messages and offers.

As we have mentioned before in this book, understanding customers is a lot more difficult than understanding products. We know that the offer dimension is fertile soil for proactive actions, as was demonstrated by the successful cases we presented in Chapter 9. However, it is also true that even sensational offers resulting from proactive market strategies can be replicated by competitors. It is the proactive company's duty to support its strategy by focusing on competitors' responses to its innovative offers, as Apple and Fiat have done very effectively to date for the iPad and Adventure concepts. On the other hand, a market strategist's understanding of consumers is something that cannot be emulated. Therefore, it will remain a valuable asset that companies can rely on to segment the market, position offers, and especially, modify consumption behavior.

Since feudal times, when bartering was the usual practice and people would say "I gave five gallons of wine for this coat,"[1] to the present day of the internet and electronic commerce, consumption of goods and services has been a rich vein for investigation, raising the interest of scholars and researchers in different fields such as marketing, psychology, economics, and sociology. Behind this interest lies a simple but important question: How and why do consumers buy?

Marketing theory defines consumer behavior as "the study of processes involved when individuals or groups select, buy, use or dispose of products, services or experiences, in order to satisfy their needs and wishes."[2] This definition mentions two key aspects of the question: the *how* (the process of selection, purchase, use, and disposal) and the *why* (satisfaction of needs and wishes). When companies jump in with the construction of proactive strategies in the customer dimension, their major challenge is simply to pay attention to this purchasing process, and its specific stages and motivations. This is a challenging and complex task because consumer behavior undergoes dynamic change. The availability of new information and knowledge transforms people on a daily basis. We are living in the era of the information consumer market. Just click on Google and you can find out a lot about virtually anything. In the knowledge economy,[3] information became a valuable exchange currency, a reference as important as time or even money. The old phrase "time is money" is being gradually replaced by "time is information."

In this context, the challenges of anticipating consumers' behavioral changes increase, and questions relevant to a company's proactive agenda are raised. How should companies address thoroughly informed customers to create new purchase preferences and needs? How can we understand future purchase motivations, today? What latent new social or economic tendency will change consumers' behavior concerning our brand and our offer? What new means of interaction between companies and customers – and among customers – will prevail in the future, as social media advance?

One among many MZs that arose in the realm of global communication between people is the boom in social networks, such as Orkut and Facebook, and microblogs, such as Twitter, which fueled considerable speculation in the management community. For a number of reasons, many companies are trying to understand the reach and strength of these social interaction mechanisms over the internet, and at the same time they are looking for ways to enter this new context. From the customer proactiveness point of view, to enter this universe with the sole intent of responding to the demands of interaction, which are dynamically generated amid the social media fuss, is not enough (see Box 11.1). On the contrary, a company must assume a stance such as that of activator companies: that is, it must generate relevant agendas to set up a dialogue with customers and anticipate changes in their consumption needs and preferences.

Box 11.1 The universe of social media and market proactiveness[4]

The boom in social media is an invisible phenomenon in the sphere of interaction between people, and is deeply affecting consumer behavior. Immersed in this new environment, when companies articulate customer communication and relationship strategies they must raise a very important proactive question: How can we, in anticipation, promote relevant commitments that are capable of generating or modifying customers' needs and preferences in regard to our brand, products, and services?

This mindset, which favors the anticipation of involvement in social media, is a potent antidote against reactive actions, which are characterized by a tendency to observe and respond only to demands for involvement. In other words, instead of passively monitoring content and reacting to web surfers' questions, a company should try to engage in dialogues that might generate positive involvement and create value – here understood as "social capital" – for both parties.

Thus, the promotion of relevant and anticipated contributions is the rule of the game when it comes to dealing proactively with social media and creating new and valuable opportunities for interaction with customers. This means that, even when it is the subject of discussions in social media, a company is not automatically inserted into the conversation. To get there, it needs to anticipate changes, creating and suggesting seductive agendas. This is only possible by means of proactive action. Responsive action, though it is worthwhile and necessary, usually does not create enough involvement to generate social capital for the other party.

As social media advance, how is your company behaving? Invoking the four types of company orientation relative to market MZs (see Chapter 1), we invite you to reflect on the following question: What is your company's prevailing orientation in the context of social media?

The *afflicted* company is a mere spectator and avoids involvement because it regards itself as unable to pursue a dialogue. In fact, since it is unprepared even to respond, it is a very long way from approaching a dialogue, and the company remains confined to silence and inertia. If you believe afflicted attitudes prevail in your company, our prognosis is not promising: the affliction will tend to increase, because the number of participants in social media are growing geometrically in all ages and social classes, legitimizing these media as channels for collective expression.

Face-to-face with the advance of social media, an *adjusted* company usually only tries to respond to the impacts created by actions by its customers, competitors, and other stakeholders when their effects are already being felt intensely. Impacted by social media, the delayed reaction of adjusted companies can only induce changes to operational processes, to product or service functional attributes, or to its communication approach to the market. In consequence, constrained by the environment, the company reactively adjusts and starts acting more transparently, though it misses out on the anticipatory contributions that could stimulate dialogue or interactive involvement. This behavior follows mainly from lack of strategic intent, at the top management level, to act proactively in the context of the reality of social media. If you think your company tends to be more adjusted, then it is not much different from most companies. This position is a weak one, however, because it does not promote involvement, an essential ingredient to change customers' behavior.

There are also *alert* companies. In practice, challenged by social media, the alert company tries to take part in the process – being present on social networks – and monitors several levels of interaction, not only to respond to demands but also to find opportunities to create dialogue and involvement with customers. In addition, the company is able to integrate its offline and online communication strategies, creating opportunities to promote interactions with different audiences and to generate social echoes that favor its corporate actions and marketing strategies applied to products and services. If you think your company is alert, this is a favorable diagnosis and demonstrates that it has sensors and is strategically attentive and permanently willing to enter into dialogue.

Finally, there is the *activator* company. With regard to social media, two differentiating abilities characterize an activator company's behavior and practices. First, it is powered by a strong proactive mindset towards social media, because it has managed to overcome what we call "anxiety for control" and succeeded in developing a "capacity for conducting." This ability goes beyond willingness and competence, to publicly and transparently pursue a dialogue. Thus, what matters for activator companies is the possibility of deliberately generating interesting facts, the insertion of stimulating themes and the creation of dialogues and interactions the company itself conducts, free from the ties and stress of trying to maintain control (the activator company knows it is impossible to control everything and everybody in cyberspace's dynamic interactions).

Activator companies embrace social media as a promising opportunity to leverage product innovation processes, inviting current and potential customers to participate, suggest ideas and give their opinions. If you believe your company is adopting activator practices towards social media, this is a good sign. Your company holds both a passport and a visa for entering the future and interacting with customers and other stakeholders in the universe of social media. The capacity for dynamically intertwining alert and activator postures as time goes by will make this precious "passport" permanent.

THE CHALLENGE OF PREVIEWING "CHANGE INSIDE CHANGE" IN CUSTOMERS' BEHAVIOR

It is clear that anticipation of changes in customer behavior is a task that demands from companies a special ability that we call "attention with refined preview." We translate this skill as a capacity for tracking and interpreting the current hellish vortex of changes, and at the same time, for creating the inspiration to preview tendencies that will model future consumption needs and preferences. It is as if a company's strategists had the unique ability to see "change inside change," and from that starting point, could preview what journalist and writer Malcolm Gladwell called the "tipping point": that is, a point at which "epidemics" occur in people's behavior. According to this author:

> *The Tipping Point* is the biography of an idea, and the idea is very simple. It is that the best way to understand the emergence of fashion trends, the ebb and flow of crime waves, or, for that matter, the transformation of unknown books into bestsellers, or the rise of teenage smoking, or the phenomena of word of mouth, or any number of the other mysterious changes that mark everyday life is to think of them as epidemics. Ideas and products and messages and behaviors spread just like viruses do.[5]

The first "epidemic" presented by Gladwell is an interesting occurrence in New York at the end of 1994 and the beginning of 1995. It involves the famous Hush Puppy shoes, icons of casual wear when introduced in 1958, with a graceful basset hound as their mascot, but whose sales had since dropped to much lower levels (30,000 pairs a year), most of them to outlets in small towns. Something unexpected happened, and sales skyrocketed, reaching 430,000 pairs of the classic model by 2005, and increasing four times more in 2006.

What could possibly have happened to Hush Puppies? To the surprise even of their manufacturers, they became objects of desire. What tipping point caused this consumption epidemic for a long-established and fading product? "Hush Puppies had suddenly exploded, and it all started with a handful of kids in the East Village and Soho,"[6] said Gladwell. It was later discovered that these kids had picked Hush Puppies because they wanted to be different, and wear shoes no one else had. The novelty attracted the attention of two fashion stylists, who used the shoes as accessories for fashion collections. Gladwell explained that "The shoes were an incidental touch. No one was trying to make Hush Puppies a trend. Yet, somehow, that's exactly what happened. The shoes passed a certain point in popularity and they tipped."[7]

Of course, every marketing strategist dreams of producing a "Hush Puppy effect" when preparing to launch a new product or when communicating with the market about an existing one. It is a fact: companies have always tried to have a strong hold on their customers (if we may use a more colloquial expression to describe attempts to educate the market). The creation of new consumption habits is a basic tool of the marketing world. In the past, mayonnaise was homemade, and there was nothing resembling the sophisticated brands of pet food that are sold today. Similarly, millions of consumers did not drink a strange-flavored beverage that was introduced in Europe in 1987 and vigorously rejected by the tasters in initial tests: but Red Bull is now one of the world's most effective brands, and sells approximately 4 billion cans each year in 140 different countries.[8] Women did not buy soap that claimed to care for their skin before Dove told them to do so. The valuable market position Dove's product achieved has now lasted for more than 60 years.

In the field of health care, people never used to take the kind of care they take today to look after their health, thanks to the communication efforts developed by companies in the health business. The challenges of marketing education are also to be found in marketing strategies and business-to-business (B2B) sales. In the past companies did not outsource their vehicle fleet management as they do today. Likewise, they did not use diversified and specialized management consultancy services, a common practice nowadays. We could say that these demands and new behaviors, in both retail markets and corporate environments, were somehow "created" by companies through their efforts to educate customers.

In the last few years, we have witnessed the emergence of new market communication strategies, which, in a certain way, recapture or "boost" the good old practice of word-of-mouth marketing. They come with the new practices of person-to-person communication known as buzz marketing, which are intentionally structured to promote products in social environments. Viral marketing actions, involving the exchange of information between users of products and services, have also gained power over the internet. The internet service provider (IST) Hotmail, for instance, offered free e-mail accounts and gained 12 million subscribers by adding this simple phrase at the end of each e-mail message sent by a registered subscriber: "Have your own free e-mail account at www.hotmail.com."[9] Such practices certainly aim at generating a consumption epidemic.

We know, however, that proactive practice involves more than surfing the waves of the present. Smarter and more skilled surfers are able to preview the coming waves and get ready for them. Consumers' needs and preferences will keep on changing forever. That does not mean, though, that more sensitive and ambitious companies will give up on designing proactive strategies. Certainly not, and they will try to foresee tipping points that could be developed into new consumption tendencies. Thus, the ability to deal with "change inside change" is a powerful weapon in the design of proactive market strategies directed at creating epidemics in the realm of customer behavior. The challenge market strategists will face in future is how to manage the uncertainties that arise in a context marked by deep changes in the way consumers think and act. Only a proactive attitude, followed by a remarkable capacity for interpretation, will enable them to anticipate the coming changes.

CUSTOMER EMPOWERMENT AND OPPORTUNITIES FOR PROACTIVE ACTION

The "digital revolution"[10] changed the world of customers, disclosing countless opportunities and providing online access to information. The new era brought a phenomenon known as "customer empowerment": in other words, the power of knowledge that comes from access to information, and the power of choice that comes from the great variety of offers available to the market. The world of asymmetrical access to information that favored companies in the past is over. We now live the era of "total access,"[11] when companies and customers interact permanently and in real time. This is an era when customers – once passive hostages to companies' marketing actions – can now start an interaction and make purchasing decisions based on abundant information that shapes their preferences and allows them to tell companies when, how, and what offers they want, and what price they are willing to pay.

Although companies lost some power when the marketing center of gravity shifted to customers,[12] they ended up getting new opportunities to interact with the market, helped by both permanent connectivity and easy exchange of information with consumers. In truth, companies have never before been so close to their customers (obviously, closeness here does not mean physical proximity, but is also important in other contexts), and their chances to feed marketing databases with strategically important information have never been so good. Thus, connectivity is a two-lane highway that can lead companies and their customers in converging directions with respect to interactive communication, favoring valuable relationships.

Vast access to information and countless offers to choose from in the market have also expanded the range of consumption alternatives experienced by customers. This reinforces their power and gives them a greater capacity for judging interactions with companies. In this context, the management of customer experiences, encompassing all points of contact – both physical and digital – with the company, is a key factor in the success of businesses.[13]

Customer empowerment can be also perceived in the innovative-customer approach, introduced in Chapter 6. Customers, who were earlier kept virtually apart from product innovation processes, or participated only passively through traditional market surveys, now want to participate actively in the creation of value in the products and services they demand from companies. Customers, who share their experiences over social networks, also want to be aware of product development processes, sharing ideas and suggestions. Thus, the opportunities for value co-creation involving companies and customers have become increasingly strong in the last few years in the domain of innovation processes.[14]

In the era of customer empowerment, how should a company act to anticipate needs and preferences? We have so far discussed four factors that leverage customer empowerment: access to information, permanent connectivity, new consumption experiences, and the innovative-customer approach. They all bring to companies willing to shape market behavior many opportunities for proactive actions. Table 11.1 explores strategic initiatives, key questions, and a few actions related to these factors, and covers what we have called the strategic agenda for customer proactiveness. We believe this agenda will open up new possibilities for market strategists' Monday mornings. As was mentioned earlier, good questions and unique insights are worth more than having the right answers to ordinary questions. Competitive convergence – a phenomenon that pasteurizes offers and customer–company relationships – happens when all competitors, trying to be different from each other, walk along the very same paths, ask the same questions, and end up becoming hostages to market patterns.

RESPONSIVE ANTICIPATION AND CREATIVE ANTICIPATION IN THE CUSTOMER DIMENSION

It is clear that to anticipate changes in the behavior of customers is a challenging task. The detection of market signs requires a radar with an ample detection field, fine-tuned to the right economic and sociocultural wavelengths. Signs that preannounce MZs in market preferences and needs can be detected only far beyond the vortex of current changes in the customer behavior. But if it does not discover signs, a company can analyze the variables that influence people's way of thinking and acting, then take a bet on future behavior and create change itself, shaping new consumption habits and choices. Finally, whether it involves detecting signs of change or deliberately creating change, the anticipation of customer behavior is still a difficult task that requires great dexterity from market strategists.

The case studies we present in this chapter show how some companies have been able to shape customer needs and preferences, achieving growth in sales, bigger market shares, and a differentiated public image in their sector.

Table 11.1 The strategic agenda for customer proactiveness

Strategy	Questions to ask
Promote interactive access	How do we promote a kind of access that represents something different for customers? • Open databases to customers. • Allow data customization: allow customers to choose their own cards to play. • Be available 24 hours a day, 7 days a week, and let customers choose their own access time.
Practice joint innovation	How do we grow an innovative-customer network? • Treat customers as insight providers, and reward them for their contributions. • Incentivize the early participation of customers in the development of new products and services. • Always invest in proactive survey practices.
Create empathetic communications	How do we create proactive empathy with customers? • Focus communications on customer needs and preferences, rather than on personal values (which are always difficult to interpret). • Educate and surprise customers when communicating with them. Messages without innovative content should be avoided. • Create relevant dialogue agendas and anticipate customer involvement with social media (it achieves little to simply respond to demands).
Guarantee a 360-degree experience	How do we provide customers with complete and differentiated experiences? • Guarantee to deliver exceptional offers (both in the core offering and in complementary offers). This is what makes customers loyal. • Take good care of all points of contact between customers and the company. Optimize the 360-degree experience. • Create a corporate culture that favors the 360-degree experience. "We are all responsible for the experience customers have of the company."

Responsive anticipation

The rapid expansion of electronic commerce is a global phenomenon: every year more and more people buy products and services through the web. Electronic commerce in Brazil, for instance, jumped from 7 million electronic consumers who bought at least once in 2006, to 23 million e-consumers in 2010, who accounted for more than 40 million orders, totaling R$14.8 billion. Best-seller categories in 2010 were home appliances (14 percent), books, magazine and newspaper subscriptions (12 percent), medicines, beauty, and health care (12 percent), data processing (11 percent), and electronics (7 percent).[15] Since at least 2002, purchasing products and services in these categories over the internet has been very common.

Specifically in the Brazilian wine market, the number of products offered over the internet is growing, especially thanks to import companies with retail stores in major cities. Although wine consumption in Brazil might seem timid when compared with other countries that have a long tradition of wine production, consumption in Brazil grew fast from 2002 to 2010, a period when fine wine imports doubled in volume.[16] It seems that some segments of the Brazilian population are gradually discovering the subtleties of the world of wine. We tend to say that the traditional and friendly invitation to join someone for a beer is gradually changing to an invitation to taste a wine. Increasingly, groups of friends from different social groups are gathering to socialize and experience a "wine moment."

Some say that wine is a "smart beverage" that, like no other, stimulates rich sensorial experiences in consumers. Such special attributes make wine a category of product whose purchase is based on information and strongly influenced by recommendations from trustworthy people. We all know how comforting it is to be properly advised by a good sommelier at a restaurant, by an expert, or by friends.

All these circumstances – which end up strengthening personal contacts at the time of choosing and purchasing wine – make us think that perhaps the internet is not the ideal channel for this product, especially when we are dealing with "standard" consumers: in other words, those who are not considered heavy users (compared with "category-specialized" customers who always buy large quantities). Thus, changing customers' behavior to make them regularly buy wine over the web is a challenging task, especially when there is such a wide range of wine on offer in supermarkets and other food and liquor retail stores. How can virtual wine shops be as interesting as the experience of buying in a specialized store that offers individual service and other conveniences? What social and cultural tendencies would lead people to the digital world when buying wine? What could a company do to be relevant in offering wine in the hypercompetitive environment of the internet, where attacks of spam intrude on millions of people's privacy every day?

With its radar well tuned to present and future changes in wine consumers' behavior, and strategically determined to offer a differentiated value proposition to the market, Wine (wine.com.br) has become Latin America's largest wine webstore after three years of operation. The company currently offers more than 2000 different wines to approximately 35,000 active customers, and every month it ships around 80,000 bottles to more than 60 cities all over the country, with a target delivery time of 48 hours. All the wine is packed in Wineboxes, a special package structured and designed by the company itself. To win customer loyalty, among other initiatives Wine offers ClubeW, currently the largest wine club in the Brazilian market. Its 8000 associates receive a Winebox on joining, with two, four, or six bottles of wine selected by Wine's sommeliers, and enjoy a 15 percent discount on the usual prices. Freight is also free for all extra orders, of any size.

The company's proactive eye is detecting signs of change in the profile of wine buyers. Strategically supported by the "world of wine in your hands" concept, Wine's bet on the webstore model goes beyond the detection of market signs that indicate lack of time, which affects most people and ends up favoring the convenience of online shopping. Wine is proactively betting on another behavioral tendency in the wine market: an increasingly large number of customers are keen to reduce the physical and especially psychological stress of buying wine, and will tend to accept value propositions that facilitate their choices.[17]

Thus, according to Wine's strategic reasoning, it is neither relevant nor productive to be present on the web and bombard target customers with serial electronic mail messages presenting attractive offers, and then wait for them to regularly click and buy (we have recently witnessed this kind of "cyber massacre" in the Brazilian online wine sector). Instead of minimizing the psychological effort demanded by choosing, this produces the opposite effect. In this context, more means less. Making more offers increases the effort customers have to make to choose what to buy, and what is worse, it does not guarantee credibility or generate intimacy with customers. That is why it sounds like "less" in the value proposition offered to the market.

Proactively moving in the opposite direction, Wine is shaping online wine purchasing behavior and offering a choice of conveniences besides the obvious time saving. The company knows very well, for instance, that customers value a sensible suggestion about what wine to choose. Therefore, a Wine sommelier is always on hand to technically explain labels or to suggest ways of harmonizing wines with food. This creates credibility and trust, besides facilitating customer selection. It is at this point, when customers are faced with options, that the company is trying to minimize the psychological effort of buying. Conveniently, the company's website architecture was designed to facilitate selection, enabling customers to sort wines by country, grape varietal, or price. Customers choose one of these options in a central spot at the homepage, and are taken to another page where only six options appear, reducing the psychic energy required to purchase. Customers can, of course, extend their search if they want to search for other wines.

Care in promotional communication with customers is expressed in the creation of simple and objective information on each wine, increasing product value and easing selection, and in-depth items such as "comments by the sommelier" and enological and gastronomical guidelines. The company also carefully manages its offers by means of smart databases, algorithms to ensure each offer is tailored to the customer's purchasing profile, and especially, being parsimonious in its sales efforts (its limits the number of e-mails it sends out to avoid over-exposure and loss of relevance). Wine's range of conveniences is complemented by an attractive pricing policy, agility in delivering orders, and a monthly publication, *Wine Magazine*, which offers technical reports and articles on wine and gastronomy.

Anticipatively responding to changes in wine consumers' behavior, Wine's web sales are increasing at a rate higher than the general Brazilian expansion in e-commerce, and it is building customer loyalty: half of its customers buy at least once a month. About 60 percent of ClubeW's 8000 associates put in additional orders every month (ClubeW's monthly wine selection is prepared by the company itself and offers a wide choice of products, including wines made in different countries and from different grape types). Wine's trajectory evidences the benefits a proactive attitude can bring to the understanding of market behavior tendencies, and teaches us how to defy common sense. A better offer to customers does not necessarily mean more promotional campaigns, more options to choose from, or intensification of communication initiatives. When a company loses its sensitiveness to aspects like these, it ends up losing relevance to the market.

Creative anticipation

When it was developing a proactive strategy to introduce Activia yogurt to the Brazilian market in 2004, one of Danone's critical goals was to show the relevance of consumer education to the offer. The Brazilian operation of this world giant of the dairy industry was facing a critical moment. Despite a substantial growth in sales after 1995 – brought about by economic stabilization and an increase in the low-income population's purchasing power – its financial margins were being more and more squeezed by heated price competition with its competitors, all of which were trying to increase share in a quickly expanding market. In 2003, for the second consecutive year, the company returned negative results.[18] Modifications were needed. To trigger change, Danone deliberately bet on changes in customer behavior and proactively started efforts to change consumption habits within what had until then been an undifferentiated yogurt category. All products offered essentially the same attributes in terms of flavor and consistency, and price alone guided purchasing preferences.

Activia, like many types of yogurt produced by Danone, offers functional health benefits, confirming the company's strategic inclination to research and develop products with therapeutic properties. Provided Activia is consumed regularly, an exclusive bacillus named Dan Regularis® helps maintain the intestinal rhythm, improving slow intestinal motility.[19] The product was named BIO and launched in France in 1987, then it was reintroduced in 1997 under the name of Activia, achieving a reasonable placing in the market. The company's strategic orientation, focused on healthy food, is confirmed by Gustavo Valle, who was president of Danone Brasil in the 2004–2009 period, and is now head of the company's operations in the United States:

> When we say "we are selling health through food," that gives us plenty of scope. It means that we will carry out research and try to develop products that improve people's health. Thus, we do not just sell a tasty yogurt, we sell functional yogurt. We educate consumers so that they understand this, and the relevance of our yogurt increases.[20]

Danone did exactly that in the competitive Brazilian market: it educated consumers in order to modify their consumption needs (Figure 11.1). This proactive strategy helped the company create an MZ in the market and change the functional-yogurt game to its advantage. This new category of yogurt was created and expanded thanks to Danone's anticipatory vision, and attracted thousands of consumers interested in the functional benefits, which had been explicitly explained by an empathic and persuasive communication strategy aimed at its target public. In the first stages of product activation in the market, the company aimed at women, who have been shown statistically to suffer more than men from intestinal problems. As time passed, Activia's advertisements started to reach other publics, enlarging the product's consumption basis.

Yogurt as a product has always been regarded as healthy due to its rich protein, calcium, and vitamin content, and had until then been consumed as a generally nutritious food. All the available products were microbiologically very similar and

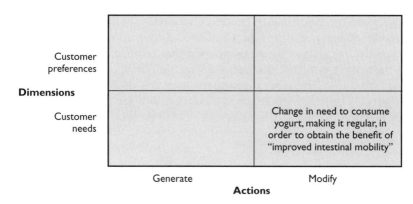

Figure 11.1 Danone Activia's generate–modify matrix

offered the same nutritional benefits. Thus, consumers' choices were guided by flavor preferences or by other specific attributes such as the presence of pieces of fruit. Other companies' communication strategies did not target consumption regularity or frequency. No one offered a tangible functional benefit that could strongly appeal to people and make them change their consumption habits. In this market context, Activia's health-promoting properties appeared as a substantial differential, but a huge market education challenge had to be tackled by Danone: people had to be motivated to consume the product on a regular basis.

Hence, to achieve success with Activia, Danone would have to invest heavily in market communications, get them right, and bet on changes in consumption habits. This was a very convenient context for the company to exert its proactive vision and try to create an MZ in the market that could mean a very positive turnaround in its business performance in Brazil. It was a real marketing challenge, as is explained by Leonardo Lima, Activia's former marketing manager in Brazil, who now supervises other functional brands for Danone's Spanish operation:

> Introducing the product to the market was not enough. We had to teach people, educate them to consume it regularly, a habit they did not yet have. It is not enough to take it one day, because it is not a medicine, not a laxative. So, we had to create a communication model based on two very strong pillars: empathy and credibility.[21]

How did Danone manage to make these pillars consistent and to proactively educate consumers? Empathy with customers was developed by adopting an "eye-to-eye" approach to communication, adopting a simple but persuasive style, focused on the high relevance of the product's functional benefits. Credibility, always an attribute of the Danone brand, was also helped by an alluring campaign named the "Activia challenge," designed to stimulate regular consumption. Adopting an audacious posture for a nutritional product campaign, Danone promised to give customers all their money back if they did not feel Activia's functional benefits after regularly consuming 15 pots. The "Activia challenge" was very successful, and contributed to boosting sales and consolidating the product's credibility. In 2006 sales grew by 70 percent, and 50 million pots were sold. Only 3000 consumers demanded a refund.[22]

The proactive efforts to educate the market that Danone developed ended up changing the yogurt purchase decision trees of thousands of consumers. Before Activia was introduced, consumers in a supermarket first chose between liquid and thicker yogurts. Then they would choose between low-fat and regular yogurts, and finally they would choose the flavor. Launching Activia, Danone was able to add a new attribute to the decision tree. In other words, target consumers now first consider whether the yogurt offers any functional benefit, and then proceed to select other attributes. In this context, in accordance with a strategy to increase market share, the company has taken good care of diversity in the Activia product line. The line has now about 40 different options, including thick and thin, regular and low-fat yogurts, in several flavors and packaging sizes.

Educating Activia consumers, Danone was able to change the rules of the competition game in yogurt markets, ultimately controlling the new functional category it created and becoming the absolute leader of the market as a whole. According to Cesar Tavares, Activia's marketing manager, the product expansion in Brazil is supported by a strategic tripod:

> The growth of the Activia brand is based on three critical success factors: first, we made intensive and assertive investments in communication, in order to create a new concept in consumers' minds; second, we offered a highly differentiated product in terms of functionality; third, we are constantly innovating the way we deliver the product functionality. We offer light versions, economical packages and diversity, in the sense that customers can enjoy the functional benefits in different yogurt formats, such as Activia with fruit pieces, or Activia with cereals and fermented milk.[23]

The proactive strategy, which reached most yogurt consumers in the huge Brazilian market and modified Activia consumption needs, was generously rewarded with growth both in sales and in profitability, reversing the company's bottom line into profits in 2006. Two years after being introduced to the market, Activia achieved a 90 percent share of the functional yogurt market, and a 8 percent share of the yogurt market as a whole. In 2010, the product still reigned alone in the functional yogurt niche and achieved a 13 percent share of the yogurt market as a whole, confirming its leading position.

Proactively acting on consumption needs, Danone created a new reality in the Brazilian yogurt market, changing consumers' minds and educating them to regularly consume functional products in a new category. In the last six years, the company has enjoyed the fruits of its successful strategy, but it is still determined to expand and strengthen the Activia brand. Mariano Lozano, president of Danone's dairy operations in Brazil since May 2009, said:

> Proactiveness is fundamental for Danone, especially because the category in which we operate still has a very low market penetration. The best way

to develop yogurt consumption in Brazil is through innovation, and brand communication is also a way to innovate, as we did when we showed people the functional benefits of Activia. As leaders in this category, our great challenge now is to raise Activia to even higher levels. Thus, besides offering flavor and format novelties, we must proceed innovating our dialogue with consumers. For us, innovation transcends the physical boundaries of products.[24]

As we have done throughout Part III of the book, we end this chapter with another successful case of customer proactiveness, to further illustrate market proactiveness in this particular dimension.

HOW CUSTOMER PROACTIVENESS HELPED TECNISA GENERATE PURCHASE PREFERENCE IN ONLINE RESIDENTIAL REAL ESTATE TRANSACTIONS AND ENHANCE ITS BRAND ON THE BRAZILIAN MARKET

It is May 28, 2009, a Thursday afternoon. Suddenly, Twitter followers are struck by a text message posted by the real estate company Construtora Tecnisa: "Now it is official! We have completed our first sale over Twitter. Long live Twitter."[25] The buyer, an executive with a technology company in São Paulo, emphasized the convenience of getting Twitter messages to guide his purchase. "It was exactly the style of apartment I was looking for, in the area my wife and I wanted. We did not even notice the construction work."[26] This landmark sale took place nine years after Tecnisa's first initiatives in the digital world.

Now we go back just ten years in time from when this book was written: we are in February 2001. Let us ask you, as a consumer from that era, Would you think of buying residential real estate through a sales channel operating over the web? You will probably answer "No." But Tecnisa did not think that way. A leading construction company, one of the largest operating in Brazil in 2001, it started to design a proactive market strategy aimed at the ambitious goal of generating purchase preferences in real estate transactions over the internet (see Figure 11.2). What could have led the company to consider this idea feasible? What signs of change in the behavior of real estate buyers were detected by Tecnisa that made it launch this strategy? What tendencies were detected in the behavior of people outside the real estate market that showed a latent preference for new channels of remote contact between customers and companies, instead of using the telephone and e-mail? Over the next few pages we will see how Tecnisa dealt proactively with these questions and impacted the market with a vigorous digital-marketing strategy.

Detecting market signs and articulating them to project the brand

In 2001, when planning its proactive strategy to enter the digital world and create new purchase preferences and alternative customer relationship formulas, Tecnisa directed its radar to detect pulsating MZs in the behavior of both real estate buyers

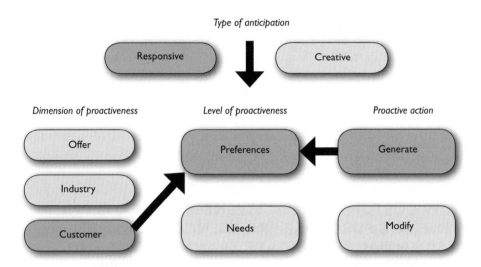

Figure 11.2 A diagram of Tecnisa's proactive action

and other individuals, scanning and interpreting signs in and outside the market where it operated (see Figure 11.3). The digital world at this time represented a promise of new ways of interaction between companies and the market. However, the internet and e-commerce still had not achieved impressive levels of expansion into the market.

After detecting signs of change in market behavior and powered by a proactive mindset, Tecnisa bet on a future where companies and customers would share new ways of contact and interaction, to the detriment of the classic way real estate was bought and sold: that is, by telephone and direct contact. Tecnisa's belief in a future alternative way of interacting with the market was supported by the strategic intention to strengthen its brand, which had limited market recognition. Romeo Busarello, executive director of digital environments and relationship with customers, has driven Tecnisa's strategy since the very beginning. He confirms the company's belief and strategic intent concerning the future of the digital world:

> The position of our brand, based on the slogan "More of the construction company per square meter," pressed us to compete for leadership in many fronts, and we really believed in the internet as a tool. Our bet was that the importance of the internet for the Brazilian market would grow at some point in the future.[27]

Another strong sign detected by the company stimulated its intention to change the rules in the Brazilian real estate market: realtors were widely disliked and distrusted. Surveys showed that customers – most of whom buy a house only a few times in their lifetime – often had bad experiences in their relationships with realtors, who usually seemed to be more interested in solving their own

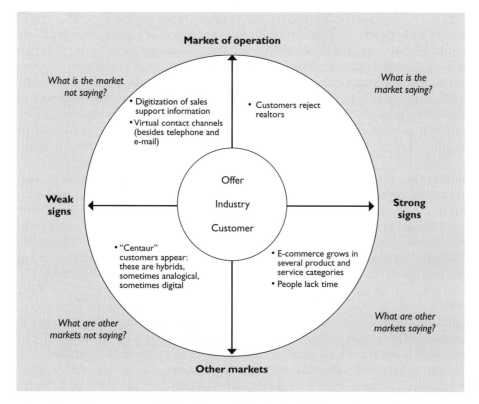

Market of operation

What is the market not saying?

What is the market saying?

• Digitization of sales support information
• Virtual contact channels (besides telephone and e-mail)

• Customers reject realtors

Offer

Industry

Customer

Weak signs

Strong signs

• "Centaur" customers appear: these are hybrids, sometimes analogical, sometimes digital

• E-commerce grows in several product and service categories
• People lack time

What are other markets not saying?

What are other markets saying?

Other markets

Figure 11.3 Moments zero detected by Tecnisa's radar

problems: in other words, in selling the property. The company has also noticed that customers tended to disregard e-mail messages as instruments of commercial communication, because of many companies' frustrating delays in answering. The market perceived the e-mail message as something that "takes 48 hours to generate an answer," a highly undesirable situation in terms of a commercial relationship.

Tecnisa has also detected signs of e-commerce growth in the Brazilian retail segment. It was a time when the first large virtual stores appeared, selling books, CDs and DVDs, home appliances, and other products. The advance of virtual interactions in the field of education did not pass unnoticed by the company either: it was attentive to the distance education offers. All this fostered the company's belief that the internet would soon be a strategic channel for its business, and that it would be possible to change customer preferences by offering a choice of differentiated ways of interacting that could smooth the process of buying residential real estate.

Interpreting the behavior of people in general and of real estate buyers in particular, the company noticed that in huge urban centers people seemed to be increasingly short of time. As director Romeo Busarello (rather harshly) puts it, "In the past, people used to spend time to save money. Now, they spend money to save time."[28] This behavioral phenomenon is an element that facilitates virtual interactions in product and service sales processes. In addition, Tecnisa's strategists, showing great sensitivity in detecting the nuances of real estate buyers' behaviors, perceived other advantages in virtual interactions. For instance, when online services offer the possibility of virtual interaction via chat, they help protect the customer, who often calls from a semi-public environment such as an office, and feels uncomfortable when others hear details of a negotiation, especially when financial aspects, such as the down payment and monthly installments, are being discussed.

Likewise, the company detected signs that customers would also soon value digital interactions because the kinds of data and information (photographs, blueprints, spreadsheets, and so on), that realtors were used to handing personally to customers could now be digitized. Strategists wonder if it is possible to transfer the whole content of our world of atoms to the world of bits. The company's perception proved right. The quick evolution of technological resources, including the emergence of broadband voice, image, and data communication, made the experience of virtual interaction between companies and customers a lot more efficient and pleasant. We know today that most people cling to the digital wave because they find it as convenient as, or even more convenient than, analogical or face-to-face interactions. An impressive example of that is the multiplicity of transactions we are able to complete by logging in to "our" bank's website.

Finally, Tecnisa's radar also detected the behavior of what it called "centaur consumers": a name rooted in the hybrid way they behave. These individuals' purchasing preferences oscillating between personal and virtual contacts. This phenomenon started timidly in several markets. The company felt that it would also be a tendency in the real estate segment; in other words, customers would tend to find the chance to reconcile the virtual and analogical worlds very convenient, as if it created some kind of synergy in the customer–company interfaces. The synergy would bring more comfort and security to the purchasing process, especially in the case of real estate, a very special product because of both the large sums of money involved, and the emotional context of deciding where to live.

Investing proactively in the digital world

All these signs detected by Tecnisa grounded the construction of its proactive market strategy, and enabled the company to anticipate changes in customers' behaviors, generating preferences for virtual interactions in residential real estate purchase processes. Thus, in 2001, Tecnisa launched its online service platform over the internet, a pioneer action in the construction segment. The company started by making an online sales channel available, with four realtors who dedicated part of their time to servicing, via e-mail and telephone, prospective customers who contacted the company through the website. Because it did not yet have the necessary culture to serve customers digitally, the company outsourced chat interactions to a specialized agency which was capable of providing a quality service. This initiative, innovative at the time, caused many internal difficulties for the company. Many realtors refused to use the internet channel, dithering between believing this new reality and staying convinced that a sale required meeting customers personally at the sales office. For the company, this behavior was related to the "comfort zone," since the selling operation would now require realtors to develop different competences.

In its first year of operation, this new online service channel generated 7 percent of sales. In 2002 this number went up to 12 percent, and in 2003 to 15 percent. This gradual evolution proved that the market was slowly changing its purchasing behavior, and accepting the internet as a commercial distribution channel. In 2005, 20 percent of all the company's sales came from the internet. In the first four years, Tecnisa dexterously surfed the "Internet 1.0" wave, where communication was predominantly one to many. In 2007, the company's virtual service platform included several service channels:

* telephone answering
* e-mail, with a commitment to answer in 15 minutes
* an online service (chat) provided directly by brokers
* active telephone, where customers enter their phone numbers on the website and the company calls them back immediately
* a novel video service, where customers and brokers talk to and see each other as in a video conference.

Brokers were available online from 8 am until midnight. The visibility of Tecnisa's digital strategy was increasing externally. Internally, the digital culture permeated many areas of the company. The initial years of digital strategy implementation produced great learning experiences and, most importantly, induced changes to people's mindset, causing them to favor digital strategies. Romeo Busarello said, "All those involved with interactive processes to deal with customers gradually accepted the idea that 'helping the purchase' was much more important than simply 'selling' a property to a customer."[29] The company was now ready to surf the second wave – known as Internet 2.0 – notable for the boom of social networks, where many speak to many. The new wave provided Tecnisa with numerous opportunities to consolidate its digital strategy and change customers behavior.

The company entered all social networks – always in a well-articulated and pioneering way – promoting intensive interaction with customers and other target publics. Proactively embracing social networks, Tecnisa advanced the strategic intention of disseminating its brand to several stakeholders. The launching of a corporate blog, in 2006, was an important event in this new stage of digital strategy. Now the company had another channel to communicate with many different publics. The maturity of the company's digital culture prevailed to prevent the blog from being censored or purged of "improper" comments. The Tecnisa blog is visited by 30,000 people a month on average. The company is now simultaneously and actively present on 13 social networks, something few Brazilian companies can boast.

As demonstrated by Table 11.2, in this era of customer empowerment, the

Table 11.2 Tecnisa's strategic agenda for customer proactiveness

Strategic initiative	Actions
Interactive access	Providing multiple contact channels and interactive database: • Customers have six access channels to contact Tecnisa: receptive telephone, online service (chat), e-mail service, video service (real-time contact), active telephone (the customer provides their telephone number over the web and the company calls back immediately, and online brokers (from 8 am to midnight). • Advanced search system available at the website with detailed information on properties, location, and identification of ten nearby institutions (schools, banks, supermarkets, drugstores, shopping centers, hospitals, bakeries etc.). • Expansion of online channels to many different platforms, being a pioneer in mobiles via mobile sites, smart phone applications, and a commercial page on Facebook.
Joint innovation	Involving clients and other publics in innovation processes: • The company offers, via the web, a collaborative space named "Tecnisa Ideas" to stimulate the public as a whole to offer suggestions in the field of construction and involving themes such as sustainability, convenience, well-being, access to leisure, infrastructure, interior design, security etc. (Launched in August 2010, the space has already collected more than 1100 suggestions.) • In 2009, the "Gerontological Consciousness" program (architecture for the aged) run on social networks raised more than 10,000 interactions and gathered 200 ideas to adapt engineering projects and make them friendlier for the aged.
Empathic communication	Creating responsive and sweeping communication with clients: • Tecnisa pioneered the implementation of a Corporate Blog, an uncensored and unfiltered interactive space created in 2006. • The company maintains intensive communication with several target publics in 13 different social networks and a proactive system to monitor all events related to its business and brand on these networks.
360-degree experience	Guaranteeing 360-degree experiences to customers: • Well-structured operational processes and strong internal culture directed to provide careful, agile and specialized services to customers guarantee an experiences better than the average in the segment. • The 360-degree experience is systematically practiced by the company and is based on a relationship program that includes 42 points of contact, from purchase (at the blueprint stage) to the handling of keys.

company maintains a very proactive stance. Tecnisa is pursuing a strategic agenda that includes relevant actions to promote interactive access, to develop joint innovation together with customers and other stakeholders, to create empathic communication projects involving several different target publics, and finally to provide pleasant 360-degree experiences to its customers, as a way to guarantee satisfaction and build loyalty.[30] Tecnisa's natural tendency to provide customers with favorable experiences is confirmed by Carlos Alberto Julio, the company's

Table 11.3 Tecnisa: capacities explored to build the proactive strategy

Capacity	Context
Capacity for innovating proactively	From the very beginning, the construction of a strategy for sales and customer relationships over the internet was strongly supported by the president and directors. Managers were encouraged to support the project, which was headed by the executive director for digital environments and customer relationship, a member of the board.
Capacity for identifying and developing proactive people	The company has been able to develop and, most importantly, retain talents in the web platform management team. Team tasks involve website administration, online media management, and monitoring of social networks. In terms of HR management, the company historically supports the development of personnel to occupy managerial positions in this area.
Capacity for dealing with risk	When beginning to build its digital strategy, Tecnisa faced the risk of rejection of the newly created virtual interaction channels by customers. Later, the intensive participation of the company in social media, including the uncensored and unfiltered corporate blog, means that it is proactively dealing with risks of excessive image exposure to stakeholders.
Capacity for dealing with error	Tecnisa was one of the Brazilian companies that pioneered the social network "Second Life," a virtual environment resembling a 3D game that simulates "real life." It was also the first company to quit and learn from this experience. Besides, when constructing its proactive strategy in the web world, the company practices an internal motto that stimulates and keeps the regularity of actions: "Do little, sell little, but learn much."
Capacity for visualizing future realities	In 2001, Tecnisa was the first company in the market to build a team of online realtors, when the internet, with 4.5 million users, was a small phenomenon in Brazil and there was no broadband access. From signs detected inside and outside its market, the company perceived a promising business future in the internet, regarding it as a potential sales and customer-relationship channel.
Capacity for managing short-term pressure	The "Do little, sell little, but learn much" motto has also helped long-term management of the proactive market strategy's construction. The company was able to grow the web platform gradually. In 2001, only 7 percent of sales originated from the internet. From 2001 to 2005, this participation grew to 20 percent, and in 2010 it reached 35 percent. The incremental scheme proved pragmatic and useful for operational processes and for the creation of an internal culture capable of facilitating execution of the new strategy.
Capacity for innovating proactively	The value proposition, supported by the corporate slogan "More of the construction company per square meter," was the main guideline of the company's innovation process which created virtual channels for interaction and a relationship with customers. In addition, the company is innovative and a pioneer in the creation of new ways of communication with the market, especially in the realm of social media, contributing to tie the Tecnisa brand to innovation, a strong factor in brand recognition by the market.
Capacity for flexible management	Tecnisa's anticipated bet on the internet required managerial flexibility to adopt new operational procedures for serving customers. There are now many different options to contact the company. The multichannel access strategy shifted internal paradigms and challenged the service patterns of the whole market segment.

former president and still a director: "We were the first construction company to create a customer relationship division to monitor all points of contact in the process of selling and delivering real estate properties."[31]

Using capacities to create changes in market behavior

Tecnisa's very successful attempt to proactively develop a digital strategy required multiple capacities. Starting from the visualization of a future reality where the internet would leverage sales and broadcast its brand, the company was able to manage the risks of excessive exposure and to innovate proactively in the new digital world. Table 11.3 presents the eight capacities explored by Tecnisa in the construction of its strategy, along with the corresponding managerial contexts.

Enjoying the fruits of a proactive strategy

Ten years after the beginning of its proactive trajectory through the digital world, Tecnisa became a national reference in matters related to the management of social networks in business environments, and the reputation of its brand, tied to the internet and to good innovative practices, is now excellent. In the last four years, the success of its digital strategy has been recognized in many different ways. For instance, in 2008 Tecnisa was internationally recognized by Google as "the world's best company operating in the real estate market in actions connected to sponsored links." In 2009, the prestigious blog Dailybits, dedicated to subjects related to the internet and technology, considered the sale of an apartment through Twitter as "one of the 20 most curious things that happened on a social network in 2009." In that very same year, Tecnisa appeared prominently in *Época Negócios* magazine's ranking of "The most hi-tech companies in Brazil", ranking first among "the companies most finely tuned to Web 2.0." In 2010, the consultancy firm A. T. Kerney, together with *Época* magazine, pointed to Tecnisa as "one of the most innovative companies in Brazil," as a consequence of its use of modern digital technologies.[32]

From the viewpoint of changes in customer behavior, the company reached the impressive level of 35 percent of sales being generated by internet interactions. Ninety-five percent of people who bought real estate from Tecnisa visited the company's website. This excellent digital performance brought financial and operational gains. In addition to being agile, and therefore, more productive, sales over the net cost, on average, one third of face-to-face sales' costs.

Customer satisfaction surveys showed rates above 80 percent in the last five years, demonstrating the high quality and consistence of services provided by the company at all stages of the sales process, in both the virtual and face-to-face contexts. Financially, in the last three years, Tecnisa has achieved net margins three percentage points above the sector's average, and net profit increased 57 percent between 2008 and 2009, and 72 percent from 2009 to 2010. Tecnisa's founder and president Meyer Joseph Nigri stated, briefly and precisely, the company's proactive posture and its ability to carry out a strategy:

Since the beginning of our history in the world of the internet, I have always believed this would prove right and would constitute an invaluable sales tool in the future. When you believe and keep good track of things, your chances of doing right are high. At the time, nobody believed us, but we proceeded and managed to innovate, with excellent results.[33]

This chapter closes the third part of the book, dedicated to the execution of proactive market strategies (PMS). Here, we discussed several strategy implementation examples that encompassed the three market proactiveness dimensions: offer, industry, and customer. We addressed different challenges faced by strategists, confirmed the good results achieved by companies, and demonstrated the benefits of anticipating changes in the market. Next, to wrap up our narrative, we address the main conclusions we believe to be relevant.

CONCLUSION

12 A Strategy to Anticipate the Future

We have reached the end of our narrative. We have tried to describe what market proactiveness is and how it works. We have introduced capacities that ease its implementation. The ideas, models, and tools discussed in this book indicate a direction: now it is time to act.

This book is dedicated to managers and was conceived to be essentially practical and avoid excessive academic material. We believe we reached this objective. Despite the trade-off between a need to be objective (fundamental in a business textbook) and the desire to say everything (in our five years of research we accumulated a lot of invaluable information), we believe we have conveyed the essential.

Let us finish the book by putting forward five issues that may help you bring to life everything we have been discussing so far. They are related to aspects that have come to our attention during the research, to reflections about reach – and limits – of proactiveness, and to interpretations and understandings which, we often noticed, do not stick to the real meaning of the proactive anticipation approach we champion.

Thus, proactive companies and their strategists must keep in mind the following.

I BEING PROACTIVE RELATIVE TO THE MARKET DOES NOT MEAN BEING NECESSARILY A PIONEER

A superficial understanding of market proactiveness may wrongly suggest that it ultimately means being a pioneer. But although proactive companies sometimes act as pioneers in the market, this does not mean that being a pioneer is a necessary condition when it comes to creating market proactiveness. Amazon.com eventually became the most important online bookseller, but the idea had been tried out two years earlier by precursors such as Charles Stack and the Computer Literacy Bookstore.[1] They were pioneers just like Yahoo! and Alta Vista, which opened up the online search engine market only to see Google revolutionize it later. Relevant moments zero (MZs) are often much more related to the intensity and amplitude of an impact than to pioneering changes.[2]

From our point of view, market proactiveness goes beyond pioneering for two basic reasons. The first is related to the application of these two approaches. Pioneering in the market is a strategy that relies almost exclusively on the introduction of new products and services: that is, on what a company offers to the market. In this context we may say it represents an offer-oriented strategy, where technological innovation plays a fundamental role.[3] Although the offer is one focus, anticipatory approaches also open two other known dimensions for companies: the industry and the customer. These are usually kept out of strategic discussions. (Our research clearly showed that the standard strategic thinking in most companies ends up privileging the offer – products and services – to the detriment of actions in the industry and customer dimensions.[4]) Hence, while companies trying to pioneer in the market focus on technological innovations in products and services, proactive companies try to find out latent opportunities involving customers and other players. Proactive managers must keep in mind that a great and radical innovation may result from a new preference created by the company in both the customer (this is the story of, for instance, Sony's Walkman, in the 1980s) and industry (as with the advent of online sales, led by companies such as Dell and Amazon.com) dimensions, without any technological advancement causing a discontinuity in the offer.

The second reason is concerned with how these two approaches deal with uncertainty. As we know, proactive anticipation is based on, first, an anticipatory response to signs of change and/or second, the creation of change based on images of the future conceived by the company itself. A company is enabled to anticipate MZs of high intensity and amplitude through its capacity for visualizing uncertain and undetermined realities and its actions (aimed at generating or modifying) on any of the described levels of proactiveness. Pioneers in the market do not always follow this path, and this explains the failure of many first movers. Pioneers often lack the capacity for dealing with the uncertainties of change, for looking for insights that may help generate innovations. Consequently, many pioneering actions end up under- or over-estimating what can be done, either falling short of or exceeding what the market is ready to assimilate. (In this particular context, the MZs radar and the future images searchlight – see Chapter 4 – help companies better align their strategies with latent changes in the market, minimizing mistakes.). This helps explain why technological innovations often do not draw the interest of consumers.

Finally, an additional fact contributes to illustrate the differences between pioneer and proactive companies. Often, pioneering initiatives end up assuming an aspect of market reactiveness, in a process called "pioneer's inertia."[5] This happens when the company is seduced by its current capabilities, those brought about by its pioneering initiative, and, for fear of cannibalizing its offer, continues to invest in technologies that already show signs of obsolescence and becomes operationally inflexible. (These aspects are addressed by proactive management, as discussed in Part II of this book.) A pioneer's advantage is not the same as market proactiveness, and may sometimes lead companies to reactiveness itself. Pioneers must be also proactive if they want to protect the advantages they have achieved.

2 PROACTIVENESS AND REACTIVENESS MAY BE COMPLEMENTARY STRATEGIES

Market proactiveness is a strategic option that companies may adopt to transcend mere reaction. This does not mean, however, that they should suddenly abandon their traditional responsive strategies. Market proactiveness does not extinguish a company's need to be alert to customer needs or to the moves of competitors and other players in the industry. The proactive approach shows, nevertheless, that an excessive emphasis on reaction can equalize all companies and lead them down the same traffic-clogged road. The more companies are reactive towards the market, the more they look alike; the more they look alike, the less differentiated they are. Just like cars that move slowly in a traffic jam, companies that only respond to markets end up hampering and hindering each other. As emphasized in the beginning of this book, the problem of market reactiveness is not the nature of the medicine itself, but rather its administration.

Consequently, we propose a strategic balance between proactiveness and reactiveness. More than necessary, this balance is a requirement of practical reality itself. No company can afford to ignore existing market conditions. Complete submission to these conditions, however, produces conformant companies. This means that each company will have to discover the best way to find room for proactive and reactive actions in its strategies. To achieve that, it is important to notice that proactiveness and reactiveness must be regarded as elements of a continuum, rather than as antagonistic poles that do not communicate with each other. A company will therefore sometimes be proactive, sometimes reactive. This may be, for instance, a consequence of the resources available at a given moment or of market contingencies. As seen, the level of proactiveness – and of reactiveness – will change according to internal and external circumstances a company faces.

A practical example of this kind of balance is seen when reactive actions are applied to support a proactive strategy. This happens, for example, when a proactive innovation to products and services is improved according to consumers' requirements. This "smart" reactive action (as highlighted in Chapter 6) was an aspect uncovered by our qualitative research involving executives from different industries. As one of them put it, "No company will ever be 100% proactive all the time. At some moments, it will have to react and make adjustments, only to be proactive again later. It is a virtuous circle where proactiveness and reactiveness complement each other."

3 THE PRESENT IS THE ONLY PLACE FOR THE FUTURE TO HAPPEN

Proactive companies do not only think of the future; they act upon it. This implies that the future is not something that is going to happen "some day," but something that is built day after day, in the present, through a company's actions. To achieve that, companies must replace their reactive way of regarding future by a proactive vision of future. A proactive look at the future requires the capacity for controlling it. In brief, proactive visions of the future are based on the idea that the future is always the end result of a collection of premeditated actions in the present. Such a challenging job requires a task force willing to plan, decide, and act to achieve the future as it has been imagined. This strategic conception, suggested in often forgotten classic works[6] on strategy, directs us to a simple – though vital for market proactiveness – vision: companies should not think of what they will be in the future, but of what they will *do*, because the future happens in the present.

4 ANTICIPATION DOES NOT MEAN PREDICTION

Proactive companies must overcome what we call "prediction equivocation." Anticipation of the future requires the application of a structured method aimed at detecting symptoms of change and at building images of it. Inadvertently – and unconsciously – this method is often replaced by opinions and guesses by managers about the future, as if they could predict what is ahead.

The prediction equivocation, in truth, reflects the tendency we have to overestimate our particular views of reality, neglecting the fact that our mindsets interfere directly in our perception of the world. As in the parable where six blind men touch different parts of an elephant and erroneously draw conclusions about the nature of the animal, we may also be misled by our perception of the future, if we base our reasoning only on our own interpretation of reality. In the world of business, this may lead to predictions like those given by 20th Century Fox managers in the 1940s. They disdained television's commercial potential because they were focused on traditional cinema. A similar mistake must have haunted the former Capitol president Alan Livingston for many years, after he decided not to promote the Beatles in 1964 because he reckoned they had no chance of being successful in the American market. Attempts to predict future may lead us to vexatious conclusions.

A very important step for companies willing to create a future with their own fair hands is to abandon the idea that predictions and projections can reveal anything accurate about tomorrow. As Mark Twain once ironically stated, "It is very difficult to predict, especially the future."

5 SUSTAINING A PROACTIVE MARKET STRATEGY IS AS IMPORTANT AS CREATING IT

A strategy is valuable for as long as it generates profitability. When most competitors are finally able to mimic or neutralize it, the strategy needs to be unequivocally condemned to the mass grave of competition and has little else to contribute. In brief, the competitive advantage that comes from the anticipation of an MZ will be sustainable as long as it resists competitors' attacks. The sustainability of an MZ may be related to two different dimensions, which we named structural protection and market protection.[7]

Structural protection is related to mechanisms involved in a company's operation and its relation to competitors. These mechanisms protect the proactive strategy adopted, making it less vulnerable to both mimicry and neutralization. There are three major sources of structural protection.

Resource control

This happens when a company has exclusive or highly privileged access to production resources (as in the cases of monopolies and dominant players). Production resources, as meant here, may be linked to supply (the company has an exclusivity agreement, enormous power over suppliers, or even incorporates the supply activity of the value chain), to operation (the company has the best equipment or professionals available in the market), and to distribution (the company has privileged access to major distribution channels or distributes its offer itself).

Patents, copyrights, and registered trade marks

These grant companies, at least for some time, the exclusive right to tap into an MZ. Amazon.com, for instance, protected itself against competitors in the industry by patenting its "one click" online shopping mechanism.[8] In many circumstances, technologies linked to MZs are protected not by patents but rather by secrecy, as with the centenarian MZ represented by Coca-Cola, whose secret formula has never been revealed.

Cost reductions

MZs of great impact on the offer and customer dimensions generate strong sales, leverage production volumes (and learning), and ultimately reduce costs. Imitators may well clone a successful MZ, but will find it difficult to achieve the cost level required by the market. Cost reductions also enable companies, when appropriate, to adopt low-price strategies to counteract any offensive against their MZs and deter new entrants from operating in the newly created market.

Market protection, on the other hand, is related to differentiation, and to brand reputation and value for consumers. There are also three sources of market protection.

Brand loyalty

Proactive companies that clearly differentiate from other players in the market gain a good reputation and consequently build customer loyalty. Even when rival companies adopt aggressive low prices (introducing a similar offer at a substantially lower price) or use extensive publicity (trying to persuade the market that their offers are superior), consumer preference for a given brand remains unchanged, as a rule.

Costs of change

High-impact MZs generate cost changes in the market. Customers will think twice before they replace their usual products and services with new ones (the offer dimension), before they change the way they access a company's offer (the industry dimension), and before they change their preferences (the customer dimension), if such changes result in financial costs (loss of cumulative discounts, for instance), psychological costs (doubts about performance or future services), or learning costs (such as time to learn how to use the new product or service, or training costs).

Chain adoption

MZs in the fields of information technology and electronic hardware often have their sustainability protected by their disseminated adoption (economists call it network externalities). In other words, the more consumers adhere to an MZ, the more difficulty competitors will have in breaking the chain that ties them to it. This is because the benefit delivered by the product will be as high as the number of consumers using it (what would be the fate of electronic mail or of cellphones if only a few people had access to these technologies?). Chain adoption was responsible for sustaining important MZs, such as the VHS video format conceived by the Japanese company Panasonic in the 1980s, and keeps on sustaining MZs like Sony's Playstation and Microsoft's operating system Windows.[9]

Finally, let us comment on probably the most relevant source of protection according to our point of view, a protection that keeps competitors in the company's rearview mirror. As we saw in Part II of this book, execution of a proactive market strategy requires that companies stay aligned with some fundamental capacities, without which the strategy would remain no more than a project. This outstanding ability to manage the capacities for market proactiveness (that is, proactive management) creates an intangible barrier against competitors. This is because capacities are difficult to imitate, especially when they constitute a cohesive and correlated whole, as in the case of proactive management. Its construction involves substantial doses of tacit knowledge and it is therefore inaccessible to rivals. But, even when they are known by competitors, practices related to capacities necessary to proactiveness are not easy to replicate, because they involve human and social aspects. It is possible to replicate the mechanisms a company puts into practice to better deal with risks or mistakes, but it will be extremely difficult to reproduce all the interpersonal relationships and individual competencies that make such practices work for the original company.[10]

FINAL WORDS

A fascinating characteristic of strategic management is that no strategy is exactly like any other. The tools and actions may be the same, but talent and skill in using them will make the difference. We are sure that each company will find the most convenient way of using the ideas described in this book to achieve market proactiveness. We believe that the concepts presented will help companies in their journey, acting as compasses, and that the examples of successful proactive companies and comments in this book will inspire companies willing to build their own futures.

Appendix

Evaluation Diagnoses: The Promark Scale and the Check-Up on Capacities

Here we present details of the tools we have mentioned to evaluate the levels of market proactiveness and of capacities for market proactiveness: the Promark scale and the check-up on capacities respectively. The Promark scale was designed to help executives evaluate a company's behavior in regard to a series of actions in the three dimensions of market proactiveness. The actions illustrate the attitudes of proactive companies to the market. The check-up on capacities was conceived to evaluate the behavior of a company relative to the eight capacities presented in Chapter 3.[1] The purpose of both diagnoses is to prompt companies to analyze their own actions toward the market and how they behave in regard to their capacities for market proactiveness. This self-analysis is aimed at helping teams establish priorities and courses of action. As first steps to apply the diagnoses, we suggest:

- The questions should be answered individually by top managers.
- If the organization has more than one strategic business unit, executives may answer referring to either the unit to which they currently belong or the organization as a whole. The scope of analysis must be clear and previously agreed upon by the team.
- Diagnostic questions must be answered considering the company's current situation, practices, and characteristics, rather than what might be thought ideal for the organization.
- The questions address characteristic practices and behaviors of proactive companies, and are evaluated according to a five-point concordance/discordance scale. Thus, extreme values (1 and 5) represent respectively total discordance (TD) and total concordance (TC). A score of 3 indicates neither discordance nor concordance (NN) with the statement. Scores 2 and 4 represent respectively partial discordance (PD) and partial concordance (PC).
- Team must discuss individual scores in a comparative way, appraising possible convergences and disparities between them.
- In the case of disparities, consensus must be achieved about the score that best represents the company's reality. This can be done either by arbitration or by calculating an average score.
- After the questions have been answered, the results should be evaluated using the Promark scale and the check-up on capacities, as we go on to explain.

THE PROMARK SCALE

Estimate your company's level of market proactiveness in the offer, industry, and customer dimensions according to the following statements.

A Offer proactiveness

In this company:	(1) TD	(2) PD	(3) NN	(4) PC	(%) TC
1. We launch products and services intended to change consumers' preferences.					
2. We try to incorporate solutions to future customer needs in our products and services.					
3. We try to generate new benefits to the market by means of our products and services.					
4. We try to change the market's standard offer by creating or modifying inherent benefits.					

B Industry proactiveness

In this company:	(1) TD	(2) PD	(3) NN	(4) PC	(%) TC
1. We try to act on all players in our segment (competitors, suppliers, and distributors) to change their structure and behavior.					
2. We estimate the possibilities of integrating supplier and/or distributor functions.					
3. We constantly evaluate the possibility of acting over the market's regulation and legislation, aiming at changing it to our benefit.					
4. We systematically evaluate the possibility of building strategic alliances with competing companies.					

C Customer proactiveness

In this company:	(1) TD	(2) PD	(3) NN	(4) PC	(%) TC
1. We work together with our major customers, trying to recognize their needs months or even years before most market players do.					
2. We anticipate current market tendencies, trying to recognize future preferences and needs.					
3. We constantly try to generate new consumption preferences and/or needs.					
4. Our market survey is aimed at finding latent needs and preferences: that is, needs and preferences consumers themselves are not conscious of.					

Evaluation of results

1 Add the scores of each individual dimension of market proactiveness. Compute the score average for each dimension.

2 Averages above 4.0 indicate that the company executes most of the actions characteristic of proactive companies. Averages between 3.0 and 4.0 indicate a less incisive action. Averages below 3.0 indicate that the company generally does not act proactively in the dimension under analysis.

Note: The results should not be taken as absolute. Satisfactory levels of market proactiveness do not necessarily ensure the success of planned anticipatory strategies. The efficacy of a proactive market strategy depends ultimately on the intensity and amplitude of the moments zero (MZs) generated by the company. This explains why many times companies have very similar proactiveness levels but completely different proactive performances. However, the Promark scale helps companies compare their practices with practices that are characteristic of known proactive companies. To generate high-intensity and high-amplitude MZs a company needs, above all, to act in a proactive way toward the market.

3 Consider the items with lower scores (1 and 2) in all three dimensions. Assess the reasons for these low scores.

4 Consider the items that scored 3 and analyze what could be preventing the company from acting in a more pronounced way.

5 Discuss possible priorities and courses of action to deal with the most deficient aspects. Consider what could be done to facilitate the company's decision to act on the different dimensions and levels.

Note: The purpose of the Promark scale is not to point to a strategic sequence of dimensions, levels, and applications to be followed by a company. As we have seen, this is a decision that must be based on the evaluation of the MZs matrix, the resources available to the company, the objectives it wants to achieve, and the contingencies it faces. Nevertheless, this analysis may help companies program possible courses of action aimed at improving their performances in specific ways, guiding initiatives in a strategic sequence.

6 An additional question could be asked: "Generally speaking, is the company proactive toward the market?" This question leads executives to consider all three dimensions together and to analyze whether the company ultimately tends to reactiveness or proactiveness in its market strategies.

CHECK-UP ON CAPACITIES

The check-up on capacities encompasses diagnoses of all eight capacities in all four dimensions of proactive management we have outlined. Trying to be as unbiased as possible, assess the following issues, in relation to the real current situation of your company.

A. Future-today management

A1 Capacity for visualizing future realities

In this company:	(1) TD	(2) PD	(3) NN	(4) PC	(%) TC
1. We usually see future realities long before competitors.					
2. We understand that it is possible to create market realities that are as yet unimagined.					
3. Top management has a vision of the future and uses it to inspire people.					
4. Everyone is aligned and committed to building the market realities we conceive.					

A2 Capacity for managing short-term pressure

In this company:	(1) TD	(2) PD	(3) NN	(4) PC	(%) TC
1. We try to balance short- and long-term results.					
2. We often sacrifice quick positive results in favor of bigger gains in the future.					
3. The criteria adopted by top management to allocate resources usually reflect a long-term vision.					
4. Short-term objectives do not hinder the search for new opportunities.					

B. Uncertainty management

B1 Capacity for dealing with risk

In this company:	(1) TD	(2) PD	(3) NN	(4) PC	(%) TC
1. We accept high risks when aiming at high returns.					
2. We encourage the development of innovative market strategies, even knowing some of them may fail.					
3. We inspire collaborators to deal with risk taking.					
4. We try to learn about risks and to determine their probability and intensity of impact.					

B2 Capacity for dealing with error

In this company:	(1) TD	(2) PD	(3) NN	(4) PC	(%) TC
1. We give people freedom to make mistakes.					
2. We are tolerant of failures and errors when they happen in the search for something really new.					
3. We understand that faults in the process of launching new products and services are normal occurrences.					
4. We do not criticize or punish people for mistakes made when attempting to anticipate change.					

C Proactive innovation management

C1 Capacity for innovating proactively

In this company:	(1) TD	(2) PD	(3) NN	(4) PC	(%) TC
1. We regard innovation as an opportunity to change the market reality.					
2. We invest in launching new products and services even if they compete with existing, still profitable products and services we offer to the market.					
3. We act to influence customer needs and preferences for products and services we launch.					
4. We believe that an innovation tends to be more successful if the market is worked on in advance to encourage acceptance.					

C2 Capacity for flexible management

In this company:	(1) TD	(2) PD	(3) NN	(4) PC	(%) TC
1. Hierarchical structure is no hindrance to creativity and free flow of ideas.					
2. We are constantly searching for change rather than trying to keep things as they are.					
3. There is room for an enterprising initiative.					
4. People are encouraged to make decisions independently, without having to ask for their manager's approval.					

D Proactive behavior management

D1 Capacity for leading proactively

In this company:	(1) TD	(2) PD	(3) NN	(4) PC	(%) TC
1. We permanently look for new ways of doing things.					
2. We encourage questioning and new ways of approaching problems.					
3. We stimulate creative attitudes and the exploration of new opportunities.					
4. We try to act in anticipation of problems.					

D2 Capacity for identifying and developing proactive people

In this company:	(1) TD	(2) PD	(3) NN	(4) PC	(%) TC
1. We invest time in selecting and hiring professionals who tend to act in an autonomous and anticipatory way.					
2. We enable people to be proactive.					
3. People who generate solutions and new ideas are rewarded.					
4. We stimulate and motivate people to be proactive, openly recognizing them when they generate innovative ideas.					

Evaluation of results

1. Add the scores for each individual capacity.
2. Use the capacity ruler (Figure A.1) to determine the degree of development for each individual capacity and the corresponding course of action. The level of management of a capacity is *deficient* if it scores between 4 and 8 points, *weak* between 9 and 12, and *vulnerable* between 13 and 16, all situations that might cause difficulties in the implementation of proactive market strategies. Scores above 16 points show that the management of the capacity under analysis is *satisfactory* and contributes to the execution and performance of planned proactive strategies.
3. Deficient or weak capacity management calls for urgent improvement. Capacities whose management is vulnerable must be developed. Capacities satisfactorily managed do not need any immediate action, but companies must constantly

monitor their level of management to keep them at this level or even improve their efficiency.

4. Check what capacities achieved low scores (below 12) and try to find out the reasons. Look particularly at items scoring 1 or 2. They disclose a company's biggest weaknesses relative to the capacity being evaluated.
5. Consider items with a score of 3, and ask why the company is having difficulties in developing these capacities.
6. Analyze what can be done to improve the capacities for market proactiveness, drawing on the practices presented in the second part of this book.

	4	8	12	16	20
Management level of capacity	Deficient	Weak	Vulnerable	Satisfactory
Specific actions	Urgent improvement	Improve	Develop	Keep/improve

Figure A.1 Capacities ruler

Notes

INTRODUCTION

1   Many different studies have provided important information on corporate proactiveness, and helped support and inspire many of the ideas in this book. Proactiveness is an encompassing and multifaceted subject which is present in many different fields of knowledge. Works that contributed to our understanding are mentioned in the notes throughout the book. We hope readers wishing to deepen their knowledge on the subject will find that these provide a starting point for future reading.

2   Some books address the subject of proactiveness with regard with corporate strategy, albeit from different standpoints. On the possibility that a company could proactively model the market and build "blank spaces" that it can fill without competition, see Hamel and Prahalad (1994). On companies' abilities to effect proactive changes in a market segment or in market fundamentals, see Kim and Mauborgne (2005). On the relevance of the proactive method in the construction of new business models, see Markides (2008).

   In the academic realm, a number of works constitute an important point of reference when the subject is the reactive character of market orientation: Jaworski, Kohli, and Sahay (2000); Kumar, Scheer, and Kotler (2000); and Narver, Slater, and MacLachlan (2004). They are a counterpoint to this approach. Finally, Birgitta Sandberg's pioneering work on market proactiveness is outlined in *Managing and Marketing Radical Innovations* (2008). She is the author who first introduced the expression "market proactiveness."

   When we use the expression "business proactive logic," we mean the common foundation that encompasses all above-mentioned perspectives: that is, the deliberate changing of prevailing market conditions. The concept of market proactiveness we conceived corresponds exactly to one of the ways companies can carry out this form of business proactive logic. Lastly, the expression "market proactiveness strategy" (MPS), which recurs frequently in this book, refers to the transformation of the market proactiveness concept into concrete and managerially applicable actions.

3   The "finger in the future" allegory was proposed by French contemporary philosopher André Comte-Sponville in *Le Bonheur, Désespérément* (2000). It opportunely illustrates the illusion of the idea of time as a linear progression that includes past, present, and future. From our viewpoint, that is a cognitive obstacle to be overcome when building a more proactive mental model. The idea that now is the only possible moment for action defies this paradigm, being rather an ability to be developed by managers willing to act proactively (see for instance Plunkett and Hale, 1982, pp. 2–3).

   It is curious that the ancient Greeks distinguished between two concurrent time measures, a fact that supports our comments. The first, *chronos*, matches exactly the objective idea of time that governs our modern civilization and underlies the manner in which we manage our daily lives. The second, *kairos*, may be understood as the "right or opportune moment." If nothing is done at this moment – in our own words, "If action is taken only after the change occurs, then it is a reaction" – destiny will find its way and nothing can be done except to respond to its effects.

The story of *chronos* and *kairos* is repeated by Daniel N. Stern in *The Present Moment in Psychotherapy and Everyday Life* (2004) – a rich conceptual collection on the idea of time and its influence on human life. Information on the subject may be easily found on the internet (see for instance "kairos" at http://en.wikipedia.org/).

1 MARKET PROACTIVENESS

1   Leakey (1981), p. 145. We now know that the first Neanderthal fossil was found in 1829, in Belgium. The find, however, was only recognized as the remains of a Neanderthal a hundred years later. Because of that, the 1856 discovery is still regarded as pioneering and a turning point in natural history. See Tattersall (1999), pp. 74–9.

2   The BBC TV series *Walking with the Caveman* (BBC Worldwide, 2003) demonstrates how ingenious the ancestors of modern humans were face-to-face with the environment, planning actions to better deal with future events. Evidences show that Neanderthals did not have such cognitive ability. (See Horan, Bulte, and Shogren, 2005).

3   As confirmed by recent paleontologic research, the extinction of Neanderthals should be regarded as a gradual process that involved many distinct and isolated populations. Thus, factors that explain the extinction of a given group may not be applicable to other groups. This illustrates the large variety of theories to explain the extinction of Neanderthals. Hence, caution is necessary when making inferences. Analysis of up-to-date scientific studies highlights the simultaneity of the extinction of Neanderthals and the ascent of *Homo sapiens*, indicating that our human ancestors' ability to plan and anticipate is a factor that should not be neglected. Our statement on the extinction of Neanderthals and the analogy with the subject of market proactiveness are based on these conjectures (see Wynn and Coolidge, 2004).

4   Gerstner (2002, p. 119).

5   Reactiveness toward the computer market was not exclusive to IBM. In 1977, Ken Olsen, founder of Digital Equipment Corporation, declared "There is no reason whatsoever for individuals to have computers at home." Ironically, Olsen was a pioneer in defying IBM with the idea of producing smaller computers, though he was not able to anticipate the advent of PCs. Texas Instruments is another company that was not able to detect signs of the PC revolution. The company did not have the ability to reproduce its success in the calculator market segment in the PC market. In the 1970s, Hewlett-Packard was the protagonist of a well-known story, when it declined to promote a minicomputer developed by engineer Stephen Wozniak. This is another classical example of the reactiveness that may affect large companies in the face of a potential change. (Wozniak ended up developing the idea together with his then-unknown friend, Steve Jobs: they set up Apple together.) At the beginning of the 1970s, Xerox did not pay attention to Palo Alto researchers who had developed the technology to produce small PCs. The graphic interface, despised by Xerox, was the fundamental element in the creation of Apple's Mac operating system (OS) and the Windows (Microsoft) OS. These examples clearly show how an excessive focus on current market patterns may blind companies to new opportunities, obstructing more proactive and audacious ideas. For more on the cases mentioned, see Malone (1997) and Farson and Keyes (2002).

6   Historical data on computer markets can be found in Malone (1997, p. 157) and Whittington (1993, p. 86).

7   Brigatto (2009).

8   This story is told by David A. Vise and Mark Malseed in *The Google Story* (2005).

9   Data on market share is from Search Engine Market Share, January 2011 <http://

marketshare.hitslink.com/search-engine-market-share.aspx?qprid=4> (accessed September 16, 2011). Data on brand value is from <www.interbrand.com/en/best-global-brands/Best-Global-Brands-2010.aspx> (accessed September 16, 2011).

10 The level of market proactiveness measured by a five-point Likert scale, in a self-completed survey. Statistics were based on answers given by more than 350 executives of 257 business strategic units in many different industrial segments. In 95.2 percent of the cases, proactiveness averages fell in the 2.5–3.9 interval. The market proactiveness general average for all surveyed companies was 3.73.

11 For further and deeper information on convergence theory and environmental determinism see Duncan (1972) and Astley and Van de Ven (1983). On the reactive nature of strategic and marketing tools, see Varadarajan, Clarck, and Pride (1992) and Zeithaml and Zeithaml (1984).

12 Drucker (1954, p. 37).

13 For an analysis of market orientation theory and its premises see Kohli and Jaworski (1990), Narver and Slater (1990), and Day (1994).

14 Whittington (1993, pp. 83 and 86).

15 See for instance Christensen (1997).

16 Leander Kahney quotes the statement in *Inside Steve's Brain* (2008).

17 This statement is traditionally attributed to Henry Ford, though the original source is not known.

18 Hamel and Prahalad (1994). Quote from the 1996 paperback edition, p. 90.

19 The term proactive comes from the English language, and according to *Webster's* dictionary was only incorporated into the language in 1933 (www.merriam-webster.com/). In Portuguese, the term was only acknowledged even more recently (in 1993, according to the *Dicionário Houaiss da Língua Portuguesa*, 2001). In dictionaries, proactiveness is defined both as an action that anticipates change (see for instance <www.merriam-webster.com>; <http://dictionary.reference.com/help/ahd4.html>) and as involving deliberate creation of changes (<www.oxfordadvancedlearnersdictionary.com>; <www.thefreedictionary.com/_/misc/HarperCollinsProducts.aspx?English>).

20 Definitions of proactiveness in organizations state that it encompasses anticipatory and influential actions on the environment. Anticipation involves a company's early response to signs of coming change, while influence is related to deliberate creation of change itself. The abilities to anticipate (act before change) and influence (creation of change) the market become clearly evident. We understand, however, that creation in itself is also an anticipatory action. In other words, proactive companies are always anticipating change, either acting on its signs or intentionally creating it. Hence, anticipation is an essential element of proactive actions, which is manifest, first in the active construction of change (creative anticipation), and second in the anticipated response to changes that are believed to be about to happen (responsive anticipation). A deeper view on the subject is presented by Johannessen, Olaisen, and Olsen (1999); and by Sandberg (2008).

21 There is a dense but informative account of Toyota's proactive action when launching the Prius in Carson and Vaitheeswaran (2007).

22 On the stance of adjusted companies, its characteristics and consequences, see Abel (1999), Harper (2000), and Miles and Snow (2003).

23 In *Peripheral Vision: Detecting the weak signals that will make or break your company* (2006), George S. Day and Paul H. Schoemaker called attention to the differentiated ability of alert companies to detect, interpret, and act in response to weak market signs.

24 Source: individual interviews conducted by the authors.

25 Fábio Barbosa, interview with the authors, São Paulo, August 13, 2009.

2   ACTION TOOLS AND MODELS

1   The inadequacy of traditional strategic tools to formulate proactive strategies – such as, for instance, the market segmentation and industry structural analysis models – is discussed in Hamel and Prahalad (1994), and more recently in Kim and Mauborgne (2005).

2   The acronym DNA refers to the English term deoxyribonucleic acid.

3   Throughout the book, the terms "industry" and "sector" are used interchangeably to represent a group of manufacturers whose products closely substitute for each other (see Porter, 1980, p. 5). Interaction between industry players and the resources involved in this interaction configure what we call the market.

4   We use the term "customer" to designate entities – either individuals (consumers) or groups (organizations) – that might potentially buy a company's offers. Thus, customer proactiveness refers to both habitual buyers of a company's products (customers) and other buyers in the market the company serves, or aspires to serve.

5   Our definition of "market" explains the exchange flow structure that encompasses, synthetically, (1) producers, (2) consumers, (3) intermediaries (wholesale, retail), (4) (material, financial and labor) resources, and (5) government (see for instance Kotler and Keller, 2006). A market, in its turn, will always be included in a wider dimension basically composed of political, economic, social, and technological forces, shaping what is traditionally called the external environment, or simply the environment (see for instance Polonski, Suchard, and Scott,1999). Hence, when we say market strategy, we mean the logical structure of objectives and plans developed with regard to a company's market, including the impact of environmental variables.

6   Strategies in all three of our dimensions can be identified in the specialized literature. In the realm of offer, they include the design of new products and services (Hamel and Prahalad, 1994), creation of a new value curve (Kim and Mauborgne, 2005), addition of new benefits to products (Jaworski et al., 2000), cannibalization of products and services (Kumar et al., 2000), changes in the standard of products and services (Hills and Sarin, 2003), and creation of a new value proposal (Markides, 2008). In the industry dimension, examples are changes in the value chain (Hamel, 1996), definition of new strategic groups (Kim and Mauborgne, 1999), changes in the composition and behavior of players of a sector (Jaworski et al., 2000), and reconfiguration of existing distribution channels (Kumar et al., 2000). Finally, actions such as changing customer behavior (Hamel, 1996), creation of new consumption demands and preferences (Jaworski et al., 2000), and creation of new consumer needs and behaviors (Hills and Sarin, 2003) are examples in the sphere of customer proactiveness.

7   The value proposal (or value proposition) refers to the "intrinsic benefits of offers introduced to the market." Benefits in turn are defined as "individual advantages or gains associated with the purchase or use of a given product or service" (see Dacko, 2008, pp. 53 and 558).

8   The word "product" can be used as the generic term to designate any offer introduced to a given market, either tangible (physical goods) or intangible (services). In this book, however, we have opted to differentiate between tangible and intangible goods, since this is common practice in the managerial and business jargon. Consequently, when we use the expression "products and services" we mean respectively the tangible and intangible dimensions of the offer to an economic sector. For a more detailed explanation, please refer to, for instance, Kotler and Keller (2006).

9   Guglielmo (2010).

10   Márcio Utsch, interview with the authors, São Paulo, January 29, 2010.

11   The notion of the industry as a unequivocal determinant of strategy was promoted by Michael Porter's *Competitive Strategy* (1980).

12   Source: www.hering.com.br/.
13   Fábio Hering, interview with the authors, São Paulo, November 16, 2009.
14   Paulo Nigro, interview with the authors, São Paulo, June 21, 2010.
15   Toyota's example is mentioned in Davila, Epstein, and Shelton (2006, p. 34). The IKEA example appears in Tarnovskaya, Elg, and Burt (2008).
16   Southwest's example was presented in Jaworski et al. (2000).
17   Example taken from Diegues and Bruno (2009).
18   Consumption preferences are an important element of customer behavior, when speculating on how it develops from a company's action (see Carpenter and Nakamoto, 1989 and Jaworski et al., 2000). The same happens with regard to needs which in their marketing dimension – in other words, representing a specific consumption desire – are also regarded as accessible to formation through deliberate strategic action (see Dacko, 2008).
19   Alessandro Carlucci, interview with the authors, São Paulo, September 12, 2009.
20   This case is presented in Markides (2008, p. 136). According to the author, the first virtual bookstore was created in 1993 by an individual from Ohio (USA) two years before Amazon.com.
21   Source: Wikipedia entry on "Twitter," http://en.wikipedia.org/.

3 ORGANIZING THE COMPANY FOR MARKET PROACTIVENESS

1   Henry Mintzberg stated that only one out of ten companies is able to implement strategies successfully (1994, p. 25). Ram Charan and Geoffrey Colvin (1999) also argued that in almost 70 percent of studied cases CEO failure had not come from equivocal strategy formulation but rather from problems in carrying out the chosen strategy. Recent surveys – such as one undertaken by the American Management Association in 2007 with 1,526 executives – found that only 3 percent of companies are able to implement their strategies (AMA press release, "Most companies are only moderately successful or worse when it comes to executing strategy, executives say," March 19, 2007). Such historical difficulty in execution is reflected by researches such as one carried out by the *HSM Management Plus* magazine (August 2009) with 520 Brazilian executives, which showed that 58 percent of all interviewees chose strategy execution as the most terrible nightmare of business leaders (<http://br.hsmglobal.com/notas/53824-quais-sao-os-sonhos-dos-lideres-brasileiros>, accessed September 19, 2011).
2   Organizational culture is understood as a set of values and beliefs that define the way an organization behaves and operates its businesses (see for instance Barney, 1986, and Deshpandé and Webster, 1989). The idea that a market-oriented strategy transcends the simple performance of actions to include a company's way of thinking is a prominent theme in the specialized literature (see for instance Narver and Slater, 1990), and is also present in the specific realm of the strategies aimed at proactively guiding the market (see for instance Kumar et al., 2000). Based on that, we mention the culture of proactiveness because we understand that a proactive strategic posture should not be restricted to a mere execution of planned activities, a reasoning that is aligned with the results of our field research with executives and CEOs.
3   The identification of capacities for market proactiveness followed the processes of specialized literature review and in-depth interviews. The importance of risk as an essential component of organizational proactiveness is described by Miller and Friesen (1978), Morgan (1992), Palmer and Wiseman (1999), and more recently Luo (2004).

The error issue and its role in the scope of proactiveness is addressed in Hamel and Prahalad (1994) and also in Kumar (2004, pp. 177–210) and Sloane (2006).

The capability of visualizing future realities as a component of a proactive culture appears in O'Connor and Veryzer (2001) and Hughes and Beatty (2005).

The notion that an innovative process aimed at changing the market is essential in the context of anticipatory strategies is explored in Carpenter, Glazer, and Nakamoto (1997), Tuominem, Rajala, and Möller (2003), and Tsai, Chou, and Kuo (2007). The positive role played by a flexible management in the scope of a proactive market orientation appears in Narver et al. (2004) and Tarnovskaya et al. (2008).

Finally, the importance of leadership in the development of proactiveness is mentioned by Morgan (1992), Kumar et al. (2000), and Carrillat, Jaramillo, and Locander (2004).

In-depth interviews revealed the adherence of executives to these capacities, upholding the legitimacy of the theoretical inventory. Another relevant finding was the identification of two capacities not markedly mentioned in the literature but strongly referenced by the interviewees: managing short-term pressure, and developing proactive people. This finding was later supported by qualitative research we carried out with about 50 CEOs, which brought out the importance they saw in targeting long-term goals and in focusing on people in the construction of a company aimed at anticipating moments zero. Studies such as those by Schindehutte, Morris, and Kocak (2008), showing the difficulty in acting proactively in a culture averse to long-term results, and Tarnovskaya et al. (2008), addressing the role of human development as a foundation to build a market-oriented proactive posture, have already mentioned the importance of capacities brought about by field research. The final list of eight capacities encompasses findings from both our literature review and our field research (on the methodological validity of this procedure, see Churchill, 1995).

4   All quotes from personal interviews with the authors, 2009/2010. Source of data: companies' websites.

5   In the descriptive research we carried out with 257 UENs, 75 percent of the indicators related to the capacities achieved averages below 4.0 (in the five-point Likert scale) and 12.5 percent below 3.0. This shows an average to low incidence of practices related to the capacities in studied companies. In contrast to the results of in-depth interviews, this fact encourages speculation on a gap between discourse (most of those interviewed in the exploratory research admitted the importance of the capacities) and practice (actions related to capacities are not a reality in the context of companies).

4   FUTURE-TODAY MANAGEMENT: BELIEVING IN WHAT DOES NOT EXIST (YET)

1   Laercio Cosentino, interview with the authors. São Paulo, January 27, 2009.

2   The term "futurology" was created by German professor and political scientist Ossip K. Flechtheim in 1943 to designate the "science of the future" (Wikipedia, "Futurology": http://pt.wikipedia.org). The end of the Second World War – and the beginning of the cold war and the arms race – increased the importance of systematic studies of the future and prompted the creation, in the 1950s, of institutions like the RAND Corporation (Research ANd Development), with clear military objectives (such as to predict, among other events, the consequences of a global nuclear conflict). It did not take long until the tools and methods developed there were employed by companies. The North American Herman Kahn – one of the most prestigious researchers at RAND – is said to have both improved and

adopted scenario planning as a business tool. Its use increased spectacularly in the 1970s after work carried out by Pierre Wack at Royal Dutch/Shell. On the history and evolution of scenarios please consult Peter Schwartz, *The Art of the Long View* (1996).

3   For a critical view on forecasting practices and their predictive nature see Mintzberg (1994, pp. 227–54) and Hamel and Prahalad (1994: see paperback 1996, pp. 83–90). To the authors, this type of prognosis is one of the major limitations of traditional strategic processes and their performance when dealing with the future's relative uncertainty. On the deterministic and predictive bias toward future and its influence on the specific context of scenario construction, see Schwartz (1996) and Schoemaker (2002).

4   Ricardo Pelegrini, interview with the authors. São Paulo, April 14, 2009.

5   Rosa (2010).

6   The tale "Funes, el Memorioso" may be accessed in Portuguese on <www.dtic.upf. edu/~joan.soler/0910/at/textos/borges/FunesElMemorioso.pdf> and in English on <http://evans-experientialism.freewebspace.com/borges.htm> (both accessed September 19, 2011).

7   Rosa (2010). Additional information on Modu's trajectory may be obtained on ≤www. modumobile.com>.

8   On the concept of residual uncertainty see Courtney (2001). Residual uncertainty is defined as the share of uncertainty that remains after all efforts to understand it have been made; it is the part of the uncertainty that always remains hidden and inaccessible. This approach defies the traditional view that considers uncertainty a dichotomous question (something either exists or not). As seen, there are different levels of uncertainty which therefore require the construction of different strategies.

9   The literature on scenario construction is vast, but a managerial perspective into the theme – which we used to support the future images approach we conceived – may be accessed in the works of Peter Schwartz (1996), Paul J. H. Schoemaker (2002), Bill Ralston and Ian Wilson (2006), and Michel Godet (2006).

10   Tyrrell (2010).

11   The attitude of proactive companies, of imagining a desired future and acting accordingly in the present, was explored by Russel L. Ackoff in a concept the author named idealized design. For a deeper analysis of this approach see Ackoff (1981).

12   This is mentioned by Paul J. H. Schoemaker in *Profiting from Uncertainty* (2002, p. 52) and by Bill Ralston and Ian Wilson in *The Scenario-Planning Handbook* (2006, p. 82).

13   The concordance criterion in analysis of the uncertainty level of events is commented on by Ralston and Wilson (2006, p. 108).

14   For a deeper view of uncertainty's different levels see Courtney (2001, pp. 15–38). There is a useful list of uncertainties related to attitudes in Ringland and Young (2006).

15   Rosa (1967, p. 147).

16   On the construction of narratives (story lines) see Ralston and Wilson (2006, pp. 125–37).

17   A dense and extensive approach to several financial analysis tools – including their specific application in the scenario context – can be found in Damodaran (2008).

18   The tension between the short and long terms is considered as one of the biggest challenges for contemporary managers. See a timely work by Dominic Dodd and Ken Favaro, *The Three Tensions* (2007).

19   The expression "impatient capital" is used by Markides (2008, p. 19). The author believes that pressures for immediate returns are a hindrance to the creation of new business models of usually slower and uncertain profitability.

20   João Castro Neves, interview with the authors. São Paulo, October 21, 2009.

21   On strategic ambidextrousness, see Tushman and O'Reilly (1996), O'Reilly and

Tushman (2004), and Birkinshaw and Gibson (2004). On the possible ways organizational ambidexterity can be activated, see Gibson and Birkinshaw (2004).

22 Research conducted by Markides and Charitou based on 68 companies that adopted a second business model in their industry shows that only 17 of them achieved success with this strategy. Of them, only ten managed the new business as a distinct business unit, the other seven holding them under the existing organizational structure. The results revealed two important issues: the difficulty inherent in the simultaneous management of two conflicting strategies, and the lack of prominence of either of the two ways of ambidextrousness – separation and integration – in the success of the enterprise. For additional reading on the subject se Markides and Charitou (2004).

23 For a deeper description of this subject, see the classical work by James G. March, "Exploration and exploitation in organizational learning" (1991). See also Kyriakopoulos and Moormanb (2004).

24 Gerstner (2002, p. 182).

25 On the role of corporate culture in the scope of innovative and anticipatory strategies see for instance Davila, Epstein, and Shelton (2006, pp. 235–60) and Weick and Sutcliffe (2007, pp. 109–38).

26 Octávio Florisbal, interview with the authors. São Paulo, July 3, 2009.

27 As previously described (see Chapter 3, note 2), our definition of organizational culture follows Barney (1986). See also Schein (1992).

28 On agency theory and the effect of non-financial measures on managers' long-term behavior, see respectively Eisenhard (1989) and Banker, Potter, and Srinivasan (2000).

29 On the balanced scorecard approach, see the seminal articles by Robert S. Kaplan and David P. Norton, "The balanced scorecard: measures that drive performance" (1992), "Putting the balanced scorecard to work" (1993), and "Using the balanced scorecard as a strategic management system" (1996).

30 The concept of sustainable gains is proposed by Dominic Dodd and Ken Favaro in *The Three Tensions* (2007) as a component essential to deal with the short and long terms in a balanced way. For the authors, companies – pressed by the requirements of immediate return – often bet exclusively on immediate gains that are not sustainable in the long run. Dodd and Favaro postulate that managers must also look for sustainable gains of longer life-cycles, the true instruments of future performance.

31 A rich and timely description of the performance measurement problem and its effects on organizational cultures is presented by Jeffrey Pfeffer and Robert I. Sutton in *The Knowing–Doing Gap* (2000, pp. 139–75).

32 Hélio Rotenberg, interview with the authors, Curitiba, June 19, 2009.

33 F. Scott Fitzgerald, "The crack-up" (1936).

34 A consistent review of incentive systems and their relation to innovative strategies (adopted as support to the approach to incentives we developed in this chapter) is given by Tony Davila, Marc J. Epstein and Robert Shelton in *Making Innovation Work* (2006, pp. 179–208).

35 Quoted by Michael J. Mauboussin in "Long-term investing in a short-term world: how psychology and incentives shape the investment industry." Available at <www.lmcm.com/pdf/long-terminvesting.pdf> (accessed June 26, 2011).

5 UNCERTAINTY MANAGEMENT: LEARNING TO DEAL WITH RISK AND ERROR

1 In our approach, we adopted the term "uncertainty" to designate the fact that, in the face of a proposition, no knowledge exists whether it is true or false. Risk will be present

whenever there is exposure to such uncertain propositions, and error happens when decisions made with respect to them prove wrong. Decisions in regard to proactive strategies (as with any other strategy) will involve a certain amount of uncertainty and risk, as well as the possibility of mistakes. (For an in-depth view of the risk and uncertainty definitions adopted here, see Holton, 2004.)

2   On the universality of the risk- and error-related organizational taboo, see Farson and Keyes (2002, p. 37).

3   Ultimately, companies and other organizations only reflect the risk taken by their agents (managers and leaders). Hence, when we refer to companies as risk takers, we assume that this stance is caused – at a higher or lower level – by the attitudes and corresponding decisions of individuals in the face of uncertainty. Consequently, and according to our conception of uncertainty management, the role of top management is fundamentally important (on this matter read for instance Holton, 2004).

4   Evidence of a negative correlation between a proactive posture toward the market and risk aversion can also be found in Miller and Friesen (1978) and Luo (2004).

5   Our approach to uncertainty management and its related capacities addresses what is sometimes called "strategic risk": that is, a kind of non-financial risk related to a company's decision to act according to a given strategy. Strategic risk in the context of this chapter includes risks associated with proactive actions related to a company's offer, industry, and customers. For a more detailed description of financial and non-financial risks, as well as the types of business-related risks, see Apgar (2006).)

6   It is important to emphasize that the risk management practices we address in this book are not aimed at constituting what is commonly known as a "risk management process" – in other words, the analysis of risks and threats related to the project management process. For an in-depth analysis of the subject see Royer (2002).

7   Sony's case is recounted by Leander Kahney (2008, pp. 200–1). On this subject see also Haire (2009).

8   The notion that individuals evaluate losses and gains in an unbalanced way is described in prospect theory, which was elaborated by two behavioral finance researchers, the Israeli psychologists Amos Tversky and Daniel Kahneman (the latter won the 2002 Nobel Prize for Economics). In brief, prospect theory acts as a counterpoint to the modern financial paradigm according to which decision makers are rational and objective agents searching for the maximization of utilities in their choices under risky and uncertain conditions (the theory of expected utility). Tversky and Kahneman observe that, in a situation that could result in either loss or gain, the possibility of loss has a much greater influence on the decision than the chance of gain. Prospect theory leads to an important conclusion: human aversion to loss often results in the acceptance of even higher risks of loss. This explains, for instance, the logic of compulsive gamblers: to avoid facing the reality of an already effective loss, they bet all their chips hoping to reverse the situation. For a deeper view of prospect theory, see Kahneman and Tversky's inspiring "Prospect theory: an analysis of decision under risk" (1979).

Loss aversion's negative effect on risk taking, on the other hand, is observed by Kahneman and Lovallo (1993). The authors state that loss aversion is a direct cause of risk aversion, and consider it a stance that favors inaction and the status quo to the detriment of change-driven actions. They also say that loss aversion is a marked variable – and very often a significant one – in organizational contexts, because of the responsibilities and consequences decision makers assume in this particular context. This helps explain why managers and executives show strong loss aversion – and consequently risk aversion – even in situations where taking a small risk of failure could lead to considerable gains.

9   On the dual nature of risk as both threat and opportunity, see Damodaran (2008, pp. 6–7 and 369).

10   The notion that in the face of uncertainty we must focus on what benefits (or losses) an action could bring, instead of on the probability of their occurring, is supported by Nassim N. Taleb, the uncertainty sciences professor at the University of Massachusetts, Amherst, in *The Black Swan* (2007).

11   Bernardo Hees, interview with the authors, Curitiba, January 15, 2010.

12   See Damodaran (2008, p. 376).

13   See Palmer and Wiseman (1999) and Damodaran (2008, pp. 6–7 and 356–8).

14   The Senna episode is described (in Portuguese) at <http://globoesporte.globo.com/platb/voandobaixo/2010/07/27/hamilton-senna-e-a-mclaren/> (accessed October 7, 2011).

15   David Apgar (in *Risk Intelligence*, 2006) states that the paradigm that risks are absolutely random and unpredictable must be overcome by managers. He shows that ultimately the outcome of few risks is absolutely random, and that building intelligence on risk requires recognizing the fact that it is possible to learn about the inherent risks in decision making. The Toyota example we use was first mentioned by him.

16   Sofia Esteves, interview with the authors, São Paulo, February 2, 2009.

17   The excessive confidence of managers in the face of risk is a behavior documented by the literature (see for instance Kahneman and Lovallo, 1993, p. 3). We observed that executives and managers are not immune to optimism and to the illusion of control, when they make their decisions in the face of uncertainty, an attitude that – curiously – seems to increase when decisions are complex and difficult to evaluate (on this subject, see Lichtenstein, Fischhoff, and Phillips, 1982).

18   Luiza Trajano, interview with the authors, São Paulo, March 12, 2009.

19   Hamel and Prahalad (1994/1996, p. 197).

20   The notion that the success–failure dichotomy is at the core of a difficulty in dealing with mistakes is the essence of a dense work by Farson and Keyes on error and its implications in the organizational context (2002).

21   On the dangers of success, see Davila et al. (2006, pp. 239–42).

22   Mentioned by Leander Kahney in *Inside Steve's Brain* (2008, p. 4).

23   The Jacuzzi and Sony examples are recounted by Paul Sloane (2006, ch.16).

24   Harry Schmelzer, interview with the authors, Jaraguá do Sul, February 26, 2009.

25   Alessandro Carlucci, interview with the authors, São Paulo, September 12, 2009.

26   See Kahney (2008, pp. 99, 232).

27   Jairo Yamamoto, interview with the authors, Campinas, October 14, 2008.

28   Wernher von Braun's history is recounted in Weick and Sutcliffe (2007, p. 50).

29   Klemp et al. (2008). On information about "right" and "wrong" errors visit http://en.wikiquote.org/wiki/Thelonious_Monk. Brazilian poet Arnaldo de Campos (2009, p. 10) analyzed Monk's words and said they inspire the creation of a "right mistakes theory" to deal with errors that may lead to new realities and, because of that, may well be sometimes premeditated.

30   Interview with the authors.

6   PROACTIVE INNOVATION MANAGEMENT

1   On the misunderstandings about the innovative process, see Davila, Epstein, and Shelton (2006, pp. xv–xvi). On the various approaches to innovation, see, for instance, Wang and Ahmed (2004).

2   Randal Zanetti, interview with the authors, São Paulo, February 4, 2009.

3   Gustavo Valle, interview with the authors, São Paulo, November 27, 2008.

4   On the definitions of incremental and radical innovations adopted in this book, see Garcia and Calantone (2002), Gatignon et al. (2002), and Davila et al. (2006, pp. 38–58). For an extensive and rich description of the different nomenclatures related to the radical innovation concept, see Sandberg (2008, pp. 52–6).

5   On "innovation culture" see Davila et al. (2006, pp. 235–60).

6   See for instance Chandy and Tellis (1998) and Christensen (1997, p. 21).

7   Throughout this book we use the terms radical innovation and rupturing innovation to mean the same thing.

8   The term "proactive cannibalism" is adopted by Cravens and colleagues to designate a type of cannibalism aimed at anticipating changes, as a strategic alternative in the ambit of innovation (see Cravens, Piercy, and Prentice, 2000, and Cravens, Piercy, and Low, 2002). This "intentional" cannibalism had already been mentioned by Mark B. Traylor (1986) as an strategy aimed at increasing a company's performance in the market.

9   Quoted by Hamel and Prahalad (1994/1996, p. 71).

10   On Apple's cannibalism, see Kahney (2008, pp. 99 and 201–2). On cannibalism at Intel and Gillette, see Sloane (2006, p. 5). On cannibalism at HP, see Davila et al. (2006, p. 277).

11   On consumers' resistance to radical innovations, see for instance Veryzer (1998).

12   On the conceptual roots that anchor our approach to market education, see two chapters in Carpenter, Glazer, and Nakamoto (1997): Stephen J. Hoch and John Deighton, "Managing what customers learn from experience" and Gregory S. Carpenter and Kent Nakamoto, "Consumer preference formation and the pioneering advantage."

13   On the concept of early adopters, see the classic work by Everett M. Rogers, *Diffusion of Innovations* (1962/1995). It is important to emphasize that there are two different classes to consider here. Innovators (enthusiasts for cutting-edge innovations and technologies) pioneer the adoption of innovations (and take the corresponding risks), and early adopters based their choices on innovators' selections. Since the former outnumber the latter, they end up becoming the real opinion leaders with regard to new offers to the market at large.

14   The importance of proactively influencing the market within the scope of radical innovation – as well as of adjusting innovations after they are launched – is highlighted by Birgitta Sandberg (2008, pp. 82–206). In a series of case studies, the author demonstrates how companies usually end up merging proactive and reactive attitudes along the process of generating, launching, and improving radical innovations.

15   On the subordination of the innovative process to the market and its consequences, see for instance Whittington (1993, pp. 79–110).

16   José Drummond Jr., interview with the authors, São Paulo, July 3, 2009.

17   Júlio Ribeiro, interview with the authors, São Paulo, July 1, 2009.

18   The inefficiency of traditional market surveys to identify consumers' latent needs was mentioned by Hamel and Prahalad (1994/1996, pp. 108–12). See also Dorothy Leonard and Jeffrey F. Rayport's seminal article, "Spark innovation through empathic design" (1997).

19   On empathic design, see Leonard and Rayport (1997). On the importance of observation to innovation generation, see Kelley (2000, pp. 23–52).

20   The logic of the innovative client as we describe it may be found in Thomke and von Hippel (2002), in Prahalad and Ramaswamy (2004), and in Von Hippel (2005).

21   On metaphoric survey and the ZMETR technique see Zaltman (1997), Zaltman and Coulter (1995), and Zaltman and Zaltman (2008).

22   As early as the 1960s, Thompson (1965) pointed out the incompatibility between

bureaucratic structures and organizational capacity for innovation; for a more recent view of the question, see two articles by Fariborz Damanpour, "Organizational innovation: a meta-analysis of effects of determinants and moderators" (1991) and "Bureaucracy and innovation revisited: effects of contingent factors, industrial sectors and innovation characteristics" (1996). On the negative effects of bureaucracy on innovation and a resulting proactive orientation towards the market, see Narver, Slater, and MacLachlan (2004, pp. 334–47).

23 Luiza Trajano, interview with the authors, São Paulo, March 12, 2009.

24 The difference we mentioned between stiff and flexible companies mirrors the classic types of organizations, respectively bureaucratic and organic. On the origins of these two structures, see Gareth Morgan's thorough *Images of Organization* (1997) and Jay R. Galbraith's *Organization Design* (1977).

25 José Drummond Jr., interview with authors, São Paulo, July 3, 2009.

26 The behavioral aspect of stiffness in organizations (and its impact on the innovation process) is impressively explored by Dorothy Leonard in *Wellsprings of Knowledge* (1995).

27 On the role of control in management, see for instance Drucke (1973, pp. 494–505). On the role of control in innovation, see Foster and Kaplan (2001, pp. 236–60).

28 The analogy between management and a conductor's performance was originally made by Peter F. Drucker (1954, pp. 341–2). There is a critical and relevant view of this analogy in Mintzberg (2009).

29 The specialized literature emphasizes the existence of two distinct types of internal competition. The first can be observed when two or more groups inside a company compete to generate ideas for new offers and technologies. The second occurs when two distinct business units (of the same company) compete for the same clients. Here, we understand internal competition to mean rivalry between individuals or teams, regardless of whether they are in the same or different business units, that is always aimed at generating proactive innovation. We are not referring to issues such as competition between salespeople for rewards and sales rankings. See Birkinshaw (2001).

30 There is an excellent survey on the deleterious effects of internal competition in Pfeffer and Sutton (2000, pp. 177–211).

31 The literature addressing coopetition is vast, but an encompassing view of the subject may be found in Brandenburger and Nalebuff (1996).

7   PROACTIVE BEHAVIOR MANAGEMENT: DEVELOPING PERSONAL PROACTIVENESS

1 The role of proactiveness at the leader and manager level has been highlighted for some time now. See for instance Plunkett and Hale (1982), Martin (1983), Macadan (1991), and Morgan (1992).

2 On the role of leadership in the context of management, see Drucker (1973); on the role of the leader in the construction of strategies, see Besanko, Dranove, and Shanley (1996, pp. 743–57); on the nature of entrepreneurial leadership, see Bennis (1994), Kouses and Posner (1996), and Kotter (1996). A deep view on leadership and its relation to management may be also found in Mintzberg (2009).

3 Our idea of proactive leadership approaches the concept of transformational (or transformative) leadership in that the latter adheres to cultures directed to anticipate the future and provoke change. On the concept of transformational leadership, see the seminal works by Bernard M. Bass: *Leadership and Performance* 1985), *Transformational Leadership* (1998), and with Bruce J. Avolio, *Improving Organizational Effectiveness*

through Transformational Leadership (1994). Specific discussions on transformational leadership and its relation to a proactive orientation to markets, can be found in Carrillat, Jaramillo, and Locander (2004) and in Beugré, Acar, and Braun (2006). There is a critical review of the concept of transformational leadership in Pawar (2003).

4   It is accepted that leaders may be more or less proactive or reactive under certain circumstances and in certain environments (depending on, for instance, the size of the organizations in which they work, their context, and the situation). In this sense, the concept of proactive leadership, as described here, does not claim that managers should avoid any kind of reactive stance, but rather that their actions should show a tendency to anticipate and to take the initiative in managerial decision processes. On this subject, see Larson et al. (1986).

5   Studies have shown a relationship between managers' and leaders' proactiveness and transformational ways of leading. The relationship between the concepts of leadership we have conceived and transformational leadership is based on these findings. See Bateman and Crant (1993), Crant (2000), and Crant and Bateman (2000).

6   Fábio Hering, interview with the authors, São Paulo, November 16, 2011.

7   See Kanter (2009, pp. 256–67).

8   Helio Rotemberg, interview with the authors, Curitiba, June 19, 2009.

9   Our model of attitudes to change considers proactive behavior as a behavior that extrapolates from fixed instructions. In this sense, it is a typical extraordinary behavior: in other words, a behavior that is not formally required by established norms and procedures. Although there can be anticipatory behaviors in the field of tasks (such as when a reactive individual anticipates machine maintenance: that is, anticipatively carries out something in itself is prescribed and expected), we believe true proactiveness takes place when people take the initiative and anticipate change beyond their formal obligations. In this sense, we consider that "extraordinary" actions provide a way of identifying to what extent individuals doing routine work are inclined to act proactively. On the nature, role, or extraordinary role of proactive behaviors, see Crant (2000); Parker, Turner, and Williams (2006), and Grant and Ashford (2008). On the importance of the "extraordinary" role as a competence-differentiating element, see Van Dyne and LePine (1998).

10   Chieko Aoki, interview with the authors, São Paulo, January 28, 2009.

11   The Pygmalion effect is an expression adopted in psychology to designate the influence of expectations on people's behavior. In brief, positive expectations generate positive performance, as when a professor stimulates pupils with positive evaluations of their capacities and they end up responding with satisfactory performances. Negative expectations can generate bad performances. The phenomenon is related, in some instances, to the concept of a self-fulfilling prophecy: that is, that what we expect to happen tends actually to happen. In the sphere of management, the Pygmalion effect refers to the effect of managers' and leaders' positive (or negative) expectations on their subordinates. Pygmalion is a character created by the Roman poet Ovid (43 BC –17-18 AD), in *Metamorphoses* (8 AD). A sculptor, he fell in love with a statue he had created. He pleaded with the goddess of love Aphrodite who, moved by the artist's suffering, changed the statue into a real woman who married Pygmalion and gave birth to a daughter. The myth tells of people's ability to act deliberately and proactively in search of their own realities.

On the Pygmalion effect in the field of management, see the classic work by J. Sterling Livingston, "Pygmalion in management" (1969). See also Eden (1984) and the Wikipedia entries on "Pygmalion effect," "Pygmalion," and "self-fulfilling prophecy."

12   Studies conducted by professors Thomas S. Bateman and Michael J. Crant on proactive behavior are seminal. See for instance Bateman and Crant (1993) and Crant (2000).

13   Crant (2000) analyzes the literature on proactive behavior, and finds different understandings about its nature, definition, and measurement. The author examines four major constructs related to the inclination to act proactively at work (proactive personality, individual initiative, self-efficacy, and ability to command), and concludes that they overlap conceptually, arguing that they share the same vision about the domains of such behavior. He also argues in favor of other individual factors that may impact proactive attitudes, such as the level of involvement with the work and the search for realization. These are factors that we know differ substantially between individuals. Finally, Crant (2000) also counts the role of contextual variables as critical antecedents of proactive behavior because they also ultimately influence a person's decision whether to behave proactively. Thus, the author's theoretical model presupposes the influence of individual and contextual factors on the formation of proactive behavior at an individual level. Although this has not been proved empirically, the depth and reach of the model contribute to the uncovering of themes common to proactive behavior, indicating that findings of different research studies on personal proactiveness in organizations are consistent.

14   Our description is based on literature mentioned in this chapter's notes, observations, and field interviews.

15   Stephen R. Covey gives an informative view of how proactive people deal with their circle of influence in *The Seven Habits of Highly Effective People* (1989).

16   On the identification of personal proactiveness, see Bateman and Crant (1999).

17   The Proactive Personality Scale (PPS) is presented in Bateman and Crant (1993). On methodological validity and application in different contexts, see Crant (2000).

18   A more qualitative and contextual proposition to measuring proactive behaviors may be found in Parker, Turner, and Williams (2006).

19   The illustrative questions are based on Bateman and Crant (1999), and on the approach to initiative at work by Michael Frese and colleagues in "Personal initiative at work: differences between East and West Germany" (1996) (see also Frese and Fay, 2001).

It is worth mentioning that the concepts of a proactive personality and initiative at work, though they have some unique features, converge to a common focus on anticipating opportunities (and potential problems) beyond mere prescribed tasks. In this particular sense, we find both concepts valid in analyses of levels of personal proactiveness (see Parker et al., 2006).

20   On this facet of proactive behavior, see Parker et al. (2006).

21   The sculpture–sculptor analogy is mentioned in Bell and Staw (1989).

22   On the environmental antecedents of proactive behaviors, see Parker et al. (2006), Grant and Ashford (2008), and Crant (2000).

23   Check out Manz and Sims (1987).

24   On the role of leadership on proactive behavior, see Strauss, Griffin, and Rafferty (2009).

25   Luiz Eduardo Falco, interview with the authors, Rio de Janeiro, July 10, 2009.

26   See de Jong and de Ruyter (2004).

27   Alberto Saraiva, interview with the authors, São Paulo, March 9, 2011.

8   BUILDING A PROACTIVE MARKET STRATEGY

1   João Guilherme Brenner, interview with the authors, Curitiba, April 16, 2009.

2   The video clip containing Steve Jobs's speech can be accessed at <www.youtube.com/watch?v=9046oXrm7f8>.

3   Rogério Martins, interview with the authors, São Paulo, November 9, 2009.
4   Interview with José Drummond Jr., published by *Época Negócios*, September 7, 2010. The report mentions the award granted to Whirlpool as Brazil's Most Innovative Company/Best Innovator by the magazine with support of the A. T. Kearney international consultancy.
5   José Drummond, Jr., interview with the authors, São Paulo, July 3, 2009.
6   Mario Sérgio A. Fioretti, interview with the authors, São Paulo, November 9, 2009.
7   Patrícia Garrido, interview with the authors, São Paulo, November 9, 2009.

9   OFFER PROACTIVENESS

1   Gabriel Madway and Alexei Oreskovic (from Reuters, San Francisco), "Novo iPad traz Jobs de volta aos holofotes" (The new iPad brings Jobs back to the stage) (2011).
2   From a description of a beginners' kit bought by George Eastman in November 1877, quoted in Tedlow (2001).
3   A reproduction of this Kodak ad can be found in Aaker (1996).
4   Information concerning TomTom's complementary services from <www.tomtom. com> and from the blog O Mundo das Marcas <www.mundodasmarcas.com.br>.
5   In his famous article "Marketing myopia" (1960), Theodore Levitt warned against the risks of such beliefs. According to him, "there is no guarantee against product obsolescence." In this same article, he points to risks associated with an excessive focus on product and production process to the detriment of focus on customer needs, mentioning examples in the North American automotive industry.
6   The segment formed by the brands H2OH!®, Aquarius Fresh, Guarah, and Schin Viva.
7   All marketing information related to H2OH!® was provided by the marketing division responsible for managing the Pepsico product, and is based on official statistics for the segment collected by the Nielsen Institute, specialized in monitoring sales and consumption data for many different retail product categories.
8   Andréa Álvares, interview with the authors, São Paulo, June 14, 2011.
9   Information on the development of the PageRank system and on Google's business trajectory may be found in Vise and Malseed (2005).
10   The value of the Google brand is US$43.6 billion (July 2011), and it comes fourth in the 2010 "Best Global Brands" ranking issued by consultancy firm Interbrand (www. interbrand.com). Google's reputation index was calculated according to the Reptrak method developed by the Reputation Institute (www.reputationinstitute.com), the same institute that yearly issues *The Global RepTrak 100: The World's Most Reputable Companies*.
11   This phrase appears in Clark and Fujimoto (1991).
12   Clark and Fujimoto (1991) analyze complexity in four types of product along two interpretation lines: the complexity of the product's internal structure and complexity in the user–product interface. "Simple" products are those of little complexity along both lines of interpretation. "Component-guided products" show great complexity in its internal structure and little complexity in user–product interface. An "interface-guided product" reveals little complexity in its internal structure and a greatly complex user–product interface. Finally, "complex products" (such as cars) show great complexity in both these dimensions.
13   All quantitative data on sales volumes of Fiat's cars and competitors were provided by Fiat Brasil's Product Directory and are based on the sector's official statistics.
14   Carlos Eugênio Dutra, interview with the authors, Betim, July 15, 2008.
15   Edson Mazucato, interview with the authors, Betim, February 18, 2009.
16   Phrase taken from <www.fiat.com.br>.

17   C. Belini, interview with the authors, Betim, April 6, 2009.
18   Windson Paz, interview with the authors, Betim, February 18, 2009.

10   INDUSTRY PROACTIVENESS

1   Daniele Madureira (from São Paulo), "Varejo eleva pressão sobre fornecedores" (Retail rises pressure on suppliers) (nd).
2   Figures from Madureira (2011). According to the article, the three giants are Nova Casas Bahia (the result of a merger of the Ponto Frio, Extra Eletro, and Casas Bahia networks) with sales of R$10 billion in 2010 (includes only two months of Casas Bahia's sales); Máquina de Vendas (a merger of the Ricardo Eletro, Insinuante, and City Lar networks), with R$5.7 billion in revenues in 2010; and Magazine Luiza (including the Lojas Maia network) with R$5.7 billion in revenues in the same period.
3   On the classical structural analysis model, see Porter (1980).
4   In *Everybody's Business* (2001), David Grayson and Adrian Hodges indicate four emerging managerial themes imposed by global change forces: ecology and environment, health and well-being, diversity and human rights, and communities.
5   These ambitious goals were established in October 2005 in a speech at the company's headquarters on the subject "Sustainability and leadership in the 21st century". Source: <www.walmartstores.com>.
6   Part of a speech by former vice-chairman Mike Duke, today the company's world CEO, at the "China Sustainability Summit 2008." Source: <www.walmartstores.com>.
7   The retail environmental impact percentages were calculated by the North American consultancy firm Blue Sky.
8   Data and information on Walmart Brasil's sustainability goals and on the "End-to-End Sustainability" project are from "Walmart Brasil: building the supply chain of the future," an executive report related to the 2010 Aberje Award (Prêmio Associação Brasileira de Comunicação Empresarial – Aberje 2010) – Category 02 – Communication of Programs aimed at Corporate Sustainability. Document provided by the company.
9   Additional information on the award and on Corporate Eco Forum may be accessed at <www.corporateecoforum.com>.
10   Maria Luiza Pinto, interview with the authors, São Paulo, December 14, 2010.
11   From material for a "Paths and Challenges" course, conducted by the bank and aimed at disseminating the company's crusade in search of sustainability among several target publics.
12   "Paths and Challenges" material (as above).
13   Fábio Barbosa, interview with the authors, São Paulo, August 13, 2009.
14   Maria Luiza Pinto, interview with the authors, São Paulo, December 14, 2010.
15   Data and information on investments and credit from <www.santander.com.br/sustentabilidade>.
16   The company website <www.santander.com.br/sustentabilidade> gives information on all national and international awards received by the bank.
17   Kanter (2009).
18   Gerstner (2002).
19   Gerstner (2002).
20   Gerstner (2002).
21   Gerstner (2002).
22   The context of the e-business strategy is addressed in a case study on "IBM's on demand business strategy," prepared by Samuel Tsang under supervision of Ali F. Farhoomand.

It is registered under the code HKU424 at the Asia Case Research Centre, University of Hong Kong.

23 Information on purchase and sale of companies from Tsang (see note 22).

24 Definition from IBM's "On demand executive guide," prepared by the company to disseminate the new concept and its applications to business management.

25 From IBM's "On demand executive guide" (see note 24).

26 Information on the application of resources in many different areas of management and on the purchase of PricewaterhouseCoopers Consulting from IBM's "On demand executive guide" (see note 24).

27 One of IBM's values is precisely this one: "Innovation that creates differentials for IBM and for the world."

28 The expression "a more instrumented, interconnected and smarter world" was first used by Sam Palmisano in a speech to the Council on Foreign Relations, November 6, 2008. This event is considered as the kick- off for the Smarter Planet strategy.

29 Ricardo Pelegrini, interview with the authors, São Paulo, April 14, 2009.

30 Naveen Lamba's statement from the "Special Blogger Series" session "Thoughts on a Smarter Planet," conducted in partnership with IBM specialists and accessible at <www.wired.com.br>.

31 Information from <www.tetrapak.com/br/produtos_e_servicos/embalagens_assepti cas/>.

32 The technical information on pasteurization and ultrapasteurization processes comes from Meireles and Alves (no date).

33 Market share information provided by Tetra Pak.

34 Paulo Nigro, interview with the authors, São Paulo, June 21, 2010.

35 Data on the growth of the Brazilian market is from Tetra Pak's website, <www.tetrapak. com.br>.

36 Mattar's statement was mentioned by Seminovos Localiza Division director Marco Antônio Guimarães, during an interview with the authors, Belo Horizonte, July 7, 2009.

37 Mattar's statement was mentioned in the Guimarães interview (see note 36).

38 Marco Antônio Guimarães, interview with the authors, Belo Horizonte, July 7, 2009.

39 Data provided by the company's Relationship with Investors division.

40 Data related to car volumes, growth rates, and other information was provided by the company's Relationship with Investors division.

41 Salim Mattar, interview with the authors, Belo Horizonte, August 12, 2009.

11 CUSTOMER PROACTIVENESS

1 Quoted by Leo Huberman in *Man's Worldly Goods* (2006). The work was originally published in 1930 and tries to explain history through the study of economic theory, and simultaneously explain economics through the study of history.

2 Definition from Solomon (2002). The author also refers to the definition of "marketing" proposed by the American Marketing Association in 2000. Another academic definition for consumer behavior can be found in Blackwell, Miniard, and Engel (2000): "activities people perform when consuming and disposing of products and services."

3 The "knowledge economy" concept expresses the idea that productive processes, as well as the distribution of goods and services, are more and more supported by activities based on knowledge. In the last three decades, following the evolution of

information technologies, the concept of the knowledge economy has become firmly established, and many authors also use expressions such as "the information society" or "networked society and economy" to designate the phenomenon.

4   This is an abridged version of an article originally published in *DOM Magazine* (Araújo and Gava, 2010).

5   Gladwell (2002, p. 7).

6   Gladwell (2002, p. 4).

7   Gladwell (2002, p. 5).

8   <www.redbull.com>, and Wikipedia, "Red Bull."

9   There is further information on buzz-marketing and viral-marketing practices in Kotler and Keller (2006, pp. 547–9).

10   The expression "digital revolution" is mentioned and analyzed by Saul Berman and Ragna Bell (nd).

11   For further information on the "era of total access" and its impact on marketing strategies see McKenna (2002).

12   The expression is used by McKenna (2002).

13   Many authors are paying attention to the subject of the customer experience, importantly contributing to the study and deep understanding of the relations between companies and their customers, and taking into account the contact interfaces between the parties in the process of delivering products and services. Among them we shall mention Carbone (2004), Schmitt (2003), Pine and Gilmore (1999), and Shaw and Ivens (2002).

14   An encompassing conceptual approach to the value co-creation process together with several practical examples involving different companies may be found in Ramaswamy and Gouillart (2010).

15   Data on e-commerce in Brazilian market is from "WebShoppers," 23rd edition, research conducted by e-Bit, supported by the Câmara Brasileira de Comércio Eletrônico (Brazilian Electronic Commerce Chamber).

16   Statistics issued by Ibravin (Instituto Brasileiro do Vinho, the Brazilian wine institute) indicate that, in the 2004–10 period, wine imports to Brazil doubled, jumping from 35.22 million liters to 70.74 million liters, in the category identified as NCM 22042100 – Other wines, grape must, Interr. Ferm. Alcohol, Containers <=2L.

17   An encompassing conceptual approach to the reduction of physical and psychological efforts in purchase processes may be found in Schwartz (2004). Contrary to common sense, the author argues that consumers with too many options need to make harder efforts during the purchase processes, with increased discomfort and difficulties.

18   Information on the growth of the Brazilian yogurt market from 1995 and on Danone's negative results is from Costa (2007).

19   References to Activia's functional properties are detailed on <www.acitiviadanone.com.br>, which says:

> DanRegularis is bífidobacterium animalis DN173010, an organism that produces Activia's probiotic effect, because it is able to travel through the gastrointestinal tract and reach the intestine in large amounts and in active form. Once there, it develops beneficial actions that help the intestinal ecosystem. This is not true for most other "live" bacteria cultures, which end up destroyed by gastric acids, differentiating Activia from other ordinary yogurts.

20   Gustavo Valle, interview with the authors, São Paulo, November 27, 2008.

21   Leonardo Lima, interview with the authors, São Paulo, November 27, 2008.

22   Data from Costa (2007).

23 Cesar Tavares, interview with the authors, São Paulo, December 13, 2010.
24 Mariano Lozano, interview with the authors, São Paulo, July 18, 2011.
25 Brigatto (2009b).
26 Quoted in Brigatto (2009b).
27 Romeo Busarello, interview with the authors, São Paulo, December 14, 2010.
28 Busarello interview, as note 27.
29 Busarello interview, as note 27.
30 All information for Table 11.2 is either from the Busarello interview, as note 27, or from <www.tecnisa.com.br>.
31 Carlos Alberto Julio, interview with the authors, São Paulo, February 4, 2009.
32 From <www.tecnisa.com.br>.
33 Meyer Joseph Nigri, interview with the authors, São Paulo, July 6, 2011.

12 CONCLUSION

1   The case is mentioned in Markides (2008, p. 136), and illustrates how often moment-zero pioneers are not those who make the most profit from the changes they created.

2   Being a market pioneer means, in brief, the entry of a company into a new market (or the unusual exploration of an existing market) before most competitors do so, typically through the creation of a new product or service. The pioneer's advantage is therefore a consequence of being able to explore, unaccompanied, a still virgin market. (It is believed that this will bring companies substantial advantages related to market share, costs of changes for consumers, reputation and brand loyalty, as well as operational benefits in connection with the learning curve, acquisition of assets and technological resources, labor force, and access to distribution channels.) Pioneers – or first movers – arrive at a market oasis before competitors, and therefore drink clean water (although we cannot neglect the side-effects that come with any pioneer strategy, especially lower-cost imitations and knowledge provided to competitors, which immediately start to work to avoid the mistakes made by the pioneer). On the advantages to pioneers, see two articles by Marvin B. Lieberman and David B. Montgomery, "First-mover advantages" (1988) and "First-mover (dis)advantages: retrospective and link with the resource-based view" (1998).

3   Although some people say that a pioneer's advantage can be gained in several ways, the specialized literature shows that the strategy is always sharply focused on products and services. See for instance Golder and Tellis (1993) and Kerin, Varadarajan, and Peterson (1992).

4   See for instance Linder, Jarvenpaa, and Davenport (2003).

5   The expression is used by Lieberman and Montgomery (1988, 1998).

6   The importance of changing the mindset on the future – seeing it as the effective result of actions taken in the present instead of as something to be predicted – was highlighted in the classic work of Russell Ackoff, *Creating the Corporate Future* (1981). For him, this open attitude to the future is an essential condition for companies trying to be more proactive in their strategies.

7   For a deeper view on strategic sustainability and its precepts, see Besanko et al. (1996, pp. 535–73).

8   Mentioned by David Dranove and Sonia Marciano (2005, p. 170). Although patents are not defense mechanisms absolutely immune to competitors' attacks (there will always be the possibility, for instance, that a patent holder decides to accept an acquisition offer made by a competitor), this illustrates how protection strategies may prolong the sustainability of a created moment zero, offering greater possibilities of gain to a company.

9   On the effects of network externalities, see Dranove and Marciano (2005, pp. 194–8).

10   The notion that capacities developed by a company are a difficult-to-imitate asset – and therefore a source of protection for the sustainability of competitive advantages – may be found in the works of Jay B. Barney (1986) and Reed and De Fillippi (1990).

APPENDIX

1   The Promark scale and check-up on capacities are based on the exploratory research we conducted: a detailed literature review and in-depth interviews with 55 top management executives from different organizations. We followed procedures found in the literature to prepare measurement scales and to check their validity. We then tested the questionnaire resulting from this exploratory phase and validated the model using confirmatory factorial analysis. Tests of unidimensionality, reliability (internal consistency), and construct validity of the scales developed indicated that the measurements were valid and reliable, ensuring the statistical validity of our scales. On the methodological validity of these procedures, see for instance the works of Churchill (1979, 1995) and DeVellis (2003).

References

Aaker, David A. (1996) *Building Strong Brands*, New York: Free Press.

Abell, Derek F. (1999) "Competing today while preparing for tomorrow," *Sloan Management Review*, Vol. 40, No. 3 (Spring), pp. 74–81.

Ackoff, Russell L. (1981) *Creating the Corporate Future*, New York: Wiley.

Apgar, David (2006) *Risk Intelligence: Learning to manage what we don't know*, Boston, Mass.: Harvard Business Review Press.

Araújo, Leonardo and Gava, Rogério (2010) "Proatividade de mercado e mídias sociais: promovendo antecipações relevantes para criar envolvimento" (Market proactiveness and social media: promoting relevant anticipations to create involvement), *DOM Magazine*, No. 13 (December), pp. 44–9.

Astley, W. Graham and Van de Ven, Andrew H. (1983) "Central perspectives and debates in organization theory," *Administrative Science Quarterly*, Vol. 28, pp. 245–73.

Banker, Rajiv D., Potter, Gordon, and Srinivasan, Dhinu (2000) "An empirical investigation of an incentive plan that includes nonfinancial performance measures," *Accounting Review*, Vol. 75, pp. 65–92.

Barney, Jay B. (1986) "Organizational culture: can it be a source of sustained competitive advantage?" *Academy of Management Review*, Vol. 11, No. 3, pp. 656–65.

Bass, Bernard M. (1985) *Leadership and Performance*, New York: Free Press.

Bass, Bernard M. (1998) Transformational Leadership: Industrial, military, and educational impact, Mahwah, N.J.: Erlbaum.

Bass, Bernard M. and Avolio, Bruce J. (eds.) (1994) *Improving Organizational Effectiveness through Transformational Leadership*, Thousand Oaks, Calif.: Sage.

Bateman, Thomas S. and Crant, Michael J. (1993) "The proactive component of organizational behavior: a measure and correlates," *Journal of Organizational Behavior*, Vol. 14, No. 2, available at <http://onlinelibrary.wiley.com/doi/10.1002/job.4030140202/abstract> (accessed date?).

Bateman, Thomas S. and Crant, Michael J. (1999) "Proactive behavior: meaning, impact, recommendations," *Business Horizons*, Vol. 42, No. 3, pp. 63–70.

Bell, Nancy E. and Staw, Barry N. (1989) "People as sculptors versus sculpture: the roles of personality and personal control in organizations," *Classic Readings in Organizational Behavior*, Vol. 33, pp. 365–79.

Bennis, Warren (1994) *On Becoming a Leader,* New York: Perseus.

Berman, Saul and Bell, Ragna (nd) "Digital transformation: creating new business models where digital meets physical," IBM Global Business Services Executive Report, IBM Institute for Business Value.

Besanko, David, Dranove, David, and Shanley, Mark (1996) *The Economics of Strategy*, New York: Wiley.

Beugré, Constant D., Acar, William and Braun, William (2006) "Transformational leadership in organizations: an environment-induced model," *International Journal of Manpower*, Vol. 27, No. 1, p. 52–62.

Birkinshaw, Julian (2001) "Strategies for managing internal competition," *California Management Review*, Vol. 44, No. 1, pp. 21–38.

Birkinshaw, Julian and Gibson, Cristina (2004) "Building ambidexterity into an organization," *Sloan Management Review*, Vol. 45, pp. 47–55.

Blackwell, Roger D., Miniard, Paul W., and Engel, James F. (2000) *Consumer Behavior*, place: South-Western College Publishing.

Brandenburger, Adam M. and Nalebuff, Barry J. (1996) *Co-Opetition*, New York: Broadway Books.

Brigatto, Gustavo (2009a) "Na era digital, Kodak busca ajustar o foco," *Valor Econômico*, Companies section, p. B3, August 3.

Brigatto, Gustavo (2009b) "Consumidor compra até apartamento por meio do Twitter" (Consumers buy even apartments through Twitter), *Valor Econômico*, 'Empresas' section, June 1.

Campos, Arnaldo de (2009) *Byron e Keats: Entreversos*, Campinas, SP: Unicamp.

Carbone, Lewis P. (2004) *Clued In: How to keep customers coming back again and again*, Upper Saddle River, N.J.: Prentice Hall.

Carpenter, Gregory S., Glazer, Rashi, and Nakamoto, Kent (1997) *Readings on Market-Driving Strategies: Towards a new theory of competitive advantage*, Reading, Mass.: Addison-Wesley.

Carpenter, Gregory S. and Nakamoto, Kent (1989) "Consumer preference formation and the pioneering advantage," *Journal of Marketing Research*, Vol. 26, No. 3, pp. 285–98.

Carrillat, François A., Jaramillo, Fernando, and Locander, William B. (2004) "Market-driving organizations: a framework," *Academy of Marketing Science Review*, No. 5, pp. 1–14.

Carson, Iain and Vaitheeswaran, Vijay V. (2007) *Zoom: The global race to fuel the car of the future*, New York: Twelve.

Chandy, Rajesh K. and Tellis, Gerard J. (1998) "Organizing for radical product innovation: the overlooked role of willingness to cannibalize," *Journal of Marketing Research*, Vol. 35, pp. 474–87.

Charan, Ram and Colvin, Geoffrey (1999) "Why CEOs fail, it's rarely for lack of smarts or vision. most unsuccessful CEOs stumble because of one simple, fatal shortcoming," *Fortune*, July 21 <http://money.cnn.com/magazines/fortune/fortune_archive/1999/06/21/261696/index.htm> (accessed September 19, 2011).

Christensen, Clayton M. (1997) *The Innovator's Dilemma: When new technologies cause great firms to fail*, Boston, Mass.: Harvard Business School Press.

Churchill, Gilbert A., Jr. (1979) "A paradigm for developing better measures of marketing constructs," *Journal of Marketing Research*, Vol. 16, No. 1, pp. 64–73.

Churchill, Gilbert A., Jr. (1995) *Marketing Research: Methodological foundations,* Orlando, Fla.: Dryden Press.

Clark, Kim B. and Fujimoto, Takahiro (1991) *Product Development Performance: Strategy, organization and management in the world auto industry*, Boston Mass.: Harvard Business School Press.

Comte-Sponville, André (2000).*Le Bonheur, Désespérément*, Paris: Éditions Pleins Feux.

Costa, Melina (2007) "As bactérias salvaram a Danone" (Bacteria saved Danone), *Exame Magazine*, November 29.

Courtney, Hugh (2001) 20|20 *Foresight: Crafting strategy in an uncertain world*, Boston, Mass.: Harvard Business School Press.

Covey, Stephen R. (1989) *The Seven Habits of Highly Effective People*, New York: Simon & Schuster.

Crant, Michael J. (2000) "Proactive behavior in organizations," *Journal of Management,* Vol. 26, No. 3, pp. 435–462.

Crant, Michael J. and Bateman, Thomas S. (2000) "Charismatic leadership viewed from above: the impact of proactive personality," *Journal of Organizational Behavior,* Vol. 21, No. 1, pp. 63–75.

Cravens, David W., Piercy, Nigel F., and Low, George S. (2002) "The innovation challenges of proactive cannibalisation and discontinuous technology," *European Business Review,* Vol. 14, No. 4, pp. 257–67.

Cravens, David W., Piercy, Nigel F., and Prentice, Ashley (2000) "Developing market-driven product strategies," *Journal of Product and Brand Management,* Vol. 9, No. 6, pp. 369–88.

Dacko, Scott G. (2008) *The Advanced Dictionary of Marketing: Putting theory to use,* Oxford: Oxford University Press.

Damanpour, Fariborz (1991) "Organizational innovation: a meta-analysis of effects of determinants and moderators," *Academy of Management Journal,* Vol. 34, No. 3, pp. 555–90.

Damanpour, Fariborz (1996) "Bureaucracy and innovation revisited: effects of contingent factors, industrial sectors and innovation characteristics," *Journal of High Technology Management Research,* Vol. 7, No. 2, 149–73.

Damodaran, Aswath (2008). *Strategic Risk Taking: A framework for management,* Upper Saddle River, N.J.: Wharton School Publishing.

Davila, Tony, Epstein, Marc J., and Shelton, Robert (2006) *Making Innovation Work: How to manage it, measure it and profit from it,* Upper Saddle River, N.J.: Wharton School Publishing.

Day, George S. (1994) "The capabilities of market-driven organizations," *Journal of Marketing,* Vol. 58, No. 4 (October), pp. 37–52.

Day, George S. and Schoemaker, Paul H. (2006) *Peripheral Vision: Detecting the weak signals that will make or break your company,* Boston, Mass.: Harvard Business School Press.

De Jong, Ad and de Ruyter, Ko (2004) "Adaptive versus proactive behavior in service recovery: the role of self-managing teams," *Decision Sciences,* Vol. 35, No. 3, pp. 457–91.

Deshpandé, Rohit and Webster, Frederick E. Jr. (1989) "Organizational culture and marketing: defining the research agenda," *Journal of Marketing,* Vol. 53, No. 1, pp. 3–15.

DeVellis, Robert F. (2003) *Scale Development: Theory and applications,* Thousand Oaks, Calif.: Sage.

Diegues, Sônia and Bruno, Léo F. C. (2009) *Eggon João da Silva: Idéias e Caminhos, a Trajetória de um dos Fundadores da WEG* (Eggon João da Silva: Ideas and paths, the trajectory of WEG's founder), Rio de Janeiro: Elsevier.

Dodd, Dominic and Favaro, Ken (2007) *The Three Tensions: Winning the struggle to perform without compromise,* Hoboken, N.J.: Jossey-Bass.

Dranove, David and Marciano, Sonia (2005) *Kellogg on Strategy: Concepts, tools and frameworks for practitioners,* Hoboken, N.J.: Wiley.

Drucker, Peter F. (1954) *The Practice of Management,* New York: Harper.

Drucker, Peter F. (1973) *Management: Tasks, responsibilities, practices,* New York: Harper & Row.

Duncan, Robert B. (1972) "Characteristics of organizational environments and perceived environmental uncertainty," *Administrative Science Quarterly,* Vol. 17, pp. 313–27.

Eden, Dov (1984) "Self-fulfilling prophecy as a management tool: harnessing Pygmalion," *Academy of Management Review,* Vol. 9, pp. 64–73.

Eisenhardt, Kathleen M. (1989) "Agency theory: an assessment and review," *Academy of Management Review,* Vol. 14, No. 1, pp. 57–74.

Farson, Richard and Keyes, Ralph (2002) *Whoever Makes the Most Mistakes Wins: The paradox of innovation,* New York: Free Press.

Foster, Richard and Kaplan, Sarah (2001) *Creative Destruction: Why companies that are built to last underperform the market – and how to successfully transform them,* New York: Currency Doubleday.

Frese, Michael and Fay, Doris (2001) "Personal initiative: an active performance concept for work in the 21st century," *Research in Organizational Behavior,* Vol. 23, pp. 133–88.

Frese, Michael, Kring, Wolfgang, Soose, Andrea, and Zempel, Jeannette (1996) "Personal initiative at work: differences between East and West Germany," *Academy of Management Journal,* Vol. 39, No. 1, pp. 37–63.

Galbraith, Jay R. (1977) *Organization Design,* Reading, Mass.: Addison-Wesley.

Garcia, Rosanna and Calantone, Roger (2002) "A critical look at technological innovation typology and innovativeness terminology: a literature review," *Journal of Product Innovation Management,* Vol. 19, pp. 110–32.

Gatignon, Hubert, Tushman, Michael L., Smith, Wendy, and Anderson, Philip (2002) "A structural approach to assessing innovation: construct development of innovation locus, type and characteristics," *Management Science,* Vol. 48, No. 9 (Sept.), pp. 1103–22.

Gerstner, Louis V. Jr. (2002) *Who Says Elephants Can't Dance?* New York: Harper Collins.

Gibson, Cristina B. and Birkinshaw, Julian (2004) "The antecedents, consequences, and mediating role of organizational ambidexterity," *Academy of Management Journal,* Vol. 47, pp. 209–26.

Gladwell, Malcolm (2002) *The Tipping Point,* USA: Back Bay Books.

Godet, Michel (2006) *Creating Futures: Scenario planning as a strategic management tool,* Paris: Economica.

Golder, Peter N. and Tellis, Gerard J. (1993) "Pioneer advantage: marketing logic or marketing legend?" *Journal of Marketing Research,* Vol. 30, No. 2, pp. 158–70.

Grant, Adam M. and Ashford, Susan J. (2008) "The dynamics of proactivity at work," *Research in Organizational Behavior,* Vol. 28, pp. 3–34.

Grayson, David and Hodges, Adrian (2001) *Everybody's Business: Managing risks and opportunities in today's global society,* London: Dorling Kindersley.

Guglielmo, Connie (2010) "Apple encerra mistério e revela o iPad," *Valor Econômico,* January 28, Empresas e Tecnologia Section, p. B2 (translated from an original published by Bloomberg, San Francisco, January 27, 2010).

Haire, Meaghan (2009) "A brief history of the Walkman," *Time,* July 1 <www.time.com/time/nation/article/0,8599,1907884,00.html> (accessed date?).

Hamel, Gary (1996) "Strategy as revolution," *Harvard Business Review,* Vol. 74, pp. 69–82.

Hamel, Gary and Prahalad, C. K. (1994) *Competing for the Future,* Boston, Mass.: Harvard Business School Press (quotes from 1996 paperback edn).

Harper, Stephen C. (2000) "Timing: the bedrock of anticipatory management," *Business Horizons* (January–February), pp. 75–83.

Hills, Stacey Barlow and Sarin, Shikhar (2003) "From market-driven to market driving: an alternate paradigm for marketing in high technology industries," *Journal of Marketing Theory and Practice,* Vol. 11, No. 3, pp. 13–24.

Holton, Glyn A. (2004) "Defining risk," *Financial Analysts Journal,* Vol. 60, No. 6, pp. 19–25.

Horan, Richard D., Bulte, Erwin, and Shogren, Jason F. (2005) "How trade saved humanity from biological exclusion: an economic theory of Neanderthal extinction," *Journal of Economic Behavior and Organization,* Vol. 58, pp. 1–29.

Huberman, Leo (2006) *Man's Worldly Goods: The history of the wealth of nations,* London: Hesperides Press.

Hughes, Richard L. and Beatty, Katherine Colarelli (2005) *Becoming a Strategic Leader: Your role in your organization's enduring success*, San Francisco, Calif.: Jossey-Bass.

Jaworski, Bernard J., Kohli, Ajay K., and Sahay, Arvind (2000) "Market driven versus driving markets," *Journal of the Academy of Marketing Science*, Vol. 28, No. 1 (Winter), pp. 45–54.

Johannessen, Jon-Arild, Olaisen, Johan, and Olsen, Bjorn (1999) "Managing and organizing innovation at the knowledge economy," *European Journal of Innovation Management*, Vol. 2, No. 3, pp. 116–28.

Kahneman, Daniel and Lovallo, Dan (1993) "Timid choices and bold forecasts: a cognitive perspective in risk taking," *Management Science*, Vol. 39, No.1, pp. 17–31.

Kahneman, Daniel and Tversky, Amos (1979) "Prospect theory: an analysis of decision under risk," *Econometrica*, Vol. 47, No. 2, pp. 263–91.

Kahney, Leander (2008) *Inside Steve's Brain*, New York: Portfolio.

Kanter, Rosabeth Moss (2009) *Supercorp: How vanguard companies create innovation, profits, growth, and social good*, New York: Crown Business.

Kaplan, Robert S. and Norton, David P. (1992) "The balanced scorecard: measures that drive performance," *Harvard Business Review* (January–February), pp. 71–9.

Kaplan, Robert S. and Norton, David P. (1993) "Putting the balanced scorecard to work," *Harvard Business Review* (September–October), pp. 143–52.

Kaplan, Robert S. and Norton, David P. (1996) "Using the balanced scorecard as a strategic management system," *Harvard Business Review* (Jan.–Feb.), pp. 75–85.

Kelley, Tom (2000) *The Art of Innovation: Lessons in creativity from IDEO, America's leading design firm*, New York: Doubleday.

Kerin, Roger A., Varadarajan, P. Rajan, and Peterson, Robert A. (1992) "First-mover advantage: a synthesis, conceptual framework, and research propositions," *Journal of Marketing*, Vol. 56, No.4, pp. 33–52.

Kim, Chan and Mauborgne, Renée (1999) "Creating new market space," *Harvard Business Review* (Jan.–Feb.), pp. 83–93.

Kim, Chan and Mauborgne, Renée (2005) *Blue Ocean Strategy: How to create uncontested market space and make the competition irrelevant*, Boston, Mass.: Harvard Business School Press.

Klemp, Nathaniel, McDermott, Ray, Raley, Jason, Thibeault, Matthew, Powell, Kimberly, and Levitin, Daniel J. (2008) "Plans, takes, and mis-takes," *Critical Social Studies*, No. 1 <http://ojs.statsbiblioteket.dk/index.php/outlines/article/viewFile/1964/1754> (accessed on May 12, 2011).

Kohli, Ajay K. and Jaworski, Bernard J. (1990) "Market orientation: the construct, research propositions, and managerial implications," *Journal of Marketing*, Vol. 54, No. 2 (April), pp. 1–18.

Kotler, Philip and Keller, Kevin Lane (2006) *Marketing Management*, Upper Saddle River, N.J.: Pearson Prentice Hall.

Kotter, John P. (1996) *Leading Change*, Boston. Mass.: Harvard Business School Press.

Kouses, James M. and Posner, Barry Z. (1996) *The Leadership Challenge: How to keep getting extraordinary things done in organizations*, Hoboken, N.J.: Jossey-Bass.

Kumar, Nirmalya (2004) *Marketing as Strategy: Understanding the CEO's agenda for driving growth and innovation*, Boston, Mass.: Harvard Business School Press.

Kumar, Nirmalya, Scheer, Lisa, and Kotler, Philip (2000) "From market driven to market driving," *European Management Journal*, Vol. 18, No. 2 (April), pp. 129–41.

Kyriakopoulos, Kyriakos and Moormanb, Christine (2004) "Tradeoffs in marketing exploitation and exploration strategies: the overlooked role of market orientation," *International Journal of Research in Marketing*, Vol. 21, pp. 219–40.

Larson, Lars L., Busson, Robert S., Vicars, William, and Jauch, Lawrence (1986) "Proactive versus reactive manager: is the dichotomy realistic?" *Journal of Management Studies*, Vol. 23, No. 4, pp. 385-400.

Leakey, Richard E. (1981) *The Making of Mankind*, New York: E.P. Dutton.

Leonard, Dorothy (1995) *Wellsprings of Knowledge: Building and sustaining the sources of innovation*, Boston Mass.: Harvard Business School Press.

Leonard, Dorothy and Rayport, Jeffrey F. (1997) "Spark innovation through empathic design," *Harvard Business Review* (Nov./Dec.), pp. 102–13.

Levitt, Theodore (1960) "Marketing myopia," *Harvard Business Review*, Vol. 38, pp. 24–47.

Lichtenstein, Sarah, Fischhoff, Barusch, and Phillips, Lawrence D. (1982) 'Calibration of probabilities: the state of the art to 1980,' pp. 306–34 in Daniel Kahneman, Paul Slovic, and Amos Tversky (eds.), *Judgment Under Uncertainty: Heuristics and biases*, Cambridge: Cambridge University Press.

Lieberman, Marvin B. and Montgomery, David B. (1988) "First-mover advantages," *Strategic Management Journal*, Special Issue 9 (Summer), pp. 41–58.

Lieberman, Marvin B. and Montgomery, David B. (1998) "First-mover (dis)advantages: retrospective and link with the resource-based view," *Strategic Management Journal*, No. 19, pp. 1111–25.

Linder, Jane C., Jarvenpaa, Sirkka L., and Davenport, Thomas H. (2003) "Toward an innovation sourcing strategy," *MIT Sloan Management Review*, Vol. 44, No. 4 (Summer), pp. 43–9.

Livingston, J. Sterling (1969) "Pygmalion in management," *Harvard Business Review*, Vol. 47, pp. 81–9.

Luo, Yadong (2004) "Building a strong foothold in an emerging market: a link between resource commitment and environment conditions," *Journal of Management Studies*, Vol. 41, No. 5, pp. 749–73.

Macadan, Millard N. (1991) "Proactive leadership," *Executive Excellence*, Vol. 8, No. 4, p. 16.

Madureira, Daniele (2011) "Varejo eleva pressão sobre fornecedores" (Retail rises pressure on suppliers), *Valor Econômico*, May 9.

Madway, Gabriel and Oreskovic, Alexei (2011) "Novo iPad traz Jobs de volta aos holofotes" (The new iPad brings Jobs back to the stage), *Jornal Valor Econômico*, March 3.

Malone, John (1997) *Predicting the Future: From Jules Verne to Bill Gates*, New York: M. Evans.

Manz, Charles C. and Sims, Henry P.Jr., (1987) "Leading workers to lead themselves: the external leadership of self-managing work teams," *Administrative Science Quarterly*, Vol. 32, pp. 106–28.

March, James G. (1991) "Exploration and exploitation in organizational learning," *Organizational Science*, Vol. 2 (Feb.), pp. 71–87.

Markides, Constantinos (2008) *Game-Changing Strategies: How to create new market space in established industries by breaking the rules*, San Francisco, Calif.: Wiley.

Markides, Constantinos and Charitou, Constantinos D. (2004) "Competing with dual business models: a contingency approach," *Academy of Management Executive*, Vol. 18, No. 3, pp. 22–36.

Martin, A. P. (1983) *Think Proactive: New insights into decision-making*, Ottawa: PDI Press.

McKenna, Regis (2002) *Total Access*, Boston Mass.: Harvard Business School Press.

Meireles, Almir José and Rodrigues Alves, Daniela (undated) "Importância do Leite Longa Vida para o Desenvolvimento do Mercado Brasileiro de Leite" (The importance of long-life milk to the development of the Brazilian milk market).

Miles, Raymond E. and Snow, Charles C. ([1978] 2003) *Organizational Strategy, Structure and Process*, Stanford, Calif.: Stanford University Press.

Miller, Danny and Friesen, Peter H. (1978) "Archetypes of strategy formulation," *Management Science*, Vol. 29, No. 4, pp. 921–33.

Mintzberg, Henry (1994) *The Rise and Fall of Strategic Planning*, New York Free Press.

Mintzberg, Henry (2009) *Managing*, San Francisco, Calif.: Berrett-Koehler.

Morgan, Gareth (1992) "Proactive management," pp. 24–37 in David Mercer (ed.), *Managing the External Environment: A strategic perspective*, London: Sage.

Morgan, Gareth (1997) *Images of Organization*, Thousand Oaks, Calif.: Sage.

Narver, John C. and Slater, Stanley F. (1990) "The effect of a market orientation on business profitability," *Journal of Marketing*, Vol. 54, No. 4 (Oct.), pp. 20–3.

Narver, John C., Slater, Stanley F., and MacLachlan, Douglas L. (2004) "Responsive and proactive market orientation and new-product success," *Journal of Product Innovation Management*, Vol. 21, pp. 334–47.

O'Connor, Gina Colarelli and Veryzer, Robert W. (2001) "The nature of market visioning for technology-based radical innovation," *Journal of Product Innovation Management*, Vol. 18, pp. 231–46.

O'Reilly, Charles A. III and Tushman, Michel L. (2004) "The ambidextrous organization," *Harvard Business Review*, Vol. 82, pp. 74–82.

Palmer, Timothy B. and Wiseman, Robert M. (1999) "Decoupling risk taking from income stream uncertainty: a holistic model of risk," *Strategic Management Journal*, Vol. 20, No. 11, pp. 1037–62.

Parker, Sharon K., Turner, Nick, and Williams, Helen M. (2006) "Modeling the antecedents of proactive behavior at work," *Journal of Applied Psychology*, Vol. 91, No. 3, pp. 636–52.

Pawar, Badrinarayan S. (2003) "Central conceptual issues in transformational leadership research," *Leadership and Organization Development Journal*, Vol. 24, No. 7/8, pp. 397–406.

Pfeffer, Jeffrey and Sutton, Robert I. (2000) *The Knowing–Doing Gap: How smart companies turn knowledge into action*, Boston, Mass.: Harvard Business School Press.

Pine, B. Joseph II and Gilmore, James H. (1999) *The Experience Economy: Work is theatre and every business a stage*, Boston, Mass.: Harvard Business School Press.

Plunkett, Lorne and Hale, Guy (1982) *The Proactive Manager: The complete book of problem solving and decision making*, New York: John Wiley.

Polonski, Michael Jay, Suchard, Hazel T. and Scott, Don R. (1999) "The incorporation of an interactive external environment: an extended model of marketing relationships," *Journal of Strategic Marketing*, Vol. 7, pp. 41–55.

Porter, Michael (1980) *Competitive Strategy: Techniques for analyzing industries and competitors*, New York: Free Press.

Prahalad, C. K. and Ramaswamy, Venkat (2004) "Co-creation experiences: the next practice in value creation," *Journal of Interactive Marketing*, Vol. 18, No. 3 (Summer), pp. 5–14.

Ralston, Bill and Wilson, Ian (2006) *The Scenario-Planning Handbook: A practioner's guide to developing and using scenarios to direct strategy in today's uncertain times*, Mason, Ohio: Thomson South-Western.

Ramaswamy, Venkat and Gouillart, Francis (2010) *The Power of Co-Creation*, New York: Free Press.

Reed, Richard and De Fillippi, Robert J. (1990) "Causal ambiguity, barriers to imitation, and sustainable competitive advantage," *Academy of Management Review*, Vol. 15, No. 1, pp. 88–102.

Ringland, Gill and Young, Laurie (eds.) (2006) *Scenarios in Marketing: From vision to decision*, Chichester: Wiley.

Rogers, Everett M. (1962/1995) *Diffusion of Innovations*, 1st/4th edn, New York: Free Press.

Rosa, João Guimarães (1967) *Grande Sertão: Veredas* (The Devil to Pay in the Backlands), São Paulo: José Olympio Editora.

Rosa, João Luiz (2010) "Creator of the USB flash drive (aka pen drive) tries to repeat success in the cell phone arena," *Valor Econômico*, November 12–15, Section Companies B3 – Technology & Communications.

Royer, Paul S. (2002) *Project Risk Management: A proactive approach*, Vienna, Va.: Management Concepts.

Sandberg, Birgitta (2008) *Managing and Marketing Radical Innovations: Marketing new technology*, Abingdon: Routledge.

Schein, Edgar (1992) *Organizational Culture and Leadership*, 2nd edn, San Francisco, Calif.: Jossey-Bass.

Schindehutte, Minet, Morris, Michael H., and Kocak, Akin (2008) "Understanding market-driving behavior: the role of entrepreneurship," *Journal of Small Business Management*, Vol. 46, No. 1, pp. 4–26.

Schmitt, Bernard H. (2003) *Customer Experience Management: A revolutionary approach to connecting with your customers*, San Francisco, Calif.: Wiley.

Schoemaker, Paul J. H. (2002) *Profiting from Uncertainty: Strategies for succeeding no matter what the future brings*, New York: Free Press.

Schwartz, Barry (2004) *The Paradox of Choice: Why more is less*, New York: HarperCollins.

Schwartz, Peter (1996) *The Art of the Long View*, New York: Currency Doubleday.

Shaw, Colin and Ivens, John (2002) *Building Great Customer Experiences*, London: Palgrave Macmillan.

Sloane, Paul (2006) *The Leader's Guide to Lateral Thinking Skills: Unlocking the creativity and innovation in you and your team*, London and Philadelphia: Kogan Page.

Solomon, Michael R. (2002) *Consumer Behavior: Buying, having, and being*, Upper Saddle River, N.J.: Prentice-Hall.

Stern, Daniel N. (2004) *The Present Moment in Psychotherapy and Everyday Life*, New York: W. W. Norton.

Strauss, Karoline, Griffin, Mark A., and Rafferty, Alannah E. (2009) "Proactivity directed toward the team and organization: the role of leadership, commitment and role-breadth self-efficacy," *British Journal of Management*, Vol. 20, pp. 279–91.

Taleb, Nassim N. (2007) *The Black Swan: The impact of the highly improbable*, New York: Random House.

Tarnovskaya, Veronika, Elg, Ulf, and Burt, Steve (2008) "The role of corporate branding in a market driving strategy," *International Journal of Retail and Distribution Management*, Vol. 36, No. 11, pp. 941–65.

Tattersall, Ian (1999) *The Last Neanderthal: The rise, success, and mysterious extinction of our closest human relatives*, Boulder, Colo.: Westview Press.

Tedlow, Richard S. (2001) *Giants of Enterprise: Seven business innovators and the empires they built*, New York: Harper Collins.

Thomke, Stefan and Hippel, Eric von (2002) "Customers as innovators: a new way to create value," *Harvard Business Review* (April), pp. 74–81.

Thompson, Victor A. (1965) "Bureaucracy and innovation," *Administrative Science Quarterly*, Vol. 10, pp. 1–20.

Traylor, Mark B. (1986) "Cannibalism in multibrand firms," *Journal of Consumer Marketing*, Vol. 3, No. 2 (Spring), pp. 69–75.

Tsai, Kuen-Hung, Chou, Christine, and Kuo, Jyh-Huei (2007) "The curvilinear relationships between responsive and proactive market orientations and new product performance: a contingent link," *Industrial Marketing Management*, Vol. 37, pp. 884–94.

Tuominem, Matti, Rajala, Arto, and Möller, Kristian (2003) "Market-driving versus market-driven: divergent roles of market orientation in business relationships," *Industrial Marketing Management*, Vol. 33, pp. 207–17.

Tushman, Michael L. and O'Reilly, Charles A. III (1996) "Ambidextrous organizations: managing evolutionary and revolutionary change," *California Management Review*, Vol. 38 (Summer), pp. 8–30.

Tyrrell, Paul (2010) "A plan for unexpected events", *Financial Times*, November, 29 <www.ft.com/cms/s/0/7ba293be-fbe9-11df-b7e9-00144feab49a.html#axzz1Ce04TRpB> (accessed April 17, 2011).

Van Dyne, Linn and LePine, Jeffrey A. (1998) "Helping and voice extra-role behaviors: evidence of construct and predictive validity," *Academy of Management Journal*, Vol. 41, No. 1, pp. 108–19.

Varadarajan, P. Rajan, Clarck, Terry, and Pride, William M. (1992) "Controlling the uncontrollable: managing your market environment," *Sloan Management Review*, Vol. 33, No. 2, pp. 39–47.

Veryzer, Robert W., Jr. (1998) "Key factors affecting customer evaluation of discontinuous new products," *Journal of Product Innovation Management*, Vol. 15, No. 2, pp. 136–50.

Vise, David A. and Malseed, Mark (2005) *The Google Story: Inside the hottest business, media and technology success of our time*, New York: Delacorte Press.

Von Hippel, Eric (2005) *Democratizing Innovation*, Cambridge, Mass.: MIT Press. Available at <http://web.mit.edu/evhippel/www/books/DI/DemocInn.pdf> (accessed April 29, 2011).

Wang, Catherine L. and Ahmed, Pervaiz K. (2004) "The development and validation of the organizational innovativeness construct using confirmatory factor analysis," *European Journal of Innovation Management*, Vol. 7, No. 4, pp. 303–13.

Weick, Karl E. and Sutcliffe, Kathleen M. (2007) *Managing the Unexpected: Resilient performance in an age of uncertainty*, San Francisco, Calif.: John Wiley.

Whittington, Richard (1993) *What is Strategy: and Does it Matter?* London: International Thomson Business Press.

Wynn, Thomas and Coolidge, Frederick L. (2004) "The expert Neandertal mind," *Journal of Human Evolution*, Vol. 46, pp. 467–87.

Zaltman, Gerald (1997) "Rethinking market research: putting people back in," *Journal of Marketing Research*, Vol. 34, No. 4 (Nov.), pp. 424–37.

Zaltman, Gerald and Coulter, Robin Higie (1995) "Seeing the voice of the customer: metaphor-based advertising research," *Journal of Advertising Research* (Jul.–Aug.), pp. 35–51.

Zaltman, Gerald and Zaltman, Lindsay (2008) *Marketing Metaphoria: What deep metaphors reveal about the minds of consumers*, Boston, Mass.: Harvard Business School Press.

Zeithaml, Carl P. and Zeithaml, Valarie A. (1984) "Environmental management: revising the marketing perspective," *Journal of Marketing*, Vol. 48 (Spring), pp. 46–53.

Index